JUDITH VO' attended sch subsequently studied architecture. She first encountered anthroposophy in 1997, and began working as a member of staff at Rudolf Steiner House in Berlin, in addition to her architectural practice. In 2004 she received the stigmata, which transformed her life. Her first book was published in German in 2005, and she now works principally as a lecturer and author. Several of her books are published in English, including *The Coronavirus Pandemic* (Temple Lodge 2020). She and her husband live in Berlin.

P. 71 - Experiece of God!

By the same author:

And If He Has Not Been Raised...
The Coronavirus Pandemic
Dementia
Descent into the Depths of the Earth
Illness and Healing
The Lord's Prayer
Secrets of the Stations of the Cross and the Grail Blood

Swan Wings

A Spiritual Autobiography

Part I
Childhood and Youth

Judith von Halle

Translated by Frank Thomas Smith

CLAIRVIEW

Clairview Books
Russet, Sandy Lane
West Hoathly RH19 4QQ

www.clairviewbooks.com

Published in Great Britain by Clairview Books 2021

Originally published in German under the title *Schwanenflügel: eine spirituelle Autobiographie* by Edition Morel, an imprint of Verlag für Anthroposophie, Dornach, Switzerland 2016

A CIP catalogue record for this book is available from the British Library

978 1 912992 33 1

Cover by Morgan Creative
Typeset by Symbiosys Technologies, Visakhapatnam, India
Printed and bound by 4Edge Ltd., Essex

Contents

PART I

Childhood and Youth

> *'Every person's history should be a Bible*
> *– will be a Bible.'*
> Novalis

'They only awoke when the fire came through the roof.' I woke up hearing these words spoken by a news presenter.

I sat on the floor of my grandparents' living room and stared at a red plastic cube in which you could stick various little geometric forms through certain openings. I looked up and for the first time in my life let my gaze consciously wander around the room. My grandmother was knitting, my grandfather was watching the news on television; to my left was a large cabinet with a few knee-high drawers. One of them was open a crack and contained some toys. If I stood up I would be tall enough to see and reach all of them.

'... They only awoke when the fire came through the roof.' The sentence by the newscaster resounded in my ears. It touched the hidden depths of my inner being with unspeakable violence and harrowing gravity.

I had obviously slept, had dreamed for around two years.

Had it taken so long before my consciousness entered my body and was no longer pushed back by it – until this consciousness itself no longer struggled against being imprisoned in the narrow confines of its dwelling?

That fire in a building that took place somewhere in Germany in 1974 and was described in the news is not in itself connected to my destiny. It was only the *words* spoken that touched upon my destiny. The words, together with the speaker's emphasis and intonation, do not only constitute the first memory of my life; they are also the first words which I heard in full consciousness, and on which my earthly consciousness enkindled. I can say this with certainty because I remember how, after that moment of my awakening, I mused with wonder about where I had been *before* – that is, during the time when my little body had already existed on the earth;

during the time when someone put the clothes on that it was presently wearing; when the hands that I was now looking at picked up the colourful toys and let them fall again. How had this body in which I awoke come here? Who or what had caused it to 'function' before? And, above all, where was *I*?

From that moment on the sentence from the news programme had stamped itself upon my mind. But for a long time I did not associate any ideas with it. Nevertheless it did not affect me so evocatively because of some idea connected to it, or a description of how the fire affected some resident of the building, or something like that. Probably I immediately forgot what the reporter said afterwards. So I don't know if anyone was injured. I have no recollection about the thing in itself. Anyway, a two- to three-year-old child could certainly not think about such things in the outer world as a grown person might. Perhaps the cause lay in that the sentence touched on something that led my groping consciousness to some completely other place and happening than what was described – namely to a place or an event connected to my own destiny.

It was completely clear to me – perhaps not intellectually, but with an incomparably greater intensity – that these words were impressed upon me so that I would *remember*. That was what those words said to me: *Remember! Awaken!*

I sensed that those words had only awakened me because I knew something of which they reminded me from a different point in time. They must have had some relation to the enormous echo that resounded in me.

However, because of all the time I was in my body here on earth during the two years I obviously *slept* through, the memory-echo must have recalled a different time, a different condition of myself. Sometime once before, I must have lived in another place with my consciousness, together with all the knowledge and memories that came about through this consciousness, and clearly *outside* of the body in which I was then living.

It wasn't primarily a case of recalling an event that happened in some distant time or other. Without question: I was to remember *myself!*

Who am I? Who, what am I really?

If I could find this out, if I could reconnect with myself – if I could become 'I' again – then everything else would arise out of the sea of dullness into which, by awakening in a body, I had just fallen – for otherwise all these questions could never have arisen.

The sensed knowledge of the fact that I had forgotten 'me', and the question where I had been, presuppose that my real being is not dependent on the place where it happens to be. Furthermore, it also existed when it was *not* in a body. So, by submerging into a body, obviously a kind of fogging-over, of falling asleep, had taken place. Although I was now awake in this body, I had forgotten where I came from. By awakening I had fallen asleep, I had lost something.

Thus awakening in my earthly body, which led to me forgetting my true self, had to be the actual state of sleep! Perhaps, though, I had not really slept during those last two years, between my birth and that moment. It apparently only seemed so to me, because now when I woke up in my earthly body among the objects of the material world, I could no longer remember the previous time, when I did *not* live in my earthly body along with the consciousness which could perceive the world of physical objects.

I felt an uneasy suspicion: the condition in which I found myself caused a curious kind of irritation – that it was not to be trusted. It had tricked me about something I could only weakly feel, something essential.

From that moment on it became evident to me – in a completely 'natural' way – that there must be two kinds of consciousness: *one* consciousness that lets me be awake *in the body*; it was not, however, able to know or to remember who I actually was and from where I came. Instead it was able to be completely awake in this little earthly body. In this state it became possible to perceive and to act; not only to perceive and to act, but also to be conscious of the perceived objects as well as my own actions within the sensory-visible world.

And then there was the *other* consciousness, and this other consciousness knew who I was and where I came from. It knew everything. I could remember all. For I myself was this consciousness. My integral whole, so to speak.

5

I realized at that moment that I had to regain the latter conscious-ness (that is, 'myself'), the real one, that I also had to reconquer it within the boundaries of my physical body, as an earthly person. For I felt that by awakening in a physical body I was somehow ter-ribly incomplete, with my real self stolen, even naked. (Years later when I heard the Biblical Paradise story, it immediately reminded me of the feeling I had upon waking up in a body. Adam and Eve's unpleasant sensation of being *naked* marked the beginning of their expulsion from Paradise and their fall to the physical earth. By tast-ing the fruit of the Tree of Knowledge, they became conscious of the earthly world, but at the same time felt naked and abandoned by it. They experienced being torn away from the highest whole, from the all-knowing consciousness.)

After waking up in a body and thinking and feeling this way, I knew at the same time that it was possible, without any doubt, to regain my integral whole, because the awakening by the news announcer's sentence was directly related to my 'old' or 'original' waking con-sciousness; that sentence meant nothing to the body-consciousness I had just attained.

Thus, with a certain calm I felt an inner certainty that the conscious-ness with which I thought all these thoughts could not be the one that had completely forgotten the answers to my questions. This new earthly body-consciousness was the one which knew nothing about me – my real me. Therefore, it is also incapable of asking the question about another existence, about another state, because it doesn't even consider that another state of being exists. It knows no other state than its own. So it must have been that *other* real consciousness – my true self – that thought these thoughts and shimmered into this earthly body-consciousness. ('Paradise' was therefore not irrecoverably lost.)

That all the answers to my questions were not available, how-ever, could only mean – at least it's what I felt then – that this 'real' consciousness was capable of expanding much further than it had done; and the fact that it had *not* done so was clearly caused by the awakening in an *earthly* body.

Admittedly, all this may seem to be an unbelievable story, or at least an astounding one – an almost superhuman intellectual performance for a two to three-year-old child. So I must add the following to rel-ativize it, or, rather, to give it more precision. What has been related here truly describes what I experienced inwardly at that time. Noth-ing has been invented. I remember it as though it were yesterday. Perhaps if one considers it more carefully, it isn't so incredible after all. They were by no means purely intellectual thoughts, so it is cer-tain that no extraordinary intellectual gift was involved. What I am trying to express in words which intellectual thinking can under-stand, and which may seem terribly complicated, did not play out in ways that intellectual thinking knows. What I am relating here in sequence came to me simultaneously. Questions and answers were together 'at once', and, in terms of time, 'lightning quick'.

Today I would say that it was 'non-representational' thinking. It was what is also called 'super-sensible' thinking – a term I consider most appropriate. It was lightning quick, free and agile – it was able to move effortlessly in one direction or the opposite, indeed in many different directions, and at the same time! – and thus was able to observe incomparably numerous contingencies, something which is impossible for discursive thinking. Thereby one might rea-sonably call my perceptions at that time 'analytical' thinking, but in the sense of a natural abstention from any personal viewpoints, and thus perhaps even abstract, but with just those characteristics which are not usually identified with analytical thought. It was fac-tual, but not 'bloodless', it was distant, but at the same time not uninvolved. Moreover, it took place with simultaneousness, that is to say, beyond 'our' time, beyond the time in which everything – every object, even every thought – seemed frozen solid. And, it was unburdened, unspoiled.

Two indispensable properties belong to this kind of thinking that until now I have only mentioned marginally, and which could put the objectivity of this kind of thinking in doubt for the rational thinker, but which in fact only make it possible. On the one hand, total impartiality is necessary for this kind of thinking. And, at the beginning of my earthly life this was given, because in this earthly life, and regarding this earthly life, I had not had any experiences. It may be an offensive idea for a rational thinker that someone can achieve a reliable thinking ability when they possess no experience with rational thinking. But unfortunately I can offer no consolation.

For it is exactly so. The basis for this free thinking was an unburdened, impartial perception or observation of the situations I encountered. And that is what happened then: I took note of this thing or that and experienced it according to the means available to the differing consciousness states of my self – completely free of previously acquired experiences and fixed ideas.

This perceptive observation was not all, however. It was, as already mentioned, only the precondition for the next step. A reflection intervened, to a large extent a neutral one, we could even call it objective, because it came from that other 'actual' consciousness which wasn't based on earthly ideas and considerations that – a rational thinker might agree – can be based on errors and consequently inexact or not applicable, for an idea does not always agree with reality.

What happened at that time was not that the earthly consciousness attempted to form some idea about the 'actual' consciousness, but the reverse: the sensible consciousness was observed by the super-sensible one. And that 'actual' consciousness soon exposed the sensible, the 'body-consciousness' one, as something incomplete, dream-oriented and forgetful.

What did this 'body-consciousness' extract from that non-corrupt 'actual' consciousness? If I try to characterize it as I experienced it then, I must speak of the second indispensable condition which makes this kind of thinking possible, and about which the rational thinker might have a no less negative impression. This special way of thinking is accompanied by certain sensations. These sensations, which only remotely have to do with what we usually call a sensation, were the actual bearers of these thoughts. The thoughts were embedded in a higher sensation that conferred upon them the certainty of truthfulness.

The decisive difference with what we usually call – and in the somewhat arrogant opinion of the analytic thinker – 'feelings', is that the sensations which were the bearers of the described thoughts were not kindled by any external circumstance from which I personally received a more or less feeling impulse with my earthly consciousness. Rather were they non-subjective sensations coming from outside my self. Although it may seem absurd, they were literally objective sensations because they – as well as the thoughts borne by them – did not come from my naturally very limited personality, namely a small child; that is, not from a physical-sensible-earthly thinking and feeling person, but from that higher consciousness existing outside my body, which was not two to three years old, but timeless in experience and simultaneously unburdened by personal sensations or ideas. They were thought-sensations, completely incorruptible compared to 'lower' or personal thinking and feeling. The sensations from without crowded in upon me and created in me, that is, in my body-consciousness, an immediate evidentiary sensation of truthfulness. It could also be called 'truth-sensation'.

These truth or reality sensations guided my being in the right direction, namely to the sphere in which the 'other' consciousness lives, which can be so objective in its thinking that I didn't have to describe my sensed experiences with the words 'I thought' this or that, but with the words: 'IT thought'. Yes, I felt an inexpressible dignity, sublimity and clarity emanating from this other autonomous, intrinsic consciousness, for I observed how 'it', of itself, thought in me virtually objectively.

Thus were the first moments in my conscious existence on earth, as the person who is writing these recollections, accompanied by a background knowledge or divining of the perhaps most decisive thought of all: *An immortal, all embracing, living, creative Majesty exists whose wisdom is limitless. An all-enfolding and pervading entity without which nothing, not a single ray of thought, is possible, let alone something of a material nature. An entity that creates everything and in which everything is nevertheless so free and uncoerced that it is self-determining and can develop in every direction.*

And all these unsurpassable attributes, about which our puny earthly words are unable to paint even an approximate picture, were completely pervaded by an impulse, by an elementally strong but at the same time extremely gentle *impulse of will* which – if I may describe what I felt then – I can today only describe as *limitless goodwill*.

It *wanted the wellbeing* of all the creatures that had been created. And such a created, creaturely being for whom the goodwill was valid, was I, my actual being.

Thus I found myself placed in the world of earthly space and time, in the world of the seen and of the touched. But in this world of forgetting one's real being I knew from the start, through what had been shared with me as sensing and sensed objective thinking, that as long as I turned to that benevolent Majesty, in whose womb I knew my actual self to be at home and secure, I would never get lost.

The foregoing attempt to characterize using words only applicable to the earthly world may seem terribly abstract, but it is in reality the opposite from abstraction. That majestic dignity and its intrinsic thoughts in which I was able to rediscover myself for several seconds, was so ineffably alive that from that moment of my earth-awakening, I have felt myself to be a 'traveller passing through', because what exists here on earth, especially the way of thinking of which many people are so proud, is so transient compared with actual consciousness, that is, with our true humanity. That first impression has not changed. On the contrary, over the years it has only strengthened.

Since that day forty years ago, it has pulled my entire being with devoted yearning for my actual homeland, for the actual homeland of us all, to that 'whole' – despite the fact that as a child as well as an adult I have enjoyed enormous delight in this earthly life and know how to treasure an earthly existence. Nevertheless, since then the irrevocable conviction lives in me that my full entirety, my 'whole', has always existed beyond this earthly existence and consciousness.

I was able to directly experience the drastic difference between the spiritual world and the sensory world, between a spiritual and an earthly consciousness, through my awakening in an earthly body. Together with this awakening in an earthly body awoke in me the yearning to become 'whole' again, and therewith the ability to greatly value spiritual consciousness, the clear and 'virgin' reality, as opposed to the irreversible relativity of the earthly. This is no trivial preference of one over the other, but it arose with complete neutrality through consciously experiencing the essence of the whole as opposed to that of the fragmented.

From that moment when I found myself on my grandparents' brown carpet, the goal was clear: the hunt began for my consciousness. Although at that time I couldn't have formulated it, I wanted to find my self's true consciousness in order to be able to expand it, until I was reunited with the benevolent creative Majesty, which was undoubtedly the homeland of my true being.

But because the newscaster's sentence not only touched me in my deeper being, but also in my 'bodily', that is, rational or intellectual day-to-day consciousness, a continuity, a kind of higher plan extending over unforeseeable time must exist. What I really was, and whence I came, must be connected with what I now found my self to be, and what I should be in the future. It should go on 'here' on the earth, in the body in which I am now placed.

Exactly *what* should go on, I didn't then know. But that previously something existed which is *to go on* was, due to the experience described, definite.

***

This 'to go on' occupied me increasingly from then on. Given the short span of earthly life, the question was what to begin with, in the sense of that continuity – in the sense of that higher plan which I was sure existed, but was unsure of what exactly it looked like. That question occupied me since that day I woke up.

One evening – I was between four and five years old, for this scene took place in the old apartment from which we moved before my sixth birthday – when I was going to bed, I tried to engage my mother in a conversation about the finitude of human existence. I lay in bed, the light had already been turned out and my mother's dark silhouette was visible in the room's open door, illuminated by the light from the hallway. She was about to say goodnight and close the door. But I still had many questions on my mind, and they had moved me for so long that no further delay could be tolerated. I wanted to know the meaning of mortality. I wanted to 'measure' the mortality in which I, with the immortality of my higher self, was immersed.

So I asked my mother how long a second lasted. She couldn't answer the question, which I cannot hold against her, because I certainly couldn't make myself clear. Nevertheless, the answer, if

I received one, was so unsatisfactory that I can't remember it. So I had to go to bed 'hungry' and find the answer in a different way.

I stayed with the problem. Sometime during the next few days I noticed a kitchen clock with its second hand. I couldn't tell the time, but was told that the faster moving hand is the one that indicates the seconds. Here was something to begin with! Eventually I had an idea: I began to try to measure the exact length of a second by adding a hum between one clock mark and the next. Soon I was able to determine the length of a second in rhythm to the second hand, between the marks, by humming and being silent. Good heavens! This life is so short! It can be measured in seconds. It plays out within what are perhaps many, but also perfectly countable, very short-lasting, closely placed units. For me it was of little importance if a life lasted 20, 50 or 95 years. I could not yet judge what 'years' were. They seemed to be ineffable and indefinitely long. This personal sensation, however – I said to myself after my encounter with the second hand – must be a trick compared to the reality. For a year consists of these very short humming sounds, these seconds, and they are, one after the other, gone at once – that is, everything that occurred during the time they lasted. However long a year seemed to me, it was a captive of the finite. The transitory here on earth was therefore inevitable as well as omnipresent, and it was really measurable. This firm inevitability and frozen rhythm was like that of the relentlessly marching second hand.

This discovery led to more musing. Not long after that episode, again during a 'goodnight opportunity', I mentioned to my mother that after the moment of birth we seem to be involved in a continuous process of dying. This did not result in a fruitful conversation either. Perhaps I remember it so well because it remained unanswered by one of my parents. I wanted to hear an adult's opinion. I would have welcomed very much what someone with experience of life had to say. But either my mother had never thought about such a question, or once again I was unable to articulate it well enough; so I was again forced to depend upon myself.

Analyzing 'becoming' and dying was one of the first and long-lasting considerations of my early childhood. With a mixture of curiosity, fascinated eeriness (because of the inevitability) and joy (for the presumption of a return path to the homeland of my true self), the thought that with the beginning of our existence on earth, that is, the moment of birth, death was preprogrammed, occupied my mind. It crept within us during birth. Death. What was this death? Because it seemed to be present in everything that constituted life, death had to be a part of this earthly life, for an earthly life was not possible without it. If, however, I had stayed back where my actual consciousness was, and where it remained when I was born, death would not lurk within me. But that had to mean that if I could find my actual consciousness again, if I could embrace it again, death would have to disappear. At least it would not be the same as what it seemed to be until then. Therefore death was in reality an experience, a question of consciousness. There it was again: the urgent need to hunt for my consciousness.

While I pondered, trying to understand, I tried to find a concept of the moment when this shimmering death would win the upper hand, that is, when crossing the threshold from one state to the other. I forced myself to also represent the fact of inevitability as a sensation. Basically, I wanted to be able to sustain the idea and feeling of inevitability. Given that death awaited me in any case, it would surely be good to be prepared, in order not to be distracted by it from the perception of what seemed to me to be essential: the re-entry into the world from which, in this earthly body, and thereby in my earthly consciousness, I had fallen into forgetfulness. For nothing in the world did I want to miss the conscious immersion in the realm of 'being-awake'.

Furthermore, if everyone, including myself, must die after such a relatively short span of time (measurable in seconds), then how precious each day, each hour, even each second must be seen to be!

It was only much later in my life that it became clear to me that the *Memento mori** from the Cluniac Reform, as well as the Masonic and Rosicrucian lodges, had no other content and no other objective than to awaken the thoughts that had moved me so deeply during my early childhood.

I spent hours with these thoughts, which occupied me for several years before other questions became more urgent, because new

---

Memento mori (Latin for 'remember that you [have to] die') is an artistic or symbolic reminder of the inevitability of death (Ed.).

experiences delivered answers (at least partial ones) to the question about my self's actual homeland.

***

But my attention to the matters of *this* side also grew from day to day. I was now at an age more appropriate for discovering the earthly world than the 'over-earthly' one. For one must arrive in this earthly world as a complete earth citizen, so to speak, and for that the undivided attention to the things of the earthly world is required. And furthermore, that phase of life requires, quite naturally, an impartial inner reception of this earthly world. This inner reception was as naturally present in me as in other children.

Full of curiosity and lively interest, I accepted the phenomena and objects of the earthly world, and grasped with wonder and joy what my eyes and other senses showed me. The rustle of leaves that in autumn lavishly fell from the trees on the streets of Berlin and through which one could wade noisily knee-deep; the unmistakable smell of the sandy ground in the *Grünewald* that mixed with pine needles and cones; the lovely song of the blackbirds on warm summer evenings; the purposeful march of the ant columns and the cumbersome path of the individual ant, which carries a twig many times its own weight with never-yielding stamina; the silky feel, similar to water, of fine sand flowing through the fingers, and the observation of how the sand's texture completely changes when it comes in contact with water; yes, how certain substances can be transformed through the addition of other substances or forces. At the age of discovery between two and six, I was also most enthusiastic about the creations of people, even if they were simple things like being fascinated by the slowly sinking snowflakes in a glass snow-globe. It's not necessary to continue describing such things, because most people can recall such experiences in their early childhood.

Most things accessible to a city child like me, however, were objects made by human hands and conceived by human minds. It was because of them that the decisive discrepancy between them and the experiences described above, in and with nature, soon became clear to me: the things made by human hands and external facilities contradicted natural laws. I also noted that nature's household interrupted the pendulum swing between life and death (my well-known

14

subject): flowers withered, apples shrivelled, became inedible, rotted, and flies, beetles, snails and birds eliminated their remains. All was subject to transience. But a magical force invisible to normal eyes penetrated the natural world, from out of which everything was rhythmically renewed. Of course it wasn't the same flowers that sprouted in spring, it was also not the same apples that were picked; they were irretrievably gone. But it was the same *essence* of the flower in the new flower, the same essence of the apple in the new apple which returned – just as surely as the sun set in the evening and rose again at dawn. Over the sporadically appearing unavoidable finality of the various forms of nature's creatures reigned in my childish heart the triumphant feeling for the rule of immortality. I knelt before the rhythm of immortality with inexpressibly humble feeling. It was a holy force, because it was beyond human ability, and my heart worshipped that force with great emotion.

At times, when I was by myself for a few moments in nature, and my perceptions were able to coincide with the corresponding thoughts about that holy cycle, I could sense each time an acting force-presence that was precisely localized in the area of the solar plexus, a point between the heart and the pit of the stomach. It was as if that 'creative Majesty' I had experienced on my earthly awakening day, previously described, had laid a finger softly but firmly on my body there, upon which my heart always gave a little jump and beat more strongly than before. And when this happened, it was like a sweet stream was incorporated in me, which my whole nature – my feeling inner life as well as my earthly body – drenched me with *life-force*. (I can express it no other way.) Because of this I realized how thirsty both my inner being and my outer being had been before. After such moments I felt in my entire being so refreshed that, often to the surprise of my parents and grandparents, I bounced around like a rubber ball for minutes at a time, and hardly anything could undermine my joy and energy on such a day. But it also had another effect, which became clearer to me little by little: the holy nourishing stream of forces was not only a fountain of youth for the physical body, it also nourished my feeling and thinking in a curious way. It was as if, through it, vitalizing and, in a certain sense, profound thoughts could form within me. Later on I found that these forces can be specifically 'managed' and used for the good. More about that in the continuation of my narrative.

The things of the earthly world devised by human heads and artificially made by human hands nevertheless followed the strict laws of nature, but the holy cycle did not. Everything that humans made eventually disappeared, be they buildings, books, toys, clothes or automobiles. Without further human assistance they could not reckon with unaided renewal. The difference was of course obvious. In the things created by humans there was no life. The human creations were not, by their nature, permeated with that magical force with which the grass, the ants and we humans were permeated. They were simply 'dead' objects. All these objects lacked that wonderful magical force that moves everything on earth that lives, and ensures that in place of the bygone a new, related being arises. It was exactly that magical force which created the observed cycle of life which gave me the absolute conviction since childhood of belonging to an immortal whole which interconnects all living things. For this force was always there! I perceived it. And if it ever became invisible to me – I was sure of this because my observations confirmed it – the cause lay in my temporary or fundamentally inadequate attention.

***

I will now try to describe the effect this force had. My observations and thoughts were approximately the following: when a dead body is seen (I only saw a dead human body later in life, but had often seen dead animals and of course dead plants were visible everywhere), then one can realize with certainty that the three body types (human, animal and vegetable) were previously filled with an invisible force, with a presence, and that the presence or occupant of the body in question was withdrawn at the moment of death. This occupant is invisible to physical eyes. But it is more powerful than anything that is visible. For when it is not present, everything visible in which it was previously present must fall to dust. Since I have been able to think, I have considered any plant, animal or human being that can be observed and touched externally as a kind of dwelling from which the actual but invisible occupant is vivified, so that it can then appear as what we generally understand as plant, animal or human. At that time it was most puzzling to me how anyone could doubt the existence, though invisible for normal eyes, of the actual occupant of the physical dwelling. Most of the people I met seemed not to recognize any existential difference between unoccupied and occupied, between dead and living matter. In any case, they basically treated themselves exactly as they treated a dead object. They occupied themselves almost exclusively with their bodily dwelling. In fact, though, every person is a living occupant or resident of his bodily dwelling. I wondered if the generally widespread fear of death was the result of most people identifying themselves as identical with their bodily dwelling; that they felt bound, their whole existence dependent upon it, or even that they confused their very selves with it. Because of what I had experienced on my awakening day, and since then have experienced again and again, it was for me without question that one 'was there', whether in a bodily dwelling or not.

But even if for some inexplicable (for me) reason someone was unaware of this fact, by the mere visual examining of a dead person compared with a live one, it is obvious that the occupant is 'at home' in the live body and not in the dead one. And whether plant, animal or human being, all are permeated by the 'magical life-force' derived from the good creative Majesty.

We could also look at it in reverse: If my consciousness, my existence as a whole, were bound to the existence of my body, then my consciousness, my earthly consciousness that is, would have had to be already present at birth. But it was not! In that case, according to the standards of the people around me, my body couldn't even have been classified as living. A citizen of the earth who is not also conscious of his earthly environment is, according to established standards, actually not a human being; nowadays he would be considered 'brain dead', as I found out later. Nevertheless, my body had lived since birth and even developed. It grew and acquired new skills. I recalled my first questions in my grandparents' living room: Who or what made my body function before I awoke in my bodily consciousness?

While I was discovering more about the earthly world, in time I arrived at differentiated basic thoughts. What I have described here, apparently the result of mere intellectual trains of thought, did not only result from a purely sensory observation of the physical world, but was also due to a completely different kind of observation of that world.

***

17

Above all, through a second kind of observation, I came to the following conviction: It was the *magical life-force* that gave me life and kept me living during the time when my consciousness had not yet entered my earthly body – and keeps me alive still. This magical life-force came from the creative Majesty.

I came to this certainty because sometimes I could see the magical life-force in everything living on earth. When I use the word 'see', an explanation is probably required, because I have also already said that this force is invisible, just as the 'actual occupants' of the various visible bodily dwellings are invisible.

What I will describe now requires that I overcome a certain amount of reluctance. For I experienced later on that if one tries to impart something about this, one is simply not believed and is accused of 'telling fairy tales'. Still worse, one risks the rhetorical counter-question: of whether one is not 'completely okay'. And when I came in contact with esoterically engaged circles and made known something of my experiences, among other inappropriate reactions an unrestrained, gawking kind of admiration resulted – this among people whose goal it is to acquire certain abilities by means of esoteric exercises, for many of whom the 'ability' described here amounts to the peak of what should be striven for. Both attitudes act as deterrents, for they corrupt the already difficult undertaking of describing super-sensible matters with words of our sensory physical world – matters which are completely 'neutral', objective, and therefore should be taken as such.

I have delayed far too long to openly convey the things I will now describe, for I have come to the conclusion that it is selfish to remain silent about them. So I will try, as before, to report from my earlier perspective. On many occasions, as I said, I was able to 'see' the magical life-force. It always happened when, without thinking of something specific, I looked, or rather stared, at something happening before my eyes. Then something emerged which I had not noticed before, and showed itself to be what I called the 'magical life-force', a constantly moving, multicoloured current.

At first I noticed it in my sleeping grandfather. It permeated his whole body, so that it seemed to be imitating his form, except that due to its movement the force was not sharply circumscribed, as the skin of our bodies is circumscribed from the rest of the physical world. I saw my grandfather in a completely different way, in a different suit, so to speak. When I followed this current, my attention was brought to the regions to which it moved and concentrated. I saw that this current of life streamed through the whole body and at certain points executed special, almost artistic movements, and in this way these points could receive what they obviously needed in order to 'function', to be alive. It acted as the drive for the working of a certain bodily area.

It was a fantastic, basically indescribable sight! However inactive and even 'dead' a sleeping person looks, when he isn't changing his position or making breathing sounds, his interior reveals a very active and variegated motion! But this motion took place according to a through-and-through orderly, meaningful passage. On the one hand, this living current was a powerful force as it flowed through the whole body. On the other hand, in certain places it formed channels along which a strong current with many side currents flowed that distantly resembled artistic Celtic ornaments, something I realized many years later when I saw pictures of them. They weren't like underground water veins however, which are mostly horizontal and therefore on two-dimensional levels. No, these channels and branches were three-dimensional and they rose – unlike water in its natural course – effortlessly sideways and upwards as well as downwards. They were more akin to fairytale-like flora, or flowers; but one could observe this kind of flora in its development, which was much faster than normal plant life. The flowers grew upwards, formed a striking shape, like a blossom, and in the next moment, with no transitional stage, namely in continuous becoming, formed a new shape.

There was clearly a plan to these currents and growths! For there were no errors in the movements, nor did they give the impression of having arisen arbitrarily or that any of the branches would run dry because it took a wrong turn. If one of the wonderful moving flowers turned back or changed course, it was because the sprouting force had already been transformed into a new bud, therewith reaching the fulfilment of its development.

The beauty of the flowers and the currents of the magical life-force were not the only elements of the motions and forms of its becoming process, but an incomparable play of colours was also part of the process. One can imagine the whole as a single magical wave of colours in the most marvellous nuances. But these colours are different from the colours we see in the earthly world. Normal colours are as a rule just as 'dead' as the objects upon which they appear. It is just *because* they appear on them that they become part of the material world, the world of the superficial, the world of the rigid. Hardly anything that we can see with our physical eye reaches this kind of colour. This should not surprise us though, for our eyes are made to observe the material world. Therefore it is barely possible to describe the colours of the magical life-force's current, because they don't exist in the world of material appearances and thus there are no corresponding words available to do so. If one says that such colours have a different brilliance and are more luminous than the colours we know, then one must add that this does not indicate that they are merely more intensive than normal colours. Rather is it a matter of the actual living essence of the colour itself. And if something of this essence died, then we would see what we know as visible colours.

If we make clear the difference between the appearance of blue – any nuance of blue – and the essence of blue, then we can perhaps have an idea of what I am trying to express here. In fact, we do have a deeper understanding of the essence of a colour, and we do provide the different colours with their corresponding attributes, which have nothing to do with their mere appearance in the material world; at least artists, who as a rule wish to attribute *more* to what is painted on the canvas than mere colours, possess this ability. Thus the colour blue that appears in the material world is neither 'cool' nor 'nostalgic', 'diving deeply' or 'calm'. But the *essence* of blue certainly is. Such *living* characteristics constitute the *essence* of colours, which have quite a different quality than normal colours, namely an incomparable intensity and at the same time an incomparable delicacy and transforming ability.

Thus the magical life-force was 'visible' in a special way, and I have already mentioned what my physical eyes did while I 'saw' it. The mentioned staring was not a forced looking at something solid. It was more an empty gazing at the exterior visible things without registering them. This was necessary in order to observe the living current. It was only in such situations that I could see the living current during my childhood. Only by the visible exterior being 'overseen' – stepping back enough – was the essential shown. And strictly speaking it was not shown to my physical eyes. It was necessary that attention to the visible exterior disappeared more and more so that something else could become visible. Because the physical eyes were no longer looking at anything, it was no longer important whether I kept them open or closed. For what I 'saw', I didn't see with my physical eyes, but with the same force which passes through our eyes when we want to see something. Except that when I wanted to purposely follow the living current further, observe it longer, this force had to be used more and more, at the same time ignoring the visible exterior with selfless will. Meanwhile in this way my own force, which I felt to be a special variant of the will, became steadily more conscious.

One should not assume, however, that one has only to 'want' it. That was a guarantee that everything would disappear more quickly from inner vision. Or rather that one's own inner vision, which can perceive the truly living, would disappear. This happened seldom during my early childhood. I attribute this to the fact that I simply noticed such things, marvelling, without any personal desire or conception or expectation. For as soon one forms intellectual concepts one falls back into physical vision. You can of course reflect upon what has been seen, but afterward. It was only much later when I discovered that it is indeed possible to have thoughts about it *during* the process. These thoughts have little in common with intellectual thinking, however. I will also come back to this later.

In any case, I can assure you that it is possible to see certain things without needing a pupil or a lens or an optic nerve, and so forth. It is possible! And I was and am certain that it is potentially possible for everyone. What hinders this kind of seeing is being fixed exclusively on only observing the visible sensory world and its corresponding representations. That is actually the only thing that prevents one from seeing the many astonishing, wonderful events and processes in and around us.

Most people are near to this seeing, but unaware of it! How many people perceive a special atmosphere when strolling through a more or less healthy forest? If they would only admit it and not feel ashamed before others – which is completely groundless – they would confirm that in such a walk through the woods they would realize that there is something else present apart from wooden tree-trunks and leaves on branches. Why do so many feel a forest as 'enchanted', 'mysterious' or also 'threatening'? Is it only their imagination playing tricks? According to what I experienced and learned, it is only in the rarest cases that delusions are the cause of such feelings. They seem more to indicate either an already present rudimentary ability, or a developing one, to perceive certain forces in nature which, although invisible, are nevertheless most likely present.

I experienced it as a characteristic phenomenon of our times, and also in the circles in which I was born, that many people no longer trust their own perceptions as long as they pertain to an area in which their earthly sensory instruments are not used. From childhood we are told that only what we can see with our physical eyes and can touch with our hands is real. Is it not a classical assurance to the child: 'Don't worry; there are no spirits!'? I found this terribly amusing. I thought: If the adults' assertion were true, humanity itself would be eliminated, for is not the actual occupant of a human bodily housing itself a spirit?

Instruments exist that can be applied for the perception of non-material phenomena and processes. One also needs a perception or sense-organ for this. We must, however, 'train' it, educate it. Nobody would expect a two-year-old child to move as adroitly as a trained dancer. Why? Because it has neither the necessary anatomy nor the sense of movement or equilibrium. At that age it has practically no experience in moving on the earth carefully, efficiently or gracefully. It 'trains' for these things during its childhood and youth. If it did not persistently practice standing, walking, keeping its balance and striving for perfection, it could never become a professional dancer. It is exactly the same for the training and use of what I will call here 'super-sensible' sensory organs.

During the following years I realized that one must do something in order to achieve advancement in this area. What I 'saw' was, after all, much too interesting and seemed too important for me to not feel the need to sharpen my 'instruments' in order to be able to go deeper into the meaning of certain things and processes. For what I saw was on the one hand self-evident: the fact that another world exists with its forces and laws in and around us. On the other hand, this fact induced many serious questions about life here on earth about which I sought answers. But this requires practice and patience. And because there was nobody around to offer me useful advice about this area, time was needed in order to find out, through my own empirical activity, how to go about educating this imperfect instrument which I would need for further observations.

***

This 'seeing' the magical life-force in a living organism opened a huge field of new discoveries and, of course, questions. It was clear to me by observing what was offered to me that the life-current's special branches or blossoms were formed at chosen points of the human body. I knew where the human heart is located from placing my hand on someone else's breast, whereby I could feel their heart-beat, and because I put my ear on my mother's or my father's breast and could even hear the heart beat; so I knew that the region of the heart is where I could perceive a particularly beautiful and pro-nounced moving formation of the life-force current. I saw that it was the magical life-force that assured the heart's motion. But because the blossom-like formations also appeared in many other parts of the body, it was apparent that something similar to a heart was also situated there. Only that these others must have been otherwise con-stituted than the heart, because their life-current formations looked so different. The word 'organs' and individual words such as 'liver', 'kidneys' or 'stomach', only meant something to me later. When I learned them though, it was immediately clear to me what they must mean. So from that time on I related them in my mental pic-tures to the concepts of the individual organs with the characteristic movement of the magical life-force in them.

In due time I was engaged in a more intensive study of the magi-cal life-force within the organs. This also involved the observation that something else could appear within the human body that acted like a congestion – similar to what happens when a dam is built in a stream with stones and branches and the water is blocked or prevented from continuing in its natural direction, so that it goes in a different one. As a consequence, however, the stream's natural pristine beauty as well as its formation and colourfulness were obscured. It was obvious that such dimness could not be caused by the magical life-force itself, but that something else was standing in its way. I realized upon seeing this that the person concerned could not feel well, especially at that place, and that due to the congestion the entire current in him was more or less strongly and lastingly impaired.

When I became aware of this my heart and my stomach contracted from sadness and regret and I wished that the magical life-force could regain its beauty in order for that person to get better. I knew: If the current's natural course is essentially changed, there is illness. However, what could be done to correct this state I did not know.

One thing was clear, because I 'saw' it often: Certain medicines which a person took against not feeling well often led not only to an increase in that feeling, but also to something so unusual that I can only describe it with the following picture. The medicine acted to cause an increased congestion in the affected organ, which in turn caused the original congestion to decrease and furthermore, that the rapidly flowing current was somewhat slowed so that the effect on the current in the other parts of the body were not as grave as before. However, I had the impression of a still greater distortion of the original condition – that there was no longer an imbalance at the affected place, but that the original distortion was corrected due to the addition of a further imbalance. By administering the medicine, one gave the motion-flower of the life-force current a completely different appearance, which no longer was as lop-sided as during the first congestion. The appearance of the lop-sided motion-flower, however, still had a similarity to the original, natural healthy state. So one could imagine how the motion-flower was originally and how it actually should be. After taking certain other medicines, on the other hand, this was no longer the case for the affected place. A completely new motion-flower was formed, which lacked the beauty of the original one. It made, rather, an unmistakably unhealthy, unharmonious, twisted impression. It also occurred to me that the changed motion-flower of the life-current was always a short distance *beside* where it was supposed to be. It was as if you wanted to ride along a street, but after a few yards it was blocked and you had to take a detour along a bumpy side-street from where you could not see what you would have seen along the first street. For this reason, I had the impression that taking certain medicine meant that the corresponding organ could not be sustained with the magical life-force as is foreseen by the creative Majesty's wise plan. But regardless of the number of disturbances in the magical life-force of the body, it was so strong that it was able to give the occupant life, or, rather, it was able to make earthly life possible for the body's invisible occupant.

***

As already mentioned, it was in my grandfather that I first noticed it; but my grandfather in a sleeping state. Mentioning this detail seems important to me, because afterwards, in my pre-school years, I very seldom perceived the magical life-force in a waking person, so it was never possible for me to follow it as steadily as in a sleeping person. And the reason was that in the waking state it was displaced by something else.

This something, which always pushed itself so predominantly into the foreground, was also invisible for normal eyes, but was also so different that it can no more be compared to the wise magical life-force than a cat to a sunflower. But someone who hears about it without having observed it might well imagine that there is no essential difference between the two forces or formations which permeate people and are invisible. Therefore I will try to describe this second force as it appeared to me at that time. It was not so consistently oriented and did not act in the least like the magical life-force. Furthermore, it seemed to me to have an indecipherable function. In any case, its function was not to provide life-force to the physical being. On the contrary. I had the impression that something is emitted by this force that disturbs the magical life-force, at least now and then. It was due to the fact that it was only several years later that I was able to simultaneously observe both force forms together and also separately, that I came to that conclusion. But according to the perspective that this second force offered, it could not be otherwise than that it occasionally acted unfavourably toward the magical life-force. (I could also call it a force-body, by the way, because – like the magical life-force – it permeates the entire interior and exterior body.) The most impressive aspect of this force, and at the same time its greatest difference from the magical life-force, was that it acted according to the same principle in respect to various people (fundamental forms of movement or directions) but in its appearance and combination it varied much more from person to person than did the magical life-force currents.

Furthermore, within each individual it was much more rapidly changing than the magical life-force ever could be. It was inconsistent, even volatile. The magical life-force always seemed to be a *tranquil* force and in a certain sense made a much more universal impression, a force which entered into people directly from the creative Majesty, from outside, so to speak, without our human activity. But the forms, the colours, the movements and the rapidity of the movements (as well as their directions) of this second force, seemed to be a living and overt image of the momentary *disposition* of the respective *person*.

It pertained directly to the *feelings* and also to what the respective person *wills*. I must qualify, however, by pointing out that this form of the will is a completely different one from what I described as the force for the 'other' kind of seeing, which normally passes through the physical eyes. Both forms of the will are almost diametrically opposite to each other. In this case it is not an actual act of conscious willing, which is what the 'other' one is. Rather, it seemed to me when I considered this second force-body that the person involved was *subjected* in his will as well as his feelings – downright *delivered* to it.

What impressed me most was seeing a person screaming furiously. It was a situation in which I stood, shocked, before a person having a temper tantrum, so that the optical impression of his normally visible outer body disappeared from view and that force-body appeared before my 'inner' eyes, making visible in an awesome, terrifying way what made that person so furious. I felt the appearance of his violent interior before my 'inner' eyes as almost encroaching, because it seemed as if the vital image of his feelings only appeared because the excessive emotional overheating had, in a certain sense, broken through my usual vision.

What it really means when we say a person is completely 'beside himself' became clear to me in an impressive way through such observations. Because it can really happen, in the case of a very angry person, that his mobile feeling-willing-forces-body extends far beyond his actual 'mass'. It could go so far that this formation, and with it the sensations of the furious person, would smash into the feeling-willing-forces-body of another person, when the furious one was in his vicinity and directed his fury at him or her. According to my observation, he *wounded* the other person if he got too close, but without physically touching or striking him. This meant that the 'wounding' really took place. It would have hit him even had he been born deaf and could not hear the ugly words thrown at him; or if he had been born blind and could not see the wild gestures and distorted mimicking directed at him.

The inner force-currents of the violent person looked like an ugly, dark, brownish red – a roaring storm penetrated with glaring but essentially dark 'flashes' of destructive waves. They were like thunderclouds which clustered in a matter of seconds and discharged into the outer world. At the same time – this was a particularly terrible and tragic view – a kind of counter-movement took place in which they turned back like an arrow that is not shot but sucked in, so that the person's inner shape darkened and somehow diminished. Thus, what he wanted to project at others disfigured his own inner self.

The feeling-willing-forces-body of a person took on an especially peculiar shape when he wanted something most urgently. I realized that it was a certain variant of the kind of will which can overwhelm. Of course this person consciously 'wanted' the object of his desire. He definitely wanted it. But this wanting, in a sense, overwhelmed him. It seemed as though he couldn't resist his wanting, which was an extreme desire. Such a person seemed to me so greedy for the stilling of his thirst that his tongue was hanging out. When later, in Latin class, I studied the saga of Tantalus in Homer's *Odyssey*, I thought: This must be a metaphor for the image the greedy person makes of himself when the object of his desire is unobtainable, and those who created this myth must have had a similar image before their eyes as I have today.

I observed an unaesthetic yellow-greenish-grey rippling of the greedy person's feeling-willing-forces current. Later on I found the word 'slug' to be appropriate for such a person. For in a sense it was the opposite of what I observed in the angry person: the angry one actively sent something out to the outer world, which immediately bounded back at him, while something like clouds of fiends, swarms of unsightly vermin, attracted from the surroundings by his fury as if magnetized, followed him. The greedy one, however, executed with his inner force something like a clawing 'gesture' from outside, but at the same time his inner greed sprouted out like slugs and thereby emitted innumerable little descendants of his own feeling-willing-forces image in his surroundings; greedy 'parasites' that quickly buzzed apart, each writhing and twitching like a tormented worm. I often observed, appalled, how such plumes of greedy feeling-willing parasites extended in a deplorable way to the 'actual' or super-sensible world like the unfiltered fumes from a factory's chimney to the earth's air. And in both cases others, who had nothing to do with the event, are nonetheless affected. That was one of the most powerful discoveries of those early childhood days which affected me deeply: the fact that our feeling and willing impulses are by no means private affairs, but that they act upon the super-sensible outer world in which we all live, just as we all breathe the same air into our lungs because we all live in the same earthly atmosphere, and therefore everything that drifts into this atmosphere unavoidably harms every person on earth.

Until now I have only spoken about how an angry person and a greedy one appeared to my inner vision. So I have perhaps left the impression that this *feeling-willing-forces-body* is a repulsive, ominous thing that solely torments and abuses us. But that is only one side of that force! The feeling-will-forces-body can also be overwhelmingly beautiful. I began my story with the unpleasant side of this force-body because my first impression of it was as I have described here. Looking back I can say that seeing these instances in my early childhood happened of itself, when the inner appearance of a person drastically changed due to his extreme emotional situation; and that was unfortunately mainly the case when this happened in a negative way.

But this force-body could also present a completely different, joyous picture as, for example, when brilliant, radiant currents emerged from the area of the heart and, finally, enveloped the whole person. I perceived his interior as the source of warming rays of sun that enlivened and gladdened what was around him, for such an activity of the feeling-will-forces-body has a direct effect on the environment. How vividly the moments stand before my eyes in which such sublime sights were given to me! When a person showed such qualities it was often due to a feeling which we would call well-meaning, loving devotion toward his environment – or when he had an especially beautiful *thought*. By means of the formation, movements and colours of that force-body, one could tell if the thought which the person had just had was beneficial for the community, or the opposite. For thoughts were not shut up in the head and hidden like the contents of a treasure chest. I realized that thoughts were in a way similar to the feeling and willing impulses we bear within us. They come from *within*, hidden from normal eyes, but they influence the *general* sphere of life in which all humans think and feel.

The more I practiced such observations, the more I was able to work further on one or another of the questions which resulted from those observations. Thus with time I realized that a beautiful thought, which a certain person had, exerted a healing influence on his feelings and on those of another person; yes, even on the magical life-force. This was the case, however, only for thoughts that had no selfish content. For example, a person who was happy with an object he had long desired to the extent that it dominated his whole being, expressed neither the thoughts nor the feelings meant here. For in this case the joyful thought would be no more than satisfaction, no more than the emotional result of receiving the desired object. But the thought that is beautiful in the aesthetically understood sense, and is not only beneficial for the one who thought it but also for the whole community – and is thus 'true' or 'correct' – could have the healing effect meant here.

An equally seldom as well as impressive event was perceiving the thinking-feeling-willing-forces-body of a person who did not display the typically extreme eruptions in his thinking, feeling and willing impulses, but rather a habitual evenness. I have met few people in my life who display such equilibrium in their force-body. They were truly exceptions, whose inner reality was no secret to the outer world. They did not necessarily have to be educated in an academic sense, but due to a certain serenity, which was in no way indifference but rather wise composure, had an overview of life's bewildering trivialities, which could only have come from a life of much experience. They exuded a breath of eternity, a breath that seemed related to the essence of that creative Majesty, whose all permeating presence I had felt since my awakening days.

A wonderful calmness and security streamed from such a person, like the proverbial rock of strength in the churning waters of earthly confusion. In certain days of my childhood I would very much have liked to swim to one of these rocks to relax and find advice, and to confide in. But the encounters with such people were too brief during my childhood. They could be counted on one hand and were not situated at a place where I could communicate more closely with them. I encountered them accidentally and saw them from a distance. They soon went into the wide world and disappeared from my view, because they went their way while I was carried along a different stream of destiny. Nevertheless I realized – and it was a great help during my childhood and youth – that such people existed; people who through some deeply inner reality were, in contrast to others, *their own masters*. Therefore, in their own circles and more encompassing spheres they exuded a beneficial balm, without being necessarily always conscious of it. I never found out if they were mindful of the 'actual' World of Reality, the world of unclouded consciousness, and if they had thoughts similar to mine about its connection with this earthly world of forgetting. Also, through their exquisitely harmonious personality, they kindled the flame of admiration and reverence in me. I wished someday to be inwardly so beautiful, but not for one moment did I consider that to be possible; the distance to those venerable personalities was too great. This was not a covetous wish, but much more a deep longing to approach the World of Reality in order to return to it, and I sensed that this would be the only way. I would gladly have remained for a longer time in the vicinity of such a person, and I would have liked to learn the secret of the objective beauty of their personal force-body.

The halos found on paintings of saints seemed to me to be a simplification or cipher among the 'knowledgeable' artists for the forces-body of particularly venerable people. (In my early childhood

I hadn't known such paintings of saints. I learned about them during my time at school.) Much later, when in medieval art I discovered the *Pantocrator* in an aureola within a so-called mandorla encircling the entire body, but emanating from himself, I was deeply moved and joyful! Many frescoes or mosaics even showed them as rays of light emanating from the redeemer, others showed them as flames, whilst still others used the colours of the rainbow – all attempts to retain the never still, alive, many-formed, multidimensional and multicoloured event for the physical eyes of the viewer.

***

I never saw such clouds of forces – whether harmonious or distorted – in the plant kingdom though. The flowers, the shrubbery, the trees were all permeated with the magical life-force, which I discovered in plants a short time after I had first seen it in my sleeping grandfather. It wasn't like an uncontrollable throbbing, it didn't show that abrupt up-and-down bubbling, like in a rapidly alternating ebb and flow – now impressively beautiful, now repulsive forms and colours – as was the case with the feeling-forces-body. The colours of the magical life-force were also different in their inner essence; not so loud, as they sometimes were in human magical life-forces, whose colours might not be more intensive than those of the magical life-force, but in their relation to each other richer in contrast – partly intrusive, partly entrancing. The observation that the feeling-forces-body doesn't exist in plants strengthened my assumption that the forces, when their shapes are overstretched, are somehow related to the depletion of the magical life-force in humans. For I could never observe a damming up or interference of the magical life-force in plants, as I had in people. Even when a plant was dying, it seemed to me that the magical life-force left it in mutual agreement with the plant's being. Although it was clearly the same source from which the magical life-force came, and which provided earthly life in humans as well as in plants, its current within the various living beings – namely within humans on the one hand and in plants on the other – was distinctly different. In human beings it showed itself as more complicated and differentiated, but also mostly less untouched, less 'pure'.

I came to the conclusion that the occupants of the various bodies were not all the same. In a plant body, only the occupant's magical life-body was present. In a human being it was trickier. Of course, the magical life-force was also present – both the plant and the human being were living beings. But the magical life-body was not the only occupant of the human body. The second force, mostly defined by feelings, was also present. And this was clearly more individual than the magical life-force. For all people were capable of a similar spectrum of feelings. They could feel joy, desire, grief, fear, anger and more, as well as the finer nuances of those feelings. But each individual had differing intensities of feeling on different occasions. What could be observed by 'other' seeing was the person's feeling-forces body, and he mostly acted according to it.

But now I would like to take a step forward, for it is my intention to proceed chronologically as much as possible and to describe my inner life at each age, according to what actually happened. That isn't so easy, for a person's inner life develops in a regular flow; grave, abrupt turning points are not everyday events. So I have tried up till now to only describe what happened before the first great turning point in my life, namely when I started school, that is, between the awakening in my grandparent's living room and my sixth birthday.

This includes – aside from innumerable other incidents from which I have selected several – all those observations that I have just summarized. And these led again to the knowledge already mentioned, that those things made by human hands differed fundamentally from naturally developed things – they were without exception *dead* objects, because they were not derived from 'occupiers' and thus could not be made to come alive. Humans could not enliven the things made by them! Thus the humblest plant – a blade of grass, moss, a sprig of cress – were in a certain sense vastly superior to the most complicated, splendidly technical, material human invention – whether a mechanical child's whirligig, a television or an airplane. There was no competition – which was for me worthy of veneration!

I vividly remember the time in kindergarten when we pushed cress seeds into jars padded with cotton wool and then gave the tiny seeds water to drink. Then we placed the jars at the window in order to expose the seeds to sunlight. The next morning, when we rushed to the windowsill, little white tails were already emerging from the seeds. And the following morning the tails bore small green leaves. Naturally, no one thought of treating a piece of plastic the same way, expecting it to become a Lego object a few days later. But if that was so obvious, why didn't anyone speak about why the unassuming and immobile, dry cress seed could become a green edible plant, whilst the piece of plastic, also unassuming, immobile and dry, remained exactly as it was before being exposed to water and light? I remember precisely how we children were gathered in a half-circle around the jars and I was trying to muster the courage to express my thoughts in order to shake the pension-aged, authoritarian teacher from her reserve, so that she would speak about the magical life-force that must be hidden in the seeds. But at that moment another child said, *'Why is the cress growing?'* The teacher's answer was (with a slight, know-it-all manner): *'Well, we gave it water everyday and placed it in the sun.'*

I was annoyed and swallowed my question. That was no answer! In any case, that obviously wasn't the only reason that the cress grew! For otherwise, if we only had to give it water and light, something man-made would also have sprouted. I was bewildered. We had been shown the wonder of life, but without having investigated its cause. This experience – that the people around me, when they got to places where they must stumble, did not seem to have developed any questions about the world's 'actuality' – followed me throughout my entire childhood and youth.

The only explanation I found for the marvel of the seed's sprouting was that in every single seed the magical life-force slumbered and was awakened by water and light. For neither water nor light would help without the magical life-force!

Because of this event in kindergarten, for the first time I undertook the observation of the magical life-force, using the cress seeds. It wasn't so easy. Nevertheless, from what I had seen before about the magical life-force in plants and people, I had no doubt that the magical life-force must lie hidden, even in such a tiny, not yet sprouting seed. And this meant that it must have descended from another once-living plant. It bore the same majestic force within as the plant from which it descended. The immortal magical life-force coursed through plant and seeds in a mysterious transition of withering and becoming. And it was also true for animals and human beings – for every being that lives and dies.

This thought then became the holiest of sentiments, and I was seized by a blessed and thankful feeling. Plants and animals, and above all we humans, were living on the earth as wanderers immersed in the world of forgetting, but eternally connected with the World of Reality – when these three spheres of being interwove with the immortal life-force of the creative Majesty which embraced all being. Thus we carry within us a spark of that light which shone upon my earthly awakening days as the lofty consciousness of the creative Majesty, and reminded me of my actual being.

At that time I experienced myself (along with all human beings) as a cocky trapeze artist, who, without being conscious and thankful for it, flies over a safety net which was created and kept taut by invisible but clever beings. But it was, as I experienced it then, an *unearned* privilege, donated by that entity which only acted for our benefit. (Later, I realized that it is man's task to gradually spread his own net. It is a net of consciousness.)

It was also what I experienced while walking through the woods. I sensed, I experienced – even though I didn't always 'see' the powerful currents of the magical life-force that vivified all the woods, from the depths of the forest floor to the tops of the highest beech trees. And through these currents, the creative entity expressed itself. The currents of the magical life-force filled the woods with the most varied kinds of life. For they also attracted other 'beings' invisible to the eye, who gladly lived in the woods. So it was always a calming satisfaction when I heard people say that during a walk in the woods they had perceived a 'mysterious' atmosphere. Unfortunately, however, such comments were never elaborated upon, although the grown-ups sensed a distinct difference between the 'dead' wood transformed by human hands into a table and a living tree, even if they were not conscious of it.

When I think back on those days of my early childhood and the path of my inner life until starting school, I realize that my inner path was different than that of many other children about which one hears, especially from those working in education. Such people often say that a small child is very close to experiencing or remembering a spiritual world, whereas the growing child gradually loses such experiencing or remembering with the years, until it no longer even remembers that it had once remembered something different. I can confirm this kind of talk through a later experience with my little foster-son. At three years of age this boy told me with great confidence, to my amazement, about his experiences in the womb.

But a year later he already knew nothing about that, and nothing similar occurred to him at a later time. Compared to this, my own inner development seems all the more remarkable. I can truly say that my attention to the world that I considered to be the actual one since my awakening day, was never lost. On the contrary, as I grew older my attention became sharper, which led to exploration of ever more areas, so that with time a monumental mountain of experiences, discoveries and new questions were raised.

Perhaps I was also a kind of unusual late developer. For there was a phase in which movement within that other world, which in earlier years occurred naturally, sharply changed and the earlier natural 'abilities' diminished for a time, before they reappeared changed or newly understood. In the course of my story I will report more about this. This phase was between 15 and 16 years of age. The relationship to the World of Reality was in no sense lost during that time, however. When I consider today the development during my childhood and youth over all, I can say that the older I became, the less perfect was my original relationship to spiritual reality, that is, in respect to the unexamined existence of this relationship. But a counter-movement ensued: the conscious, willed occupation with partial aspects led to more precise partial results, which gradually merged into a more perfect whole, so that the older I became the closer I came to my original goal, namely to 'myself', to my 'actual' consciousness and therewith the World of Reality itself; for only with one's own actual consciousness can one enter the World of Reality.

For clarification of how lively the World of Reality was compared to the world of illusion for my childish perceptions during that phase, I will describe an episode which happened in kindergarten when I was about four years old. At the centre of this incident was the teacher already mentioned above. She was a very strict, authoritarian old woman who could, however, also be friendly or even gentle to a few favourites. She made no effort to disguise her sympathy for those other children. I didn't understand this strange behaviour and, with time, I had the feeling that it was very unfair and unjust, for with the best will I could not understand from the purely exterior appearance of this or that child why her sympathy was directed at those children and not others. I clearly did not belong to her favourites, but neither was I one of those whom she obviously could not stand at all. I felt very sorry for those children, and I wonder if they carried something from their oppressive experience into later life.

One day it came to an argument between her and a little boy who was one of those pitiful creatures that she had it in for. I don't know what the boy did to annoy her, but she screamed at him with a shrill voice that took my breath away. At first he cried, then also screamed. I stood rooted at the scene when suddenly the image of her feeling-willing-forces-body appeared before my vision. Everything happened at once: She grabbed the boy by the arm and dragged him to the lavatories. Once there, she locked him in a toilet stall where he would not be seen by her and where he was to cry himself out. At the same time I 'saw' what was happening *in* her, but not only her *feelings* – which were also clearly evident to the outer world – but I 'saw' her *thoughts*. Her thoughts were just as real in space as her physical form and actions. They were there! And shortly before she grabbed the child her soul-force-body, which had expanded into a fear-drenched gigantic monstrosity, developed an almost irresistible thought which sank down into her darkened, magical life-force-form. I saw her cruel thought take form: 'Now I'll paste the damned brat's mouth shut with tape. That'll teach him a lesson!'

I was agitated when I told about this shocking event at home. My mother was understandably appalled and she confronted the teacher. But during the discussion the teacher was able to find various witnesses that she had not pasted the boy's mouth shut. I was supposed to have 'excessive fantasy' – and that must be stopped in education as soon as possible with forceful measures. My mother felt understandably disgraced. Not only did she fall for a fantastic story and was given a better one by the teacher, but her own daughter was also a liar! But the defining consequence of this experience was not the ugly rebuke that followed, but that in a bitter way I had learned a very important lesson. One must learn to differentiate between what is revealed by inner vision and what takes place before the physical eyes. I understood that it is not one and the same if someone thought about something or if she carried it out. In the 'other' world a thought is just as real as an outwardly accomplished deed. It changes from a 'thought-of' fact to an actual fact. I have already mentioned that I had often inwardly experienced how the feeling-forces-body of a person could approach another person too closely, could assail him, without the angry one laying a physical hand on him. It was a real abuse of the feeling or soul-force-body – and above all of the magical life-force-form – of the other person, which had a destructive effect. It could make the person physically ill, even if the attack on his consciousness was not a lasting one.

But I couldn't tell my mother about any of that. The situation was already too complicated, or, rather, apparently clear: I lied or, in childish delusion, had greatly exaggerated and thus accused a blameless person, a person of authority no less, of a terrible transgression which, had it been true, could have had serious consequences for her future as an educator.

But a sense of having been misunderstood and unjustly treated was not what I felt. I was very contrite. I was terribly ashamed of what had happened, for the last thing I wanted was to accuse another person of something she had not done. Until then I simply hadn't understood clearly enough what relationship a person's inner life has with the appearance of his self in the outer world. In everyday life his inner deeds, which means his true thoughts and feelings, could be hidden behind a physical 'non-deed'. But in the spiritual World of Reality, nothing can be hidden; the thought is the deed there. And so what appeared to me was what was hidden in the physical world behind the 'non-deed': the actual lie.

But now I had a new problem. I felt guilty as a citizen of the sensory everyday world. According to the laws of this world I had not told the truth but had said something untrue, and therefore had lied. In the sensory everyday world only the sensory counts. And I had not really seen the teacher paste the boy's mouth shut. And because of that I felt very guilty, and it was terribly embarrassing for me to have to meet the teacher again the next day. Strangely enough, what I feared didn't happen – that she would consider me one of her 'enemies', one of her especially unloved children. I am not sure why that was so. Perhaps what my mother told her about her presumed attack perplexed her. She knew very well what she secretly wanted to do to the boy during that scene.

This affair was – however unpleasant – important to me. In the future one world would have to be clearly differentiated from the other world, and treated accordingly. The laws of this earthly world demanded it.

***

Shortly before my sixth birthday – a few months before I started school – we moved from our old home to a new one. It was also in a green part of the city, but the access was more direct, because we now lived on the ground floor. This move, an outward event, marked an inner turning point.

During the first years of life, my experience of the actual world and my experience of the everyday physical world ran alongside each other more-or-less free of friction, because both were equally astonishing and were therefore mostly accepted without judging. But at around my sixth year I began scrutinizing what I saw in one and then the other, and this increased more and more in the following years.

Whereas at first the observations were judgment-free, with time something was added. Because I observed things in two different areas, I gradually began to compare these observations and to seek the mutual relationship. This was necessary, because as these were observations of one and the same being or consciousness, the threads also came together at one and the same point.

The older I became, the more I experienced the discrepancy between those two worlds, sometimes painfully. One of the worlds, the one on this side, was permeated by the other one, but didn't recognize it, and for that reason looked and comported so differently.

Sometimes the earthly world seemed to be a cosmos in itself for which peculiar laws ruled – laws not posed by nature, but by some person or other, at some time or other. Of course I was fully integrated into this everyday life, but occasionally, and with time more frequently, there were moments when this cosmos seemed very outlandish. One was so busy doing all kinds of things in order to comply with these laws. For example, in the morning after getting up: brush your teeth, wash, dry, get dressed, brush your hair, carefully make the bed, prepare the kitchen for breakfast, eat breakfast, rearrange the kitchen… to mention only the most basic morning ritual. I realized that it made sense to wash a fork after using it and to put it back in its proper place in order for it to be readily available for use when needed again. But basically it seemed unimportant if the fork was washed immediately after use or before the next use, or whether it was placed to the right or to the left of the knife on the table. Yes, as opposed to that other world it was ultimately immaterial whether one carried food to the mouth with a fork, with a spoon or with a hand. Most of the time was occupied with innumerable unimportant rituals. And sometimes I feared that my life, and that of my family members, could pass without having dedicated to the actual world even a fraction of the time and attention that we do to earthly, everyday life.

I can't continue here without interposing an incident which set the course for the further handling of my experiences (regarding the 'actual' World of Consciousness) and my corresponding thoughts. I had learned to read some time before starting school. In order to encourage me to learn to read, my mother announced that it would be embarrassing to start school without knowing how to read, because other children would probably know already. There were surely other ways to instill enthusiasm for reading, but this method was very successful. I felt ashamed not to have myself thought of learning to read in order to prepare for starting school. So it went quickly. I remember one day sitting across from my mother at the dinner table. She wrote one word after another on a sheet of paper, turned the paper toward me, and I read the word out loud. I had a lot of fun with that game, especially when the words got longer and more complicated and I was able also to master that challenge. Once the telephone rang and my mother answered it, but continued to write down words during the conversation. Suddenly she said proudly and with a shrill tone, 'Now she reads the words upside down'. I remembered that sentence, because I was very glad to hear such recognition from my mother, and before an unknown grown-up!

Being able to read – although I certainly didn't begin to digest world literature! – was the starting point to a very differentiated development of my inner life. With this step something was activated which I would like to call, the ability to realize what could be learned from without and the comprehension of someone else's thinking. It extended the horizon to another level, whereby stronger contemplation resulted. Thus the new form and involvement with the outer, but still abstract, outer world resulted in the above mentioned differentiated development of my inner life.

At around that time I first came into contact consciously with the concept of religion. I was given an artistically illustrated children's Bible as a gift, which I read with great interest. I learned of concepts like 'God', 'heaven', 'angel', 'soul', 'pray', 'holy' – or at least I began to think about their meaning. That may sound strange. But what I had previously encountered *inwardly* about religion was from the 'pagan' world. It was only around the time of my sixth birthday that I began to associate certain religious concepts with incidents and beings which I had experienced inwardly. I was not always successful, however. Since that awakening day, my inner self was deeply pious, in a naturally religious mood, so to speak, because of those experiences. But this mood was not the result of some religious-confessional education – that is, from an exterior source. It was the result of my own inner experiences. And these were not always in agreement with the religious concepts – or in any event, what had been made of those religious concepts.

A word with which I had no difficulty was the word 'God'. What people called 'God' and also what Genesis described could only mean the immortal creative Majesty, whose all-permeating existence one could sense every day, and before whom my whole heart, my entire being, bowed. Now there was a name for this all-powerful, all-wise, beneficial entity: 'God' – although his name was also called ineffable, because some believers wished to reinforce his holiness. The word 'holy' was also quickly comprehensible. And I could also call 'holy' my understanding of 'God', who was 'holy', and my thoughts about God, which sprang from the *actual* consciousness shining into the murky sleepiness of earthly consciousness.

The word 'heaven' in the religious sense wasn't so easy. I had often heard heaven referred to on the radio as the setting for weather forecasts.* I heard, 'The heaven [sky] is mostly cloudy today', as part of the news. Also, when I asked why the heaven [sky] was blue or what was behind the heaven [sky], I received only prosaic answers such as: the heaven [sky] looks blue through the clouds because cosmic space behind it is black. In space there are other planets besides our Earth, and between the planets there is nothing – not even air. There was also quite different explanation, which obviously came from a religious context, for it was said with a dignified expression, probably meant as consolation: *'When a person dies, he goes to heaven.'*

This sentence occupied me intensely. There were several reasons for this. I tried to make sense of how someone can give one explanation as well as the other without stumbling on their thoughts. I came to the conclusion that the phrase about a dead person going to heaven was not taken seriously. In reality, people believed that as much as they believed in Santa Claus. For such a phrase was only used when it was the only available consolation for the loss of a loved one; it also brought the conversation about the loved one quickly to an end. This explanation seemed like a cheap consolation to me, because if what was meant was the concept of heaven as an airless, black cosmic space with planets flying around it, the phrase could not be taken seriously. In any case, it did not seem much of a consolation to me. Clearly, this was how many people handled the inevitability of death: in everyday life heaven [the sky] was an airless black space, and another heaven served only when a loved one was lost. But according to information received in answer to my questions, this other heaven could not be described more closely. I only learned that God was supposed to live there with many angels. And that's where we would also linger for all eternity after death. What a ghastly idea! *For all eternity.* Eternity meant a condition that would never end. *This* existence after death seemed to me to be an awful punishment. Was I never to leave that heaven? To simply be there for all eternity? Why? An ultimate penalty imposed by God? No! It couldn't be that – not what 'my' God, the Majesty who wishes well for all creatures, would let happen to us human beings! It could not be

---

* Translator's note: In German there is only one word, *Himmel,* for both heaven and sky.

41

that! I spent many nights with nightmare-like feelings, because that idea, which one was supposed to believe, was so terrible. It is not true that at six years of age one either unquestioningly accepts such explanations or dogmas without batting an eye, or brushes them aside as though one never heard them. Children are deeply influenced by what adults tell them about the world.

***

I tried, therefore, to advance in a different way with the concept of heaven. For example, it brought me to think more about the 'air-free' question, and I finally found a conciliatory element, a kind of bridge between the earthly material and the religious viewpoints. I said to myself: Maybe this cosmic space has something to do with the heaven in which God is supposed to reside after all. For if when I die I enter again the World of Reality, the world of the actual consciousness of my self, that would mean unification with the creative Majesty, with 'God'. But the sphere in which I perceived the activity of the creative Majesty was independent of earthly things. God interweaves in everything earthly, but he himself – as creative Majesty of the earth – was not dependent on it. His living essence, his power, I had perceived in the magical life-force, which also interweaves in us humans and vivifies our physical bodies. And although the physical body breathes in air and needs it to live, the magical life-force is not dependent on air. The magical life-force only enables the body to breathe in the air. For without it, the human being could not breathe. But my actual consciousness, which also must have existed earlier – as I realized on my awakening day – was *independent* of the place where it happened to be. It also existed when it was not in my physical body – like when it was sleeping, when one is not able to perceive earthly things, because one is not 'at home', that is, not in one's physical body. Thus my actual self also needed no air. On the contrary: where my actual self was at home, there was no air. For one needs it only for the earthly body. And also the feeling-forces-body – which, by the way, I had gradually come to assign the concept 'soul' – needed no air. It moved in a completely different sphere. It was itself a different sphere or level of human existence. So it was quite possible that the 'heaven' in which one entered upon dying was 'air-free'. Only I couldn't imagine that planets, and certainly not satellites and rockets, were flying around in this heaven – in the heaven of full consciousness interwoven with creative Majesty.

I couldn't resolve these contradictions. In any event, due to the concept of heaven and its definition, I ran into the great discrepancy between the *earthly-material* worldview and the *religious* one. Neither one seemed entirely correct to me, for they both lacked something essential. The earthly-material lacked the recognition and necessary devout feelings for the immortal creative Majesty and its commitment to us: our actual consciousness, our true selves. On the other hand, the religious viewpoint lacked the passionate urge for systematic research and discovery of the exact conditions of super-sensory and sensory existence.

The religious concept with which I could at least begin with was the word 'angel'. When the word angel rang out I imagined the chocolate figure packed in aluminum foil that I saw around innumerable Christmas trees placed in department stores weeks before the holiday, or for sale as pictures in postcards or kitschy ceramic dolls, namely figurines of little naked baroque statues with shocks of hair and stubby wings on their backs. (Had the artist Raphael imagined what would be made of his *Sistine Madonna* five hundred years later, he might have dispensed with the two dainty little boys on the lower border.)

Anyway, it was a long time before it dawned on me that what came before my heart and inner eye on certain occasions as a spiritually powerful entity could well be named 'angel'.

Unfortunately, I could seldom find anything in the outer world that was in agreement with my own inner experiences. Old Testament stories that described how the patriarchs and prophets of ancient Israel communicated either with angels or even directly with God came closest to being helpful. I had never experienced that. 'God' himself had never spoken to me. And the angel speaking in the Old Testament stories was impressive, but was also not what I encountered. A few years later I realized that I had taken the passages much too literally and that they were only appropriate for earthly-sensory events. It also may have had something to do with the text in my secularized children's Bible. Naturally the angel did not 'tell' the prophet Elijah in his mother tongue (ancient Hebrew) to go to the king of the Moabites and state this and that, but Elijah was 'told' in a different way, and that way could have had something to do with what I experienced.

But then, around the time when I began school, I found no reference point to what had been communicated to me, and I felt that to be more and more unsatisfactory. It was namely the time when I was developing a deeper relationship to the all-wise, benevolent, creative Majesty, whom I more and more often called 'God'. I could not shake off the question of where the magical life-force came from and where I came from – where we all came from. It was not an intellectual question, but a truly heartfelt one.

One night I received an answer. Until that day I had perceived the creative Majesty just as I have sketched it here: as the hidden cause of the life-force in other living beings as well as in my conceptual discoveries concerning my 'actual' self, my consciousness. That night, however, a portion of that world – which can open to one if the truly essential things become an affair of the heart – was 'shown' to me. This can happen if one asks a question from the deepest impersonal need, and is not so presumptuous as to think that all questions can be answered by one's own reason – that is, without help. In this respect I had enormous luck. Such hubris did not occur because my young age prohibited it, and the defining impressions and experiences of my entire life precluded further temptation in this direction from the beginning, for the childish experience of the creative Majesty and its world planted an incomparable humility and reverence forever in my heart. Not once did I feel that the creative Majesty demanded such humility. And this grandness, never to demand humility, only increased my humility. Only it's not a contrite humility, but a fully joyous one.

That night I got a glimpse of what human consciousness is, that consciousness that can remember itself. I, meaning my consciousness, my actual self, moved in a non-spatial, infinite (not threateningly large, but simply infinite) sphere in which each thought 'lived'. And these living thoughts came from other 'selves'. I swam, as it were, in the thoughts and at the same time in the other selves. Thus I participated directly in the thoughts they sent out. The selves were in a certain sense their own living thoughts. Due to this participation, I was (that is, my actual self, my consciousness) a living, thinking, being within the selves and thoughts. I was like a single ear that listened to the living thoughts which went through me and, as strange and improbable as it may sound, in this way I participated directly in the all-embracing wisdom of the creative Majesty. The cosmic thoughts on the cosmic 'construction' of the world edifice passed through me, were present in me. I 'understood' – directly experiencing – what the 'actual' consciousness is.

This seemed to be an infinite artistic carpet woven from innumerable living threads. Everything created, every being, whether visible or invisible, every improbable feeling, every slightest or ultimate thought, originating from any being, and every deed implemented, as well as the unbreakable cosmic laws, the cosmic facts – they all comprised single threads in the carpet, in whose spiritual weave even a grain of earthly sand was given an indispensable task. If one pulled on a single thread – which occurred continuously, for all was living – it would have an effect on the whole carpet. Everything hung together and was multidimensional! The carpet is only an inadequate image. Everything hung causally together, and for all time. It was clearly shown that when you make this or that decision today, as trivial as it may seem to be, it is not your affair alone. It has – even if you cannot see the connecting threads with your everyday consciousness – consequences in the whole cosmos of being; and the echo within the cosmic edifice is such that the future is also shaped by it. And I saw how every decision also has deep roots in the past, so that future and past are held together by present human conscious thinking. But that was only a hint, an insight in the temporal and causal processes on earth, the transient world. There, where my actual consciousness sojourned that night, everything called past, present and future on the earth was a single non-temporal, super-temporal essence, like that carpet in which everything is so interwoven that one cannot claim that one thread is more or less important, more 'past' or more 'future', than another.

It was the *higher plan* that I encountered, the existence of which I had already somewhat surmised, and which in that state of consciousness I could easily observe. That night I was 'wise' – in the higher sense truly wise – for I was allowed to participate in the higher thoughts in which I swam. Every question that arose in me was immediately an answer. I didn't have to exert myself, it was simply how it was.

But I always had the impression that I was only allowed to visit in this way on *exceptional* occasions. Internally I realized that every person, including myself, received a 'gift' as a created being; but that I would have to contribute something in order to activate this gift – to prove myself worthy by wanting and learning to someday *permanently* achieve that all-wise consciousness.

When I woke up in my earthly consciousness the next morning, I had forgotten the content. This earthly consciousness was truly a world of forgetting! I greatly regretted that I could recall nothing of the world's magnificent structural design. But what remained indelibly in my everyday consciousness was the *impression* that the World of Reality, and my visit to it, had made. It was the impression of truthfulness. This truthfulness had hardly anything in common with things or events that we consider truthful with our earthly understanding. Words fail when, after a visit to the World of Reality, one wishes to describe God's truthfulness for normal understanding. There is absolutely nothing about it one could object to. It is limitless, immanent and at the same time indescribably beautiful. Although it may seem absurd to everyday comprehension to describe an abstract concept like 'truthfulness' as 'beautiful', the truthfulness of the creative Majesty *is* really beautiful; for the concept 'beauty' has an entirely different, absolute meaning in the World of Reality and Truthfulness, because of not being subjective.

From that day on I was more inspired than ever by the thought of bringing the world of forgetting, in which we live, closer to the World of Truthfulness and Reality. And I could only accomplish that by first trying to approach the World of Truthfulness and Reality myself. But how terribly difficult that was! Where should I begin? I remembered the living thoughts of the very self who had inspired me that I should do something to use my gift that the creative Majesty had implanted in me so that I would remember the real world again. But what kind of a gift was it? It would be impossible to use if I hadn't even discovered what it was yet.

I stood before a great dilemma. Once again it became clear to me by means of an occurrence, this time a super-sensory one, that I should *remember*; remember my actual self, which could live within the creative Majesty wisely, knowledgeable of itself and all other facts. But *how* should I begin?

I decided to ask an adult. Until that moment I had not confided with another person about my many observations and the resulting conclusions and questions. Something stopped me. I had of course realized that no one ever spoke of such things. I explained this strange circumstance to myself by assuming that 'one' simply didn't talk about such things. I presumed that the silence about the other world was a kind of known and observed codex, the sense of which I didn't understand yet, but which had to be observed. On the day after my visit to the World of Truthfulness, I plucked up courage and spoke with my mother about it. I wanted to know what I should do in order to be able to return to the state of consciousness or existence experienced on the previous night.

I no longer remember exactly how I expressed my concerns. I don't think I was even able to express my actual concerns. I began by describing the enormous experiences bestowed upon me. My mother was probably greatly surprised by this surely clumsy attempt to explain. Today I think: Who is prepared to hear such things? She surely didn't mean to hurt my feelings. But her reaction was the decisive cause for my never again mentioning my inner experiences to another person, from that day until I was twenty-six years of age.

I had just begun to explain when her reply cut off my words as by a sharp knife. It was made clear to me, with a short and unmistakable statement, that such crazy ideas would not be tolerated, and that my derailment was probably the result of my relationship with her eccentric-leaning mother-in-law. Thus was the affair closed for my mother, and I can well imagine that she doesn't even remember the scene today, because for her it was simply unimportant.

But her reaction was a real shock for me – which naturally my mother didn't realize. Because of the content of her reply and the manner in which it was given, three facts were immediately obvious: Firstly, the reaction was – although not meant to be hurtful – basically destructive. As I later thought back on what had happened, I realized that I was not at all offended. It was much worse than that! What really shocked me was that what I – especially in my nocturnal experience – recognized and revered as the holiest 'sanctissimum' (this pleonasm may be excused because it fittingly describes my feeling then) was so abased, degraded and not taken seriously that is was effectively mocked. That reaction seemed to be an unforgivable desecration of the divine entity to which my mother and the whole world owe their existence. Without its will and force, man would not even have a mouth with which to mock. I felt that the reaction was directed against what was the most precious, noblest and fairest; against what was higher than human reason can comprehend; against what one should only show the most profound respect. And for this reason I swore that never again would a word about my experiences, impressions and questions concerning God's World of Reality pass my lips. I made this oath in order to protect the sanctissimum from the obviously 'unknowing'. I remained true to my sombre oath for 20 years.

The second fact which became clear to me as the result of this scene was that the people around me had no similar experiences, and therefore had no thoughts similar to mine. The World of Reality was hidden from them; they had forgotten it. There was no codex of silence! They simply knew nothing of that world. I considered my mother to be a not untypical representative of my human environment, from which her singular reaction reflected a general attitude. None of the others spoke about the World of Reality either. And even if my mother was the only one who had no such experiences and others around her did, she would surely not have reacted in that way because she would have heard something about super-sensory facts from others. No, it was evident: people 'saw' neither the magical life-force nor the soul-force-body; they did not encounter – at least not consciously – the other selves who live in the World of Reality and Truthfulness; they didn't recognize the cosmic carpet in which every being and every fact is interwoven with its own meaning and effectiveness; they didn't sense that they themselves were 'higher' selves in that World of Reality – that their actual consciousness lives there, waiting to be reunited with them. At that moment it became clear to me that to continue living on this earth was going to be a real challenge. In order to 'survive', from then on I would have to act as much as possible as someone who was expected *not* to make the observations which I *did* make.

And therewith the third fact became obvious: what I called 'the World of Reality' was considered to be pure invention due to personal conceit. Nevertheless, I did not for one second think that I had erred – that the insinuation was perhaps justified. As I write this, I already hear the critical objections, which can perhaps be summarized by the assertion that it's a sign of insanity which the insane one does not realize as such; or that the judgment about my experience is erroneous because I did not question it. But I can and must live with such criticism. Whoever has once entered the World of Reality, or has only a hint of contact with it and its creative power, knows the phenomenal difference between a mere representation and an encounter with the reality. Even if it was a representation in which one was deeply involved, it could never convey the self-evident nature of the reality and truthfulness as only the reality and truthfulness can. So *in that sense* my mother's reaction didn't irritate me. But it led, as I said, to my keeping my inner life strictly closed to the human outer world from that day on. (After such a grace-filled, self-evident experience, someone who would question the existence of the World of Reality and its consciousness-being is seriously – namely in the soul-spiritual sense – *sick*.)

A result of this event was also that I invented a name for the earthly world of everyday consciousness, from an admittedly growing sense of frustration: the 'day-theatre-world'. This world of everyday consciousness in which one lived, mainly during the day, was like an absurd theatre as opposed to that spiritual world in which I could 'enter' undisturbed, mostly during the night. What I experienced in the World of Reality was undoubtedly much more real than anything that could even exist in the earthly world. In comparison, the earthly material world seemed to me like a gigantic illusion, like a mirror-image as opposed to the reality which made the mirror-image possible. No, often more like a distorted mirror-image of reality, for the actors in the play didn't even realize that they were in a theatrical production. They moved in a world of illusions, but they created concrete facts which had consequences in the World of Reality.

At this time, therefore, I could not recognize much that was going on around me as having any connection with my hunt for actual consciousness or existence. Nobody except me seemed to be hunting for it. I felt that the most important thing of all, the hunt for reality, was not unfolding – at least not in my immediate surroundings. Life began in two worlds, and soon I became a master of adaptation, a chameleon actress on the corrupt stage of the everyday theatre.

***

Due to this situation, a conflict gradually arose between me and the Day-Theatre-World's 'actors'. The most important of these were my parents and grandparents, but also teachers and acquaintances – in other words those adults who to the child – to me – represented authorities.

At first the question essential for my inner conflict was not very clear, that is, what the object of my subconscious question really was – i.e., the observation of our *actual humanity*.

Something in me kept returning to the riddle of the observed 'soul-force-body', which often overlapped with the magical life-force-body and depicted a true, vital and therefore continuously changing picture of fluctuating human wishes and feelings.

I have already mentioned that I had earlier seen the soul-force-body as someone *'flying off the handle'*. This expression related directly to the soul-force-body, for one could really see in the human forces a 'flying off the handle' – also, a herd of wild horses that stormily flies off in all directions. But I also discovered the opposite case, whereby the human forces offered a beautifully formed aesthetic image. A person with such a soul-force-body was naturally in a correspondingly balanced and peaceful state of mind. With special people – such as I have already mentioned – their soul-force-body, their soul-image, was almost always beautiful, and the reason lay undoubtedly in the fact that they were always *masters of themselves*. They were not overwhelmed by their wishes and feelings, which did not become at all vehement, unlike what generally happens with most people.

But what did it actually mean: that a person is not overwhelmed by his feelings or (in the opposite case) he flies off the handle or is distraught? Who was this 'he' who was not overwhelmed? Who was 'he' who flew off the handle or was distraught?

I had previously observed how the currents of the soul-force-body acted in two people according to the same principle, which meant that certain feelings, like anger, sadness or joy – also certain nuances of colour and movement patterns, as well as movement

50

directions – was caused by the soul-currents. But the older I got – and this question began to persist at the beginning of my school time – the greater became my motivation to find out what it actually was that enabled us not to lose our composure. I didn't wonder about this in a strictly scientific sense, that is, I didn't undertake to solve the problem on the basis of a formulated question, but it bothered me simply because of my observations. For I could (with the already described 'technique' of the other 'seeing') directly discern that the soul-force-body acted in a fascinating way at the moment when the person made the decision not to allow their feelings or wishes unbridled free rein. It was as if the ruler of a foolish population gave an order, which they then all obeyed. Thus, it all depended on whether the ruler of the soul-force-body appeared or did not appear. Or formulated differently: whether this 'ruler' *slept* or was *awake*.

It was this discovery that built a path to the impression first gained on my awakening day, that the 'earth-body-consciousness' is, as a rule, a sleeping one, because the 'ruler is not at home' – namely, our actual awake consciousness is not together with it. This actual consciousness of our self, which one acquired when awakening in the World of Reality and Truthfulness, meant that the ruler of the foolish population must be consciously within. And the 'fools' were our feelings and wishes that we did not bring to consciousness! They always cavorted and vagabonded when the ruler was not at home. But when he was, they could be personable, neat and eager to learn.

This observation brought me to the just mentioned inner conflict with those who were my educators and whose decisions and instructions I had to respect – actually much-loved people – who therefore acted as my role models. Of my close family members, namely my parents, I almost daily came up against the invisible true image of their spiritual bodies, which arose when the ruler wasn't at home – when the fools, that is, my parent's craved needs, were allowed to enslave them. During my entire childhood, both parents were heavy smokers. Not only was the foul-smelling smoke most unpleasant, but also, and above all, was this weakness in respect to the object of their craving: the cigarette. I 'saw' how my parent's soul-force-body bloated when their craving for a cigarette increased, how it released an unbelievable potential. Its image could be compared to a trembling and snorting dragon, blind with greed, that has only one thought: to get what it wants – but goes crazy when it can't have it immediately. It was shocking to see how the actual human being, the 'ruler' who should keep order at home, was clearly very weak; could think of nothing better and made no effort to go back 'home' and rein in the dragon's fools. And I also discovered that this habit of the soul-force-body left something like an 'imprint' over the years, so that I perceived something in the magical life-force-form that I find difficult to express in words. From it streamed something back – clearly from the continual yielding to the desire to smoke – which could be called the power of habit. It imprinted a shadow in the magical life-force-form and, through this, a counter-image which was more powerful than the form which had created it, namely the soul-force-body. By means of its continuous prevalence, a wild power was exerted from the sphere of the soul-force-body on the transformed magical life-force-form which caused it to dance like a marionette, so that the 'ruler at home', the actual human core, seemed to be totally lost.

This was a pitiful sight, but as a child it mostly awoke in me a strong dislike. I felt repelled by it, but I felt more repelled by the weakness which was evident at such moments in my parents – the weakness of not being the ruler in one's own home. It was embarrassing; I was ashamed before the spiritual world by my parent's weakness. I was ashamed because they seemed to have surrendered their higher consciousness, and therewith their higher will, when it came to smoking. (As vindication, it should be mentioned that in later years both of my parents found the will to stop smoking permanently. And the transformed magical life-force-form also learned to stop demanding that the soul-force-body eliminate the addiction.) Nevertheless, during my childhood and youth, the smoking was a constant companion and thus a recurring reminder of the actual decline of my parents' human core. Because of this, a serious conflict of authority arose within me, which I never revealed, because it was clear to me that I had to respect my parents.

For me, the real authority was the person who was a master at dominating himself. And not so that he had to continually struggle against his lower nature (struggling could only be the first step), but one in whom conquering his lower desires had become a consciously acquired power of habit. Therefore, the highest authority for me would be the person who did not have to fight back mightily against the challenge to his soul-force-body, because he – his actual self – had already liberated himself through inner maturity.

An example was the cascading effect in the 'invisible' but *actual* human being – the actual self, who was conscious of himself and thus the 'ruler in the house'. This *core of the human being* could act in a corrective way on the *soul-force-body*, which in turn gave the *magical life-force-form* a beneficial and supporting impression. When this happened, the *physical-material body* was also protected from all kinds of disturbances, because the magical life-force-body could care for it undisturbed. At the very top stood this actual self, whose home was in the World of Reality and Consciousness. This was the actual 'higher' human being. Conversely, a rising cascading action was seen when one followed the disturbing forces. The needs which led to disturbing the highest 'occupant' often had to do with purely physical existence. A foreign power acted on the magical life-force, which made the soul-force-body its marionette. And this let the soul-force-body take on overly exuberant conditions, and a disastrous interplay followed between it and the magical life-force-form, until the actual human being seemed to abandon its corrective function.

So there was a *third* living form in us humans besides the magical life-force and the feeling-will-forces-body (the soul). In our physical body the actual ruler also resided: our higher self, the *core of our actual human being*. And this was able to make conscious decisions and resolutions. I recognized here a totally different will than the one in the feeling-will-forces-body or the soul; namely the will to be not obliged to will something!

Unfortunately I could not 'see' this *human being core* as I saw the magical life-force-form and the soul-force-body. Nevertheless it – this invisible highest entity – was definitely present. And I gradually came to realize what it was: If I wished to name my actual humanity, I would have to point to this 'core of being', which was none other than 'I'. It was a few more years before it was directly perceptible to me. Nevertheless, even then it was clear it existed, for the *consequences* of its *action* or *lack of action* were visible. I could 'see' what happened when it remained passive. And I also saw what it could do positively. Only *it* made each individual person unique.

It was in this context that I pondered the religious concept of 'temptation', which had too moralizing a character in the confessional context. For me a temptation was a challenge to be defeated, over and over, until it surrendered. That seemed to be a temptation that made sense. I found that a temptation could have quite a useful meaning on the way to a soul's maturity. Expressed differently: The value of an inner and an outer act is only really present if the person could resist a temptation; if he decided 'correctly'. If on the other hand there was no possibility of falling into temptation, every good deed would be a boringly obvious matter, without the insight of the person involved.

If, because of my observation of my parents' changed 'invisible' forces-body-forms, difficulties arose in seeing them as role models, my observations and resulting insights also had a positive result: In my whole life I have never even touched a cigarette, let alone any other addictive or narcotic agent. It was impossible for me to betray my own self, my true higher human being, by voluntarily (or more likely thoughtlessly) allowing it to descend to the level of a jumping jack of its lower desires.

***

When I was six years old, something entered my life that was to become one of the most dependable supports on the arduous path through that world that had forgotten itself, and in which I often felt like a thirsty stranded person. What enriched my daily life in that world beyond measure was music.

Thankfully, my parents had already exposed me at kindergarten age to musical training in a more-or-less well behaved group of about 15 children in the Charlottenburg music school. Besides singing – which I had already learned from my mother and liked – we learned to play simple tunes on a small xylophone with red metal keys, that encompassed around one and a half octaves. Making tunes, the possibility to produce various sounds to one's heart's content, gave me great pleasure. By contrast, I took the drum and triangle and tapped them when they were given, but otherwise left them alone. Reading notes in treble clef was also taught and practiced.

My enthusiasm for more complex music, especially classical music when it was played on the radio between the usual popular hits, or on Sundays after breakfast when my father put a record on the phonograph, was not hidden from my parents. I also kept saying how much I would like to learn an instrument. But not any instrument; I wanted to learn to play the piano.

During Advent, which followed my sixth birthday, the doorbell of our apartment rang. My mother stormed into my room and told me, somewhat harshly, that I was to stay in it. She would tell me when I was allowed to leave. In spite of the closed door, I heard her telling the visitor to please take the object 'down below', which meant the basement area belonging to our apartment, where my father's study was also located. I knew immediately what was to be brought below because there was no room for it above. My happiness could not be expressed in words. I can only say that I had never felt such happiness until that day, and even until today I have never felt such joy over a material object as I did on the day my piano was delivered. I jumped on to my bed and put a pillow over my mouth so my cry of joy would not be heard.

The days until Christmas would have been hardly bearable if I had not been such a passable actor on the stage of the 'day-theatre-world'. I could not let it be known that I already knew what was 'down below'. It was supposed to be a surprise and I did not want to deprive my parents of the satisfaction of experiencing how happy I would be at receiving it, the fulfilment of my most heartfelt wish.

Soon thereafter I had my first piano lesson. It took place in a music school in Wilmersdorf, in a huge empty hall at one end of which was a solitary piano. At that piano sat a wonderful young teacher. When she began teaching me she had already finished her musical studies majoring in piano and was studying theatre at the Berlin Academy of Arts. The way she approached and introduced me to the world of musical sounds as well as technical finesses, in order to coax relatively good sounding melodies from the piano, was unique. The best part was when, at the end of the lesson, she composed pieces to practice. Her pieces were better than the usual children's practice literature, because they were aimed exactly at my current development and were at the same time creative and witty. She animated me to practice, which did not feel at all like practice, but as play, 'playing' music. Each piece had an onomatopoeic title, for example 'Gustav with the Horn' (the squawking drum!), 'Dottie and Anton', a piece with dotted notes and rhythms, or 'Trees in the Rain', a piece to be played in soft staccato phrasing, like raindrops falling from leaves. I remember a piece called 'Black Sheep' in which only (almost) black keys were used, with the warning: 'attention, a white key has been smuggled in', and another with the title, 'A smiling and a crying eye', denoting the change from major to minor keys. The notes were always adorned with appropriate, funny and skillful sketches, as was my notebook. Her explanation for the full and half-rest symbols was especially expressive. Who notices off hand if the bar for the full-rest sign lies on the note line or hangs from it? A whole ham was drawn in my notebook that hung from a meat hook (from the note line) and alongside it half a ham that lay on a board (on the note line).

No one else in my childhood impressed me with such creativity and imagination. I absorbed her suggestions like a sponge. I blossomed through her. She soon wrote out my first self-composed piece for me, which we called 'Brummel-Bummel-Hummel-Train'. For a short period, a person entered my life with whom I had hardly any contact beyond the weekly piano lessons and therefore never found the opportunity to share my experiences and questions, but whom I felt was totally natural and authentic. It was a great loss for me when she moved to Hamburg a few years later.

Perhaps my account is somewhat rambling, but this kind of imaginative devotion by a teacher was really a great and beneficial exception during my childhood. Naturally, it impressed me very much, and illustrates how important it is for a child hungry for spiritual nourishment to receive it. Moreover the lessons – and this is why I have mentioned this episode – had the effect of awakening my musical ear and sensibility. As early as the second lesson she wrote a single-line piece for me that contained all the note values up until the eighths as well as various rest lengths. Above she wrote: 'Listen! Not count!' This listen – the careful listening to the essence of the piece – was not easy. And even today I think that it is fundamentally most important if one truly wants to feel the music. Not counting, not technical knowledge. When one really listens, one feels the music as it really is and the counting – or, rather, the rhythmic precision – comes of itself. I basically played everything from memory, and also many new things by ear. Naturally, that had the disadvantage that I became a miserable 'player by note', to the point where my piano teacher, unnerved, held the piano lid close over my hands so I was forced to read the notes. So finally I did not become an 'active' musician, although I continued to have lessons until I was 16 and have continued to play by myself. Instead, I became a passionate 'passive' musician in the sense that a completely new, incomparable world opened to me through listening to music – a world that made it possible to come into contact with the World of Reality in a different way.

Real listening is also a truly active process! One must not merely be exposed to it, but must enter into a reciprocal relation with what is behind the music, so to speak. I experienced music – and in order to avoid misunderstanding I must add that I only listened to classical music – as a perceptible gift from the World of Reality, from the world of creative Majesty, in which the wisdom-filled cosmic plan was woven. Thus, music was a bridge between the spiritual and earthly worlds, a bridge that was accessible from both sides. It let a whiff of God's breath into everyday consciousness, sweet and comforting, lovingly admonishing, reminiscent of the World of Reality in which the benumbed heart could be alive again and truly *feel*. At the same time it let the nostalgic heart cross the delightfully sonorous bridge to the home it so yearned for. To me it was as though music, through the physically perceptible tones, created a place on earth where the World of Reality opened a 'campsite'. At first I feared that it would be a transitory campsite, which the fickle flurries of the sensory world would soon sweep away along with the divine messenger's gift from the World of Reality. After the last note fades away, the boisterous everyday world, with its tumultuous noisy trivialities, would swallow the just created living magic. But I soon realized that the campsite could be built on solid ground within the earthly world, if the music awakens true life-forces in the hearts and thoughts of its listeners; if, over the bridge of music, the spiritual world is able to drop anchor in the hearts of human beings. Then, the divine messenger's gift would not be lost. It was then not only enduring, but made life easier for one, without the need for interchange with others about the essential questions of existence. Still more, one could even give to the world something of the invigorating spiritual repast which had been received.

I have my parents to thank that they took me to concerts already when I was in primary school, often to the Berlin Philharmonic and the opera. A little later, I could accompany friends of my parents or acquaintances. I also had free entry to the Philharmonic through a classmate's father, who played the violin with the Philharmonic but could not make his own daughter like classical concerts. Despite regular visits to concerts, my daily routine would not have included music if I didn't have a record player in my room. My piano playing was not sufficient, and I couldn't improve much because every time I touched a key, a cranky old battle-axe in the floor above ours banged with a metal object on the radiator pipe that extended down to my room. My first records were *Yehudi Menuhin Describes the Orchestra's Instruments*, Sergei Prokofieff's *Peter and the Wolf* and (my favourite) *The Carnival of the Animals* by Camille Saint-Saëns (comments by Loriot). These choices were useful for learning and sensing the characteristics of the instruments, differentiating them, and perceiving their effects when playing together.

It must have been at the beginning of the eighties when I received a cassette recorder as a present and my first cassette: Tchaikovsky's *Sleeping Beauty* and *Nutcracker*. I remember my disappointment at first when I realized that the recording did not include a commentary on the music and its history. But when I played it again I was greatly surprised: the music related everything, *even more* than could be expressed in words. Soon it became clear that a commentary, arranged by a commentator, would be a subjective barrier to what the music really had to say; furthermore, spoken words between the individual movements would perturb terribly the music's flow. I began to appreciate the value of orchestral music.

It wasn't long before I was given a Walkman, although compared to today's standards of quality, it was practically of Stone-Age primitiveness. Being able to play cassettes 'on the go', however, was an enormous enrichment for me, because through the earphones – without being bothered by noise from without – I could freely repeat and study certain passages which would perhaps not be of interest to someone else. I could finally be alone with the music. I didn't play the whole cassette on the go – only later at home, whilst I sat in bed. For hours on end. Until late at night. My cassette collection grew quickly. Some Bach and Brahms constituted my 'passive repertoire'. (Unfortunately I didn't know early music, like Renaissance music, and when I first heard it I felt that something that was indispensable for my inner life had been withheld from me.) In my early childhood classical, followed by baroque (in second place) and romantic (in third place), were my absolute favourites – and as their representative, ahead of all other composers by an unrivalled distance: Wolfgang Amadeus Mozart. It goes without saying that the pleasure given by music from a Walkman was relative, and when I was again in the presence of a live orchestra, it was as if the gates of Paradise had opened. The technical medium was more a 'crutch' which enabled me to get to know various composers and their inner worlds. One had to let the music speak for itself.

When I speak here about 'worlds' which were opened to me by hearing music, it is not just a means of expression to emphasize my enthusiasm. It is much more about how music expressed, in a wonderful way, the composer's world. I 'understood', for example, how people lived, thought and felt – perhaps in a more authentic way than through history lessons – during the era in which the composer of a certain piece lived. I then deepened my impressions during the day by referring to all kinds of books and magazines. I studied how people dressed, how they acted, whether they were times of peace or war, whether there was a king or an emperor, what one would have seen with the eyes of those times: the cities, the architecture, the scenery. I buried myself in the complex expression of life in the particular era, and when during the following nights I listened again to the music of that time, I was myself well-nigh a resident of the relevant country and time. Through the music, in my imagination I lived together with people in near or distant cities or countries from past times, which became present again in my thoughts, and in which I was completely immersed.

In Händel's *Music for the Royal Fireworks*, great gondola-like, lavishly decorated boats of the English court glided along on the glassy smooth Thames, under a deeply black starry night. The truly royal music from the orchestra, dispersed among various boats, rang out over the river banks lined with people and illuminated by torches, deep into the streets and over roofs and church towers. Only during the pauses between movements did I hear the water lapping against the bows of the boats, the beat of the oars and the gay babble of the onlookers' voices. With the introduction of the fourth movement, La Réjouissance, I saw the colourful fireworks illuminate the sky over London, the sparks of which fell into the river, and I imagined the boom of the artillery that I heard was at the behest of the king, in order to announce the birth of the heir to the throne. I felt the joy, the enthusiasm and the emotion in the hearts of the people at the arrival of the prince. I admired the noble gentlemen with their powdered wigs and brocaded costumes and the accompanying noble ladies in their wide, heavy dresses, as well as the simple people in the streets with their heads thrown back, staring at the superb fireworks, sometimes whispering in amazement, sometimes uttering loud cheers with delight. Certainly, it was all merely imagination. Nevertheless, my imaginative stories were based on realities deriving from that era and preserved in music. They were packed in small packages and tied up, but one could easily take them out again with the music and awaken them to life. Only then did the recordings become music in the actual sense.

During that early time Mozart was my one and only. I buried myself in his biography like in no other; I read various monographs and his letters. I also began to study and compare the handwriting of several 'great' people, observed contemporary portraits for hours and attempted to obtain a true idea of how such people – especially a Mozart – must have acted and spoken in everyday life, under white makeup and powdered wigs and Sunday suits, sitting for portraits. But it was mainly the music that revealed to me the actual histories, namely the thoughts and feelings of the composers and their experiences in the *World of Spiritual Reality*. This is where significant differences existed! Whereas many composers provided information about the era in which they lived, their personal moods and thoughts about the world of the past, which was without question informative and entertaining and perhaps now and then touching, few others had anything else to offer – namely direct, conscious and thus 'higher' experiences with the *World of Reality*. And it was these whose music was awarded the eternal seal of approval – of eternal 'validity' and truthfulness – by whose music not only the listener's soul-force-body, but also his immortal human core was affected. No offence meant, but from a Johann Strauss (irrelevant in this case whether father or son) the listener immediately receives an impression of the social environment and habitus of the times. But, with due respect, what is a Jean-Philippe Rameau compared to Johann Sebastian Bach? Or even a Johann Nepomuk Hummel compared to Wolfgang Amadeus Mozart? Whereas with many composers, who also touched my heart, 'something' happened now and then, for the other *few* it seemed hardly possible for them to produce anything that was not perfect. It seemed as if some of the more-or-less famous composers had once been sprinkled with inspiration by a peeved angel, whereas the 'greatest' must have 'seen' God himself. For them, the outer sound was an image of the inner sound which they heard with *super-sensory* ears, and delivered a metamorphosed portion thereof for the sensory world. Through such sounds, I could recognize the World of Reality and Truthfulness as I had encountered it. And I felt that the truly great composers must have experienced it and suffered, because their music – which we consider perfect – could never be a *perfect* replica of spiritual sounds. Nevertheless, of the whole harvest they were able to collect at least a small but real life-containing portion of grain. What was so special about the grain from the golden acre of the divine world was that it had passed though the composers' *actual core of being* and was therefore individualized in the most beautiful way. Thus, from the general objectivity of the World of Reality came an individualized objectivity through authentic art. And that was a conscious act of the individual human core of musical genius!

Mozart knew something about the great, wisdom-filled divine cosmic plan – that was clear to me. Otherwise he could never have composed his Jupiter Symphony. The goal of the divine cosmic plan is the fraternal union of all beings into a harmonious whole; a whole in which one's individuality does not perish, however, but rather one which can only come to pass through the individuality of the individual, and only when human beings re-encounter their actual selves – when they become conscious of their actual human core and therewith acquire the force to transform themselves and their world in the divine sense. I perceived that the Jupiter Symphony's music told of this. Yes, it told of the future: of the accomplished transformation, of the cosmic plan's fulfilment. The symphony's last movement begins quietly; one could almost call it melancholic if the foreshadowing of fulfilment were not contained in the gentle opening bars. Some small doubts traverse the exposition about whether the noble goal can be reached. But the sublimity of the spiritually divine human being finally prevails. It is born and celebrates in triumph the human fraternal covenant – not decreed from without or bigoted – which builds a new world in the Realm of God's Reality.

For every situation which my inner life lived through, Mozart gave me something appropriate. Whether it was the *Clarinet Concerto*, with its yearning, modest lament in the second movement about the loss of our divine home, or the demand by God's strong hand for Don Giovanni's accountability: an amusing divertimento upon hearing which one wanted to go faster and faster around in circles; his so youthful seeming *Concert for Two Pianos*, which when hearing I always saw before me Salzburg's old city with its cobble-stoned alleys and its clattering coaches, or his unfinished *Requiem*, which so relentlessly applies pressure on the conscience, as though a divine cosmic judge is preparing to weigh the soul on his scale, while the latter – conscious of its transgressions, seeing the meaning of existence – wakes up when it is too late for repentance. Nevertheless, blind from tears of emotion, and despite being undeserving, he receives total absolution through the creator's love. That's how I lived through some of my childhood years, in a certain sense at Mozart's side. (I hope he can smile at this.) For we had at least one thing in common: we both obviously loved the Realm of Reality, the realm of divine perfection, but at the same time we also felt ourselves sent by the higher plan to this world, to this side, and therefore belonging to it – which follows from his words: *'To gain heaven is superb and sublime, but also on the earth it is incomparably beautiful. So let us be humans!'* Yes, I wanted to be a human being, in the sense of the higher plan. The earth was truly 'beautiful' to me through the untouched-by-humanity nature on the one hand, and on the other hand the embellishments conceived by humanity, which could reach almost every field of the sensory world, such as music, poetry, painting, architecture, landscaping – even the exterior appearance of the individual, like his clothing. I believed I understood that the creative Majesty expected from us human beings – in an extraordinarily uninhibited way – that we *'subdue the earth'* in *this* sense. And I felt that this divine expectation, to be brought about by us, was given to the healthy human being at his core, so that he would strive for this goal from within. I began, not least by the conscious perception of the beautiful and of created beauty, to have tentative feeling-thoughts about humanity's purpose in life, and believed therein to find the use of the 'gift' which was spoken of to me by spiritual beings upon my first conscious visit to the World of Reality.

So, of all the composers I knew, Mozart stood closest to my nature. I wasn't mature enough for Bach. I sensed something, but couldn't quite assimilate it. From Bach resonated a robust cosmic truth from the depths of the past, from the depths of eternity, like an immeasurably venerable Father-God mood.

But I loved the son, the son with whom I played, with whom I could laugh and weep. As a child I loved him so much that I wanted to marry only him, and because he died in 1791, I decided never to marry – which was a good excuse for someone who basically couldn't imagine marrying. To a certain extent, I felt under his protection and wanted to express my devotion to him by studying at the Salzburg Mozarteum at least until the year 1991. That would guarantee his further protection or another life with him that extended beyond the year '91, the year of his death. I don't know how I got this strange as well as absurd idea. Anyway, the protection was obviously taken over by other spirits, or it was bestowed by him without my studying music in Salzburg.

Music was an essential, faithful companion of my childhood and youth – and a CD player was not always necessary to hear it. I also heard it internally. It was possible to internally reproduce a three-movement violin concerto by Mendelssohn or the entire *Messiah*, which resulted in an incomparable 'listening' experience, because in this way I enjoyed the privilege of being the director, the orchestra and the soloist.

As I grew older, my own pieces arose in my mind. One could perhaps not call them 'compositions' because they were not built systematically, nor were they ever written down. They were improvizations, but concrete and partly complex improvizations. Sometimes in a dream I heard a complete orchestra piece from A to Z. But I couldn't write it down. I sometimes wished that someone would invent a device that could transfer directly to it musical thoughts – that is, the music resounding in a person's interior. Then, some of the pieces might have been salvaged. Through the complete dedication to music, and perhaps also the impossibility of freeing it from within by writing it down, it sometimes reached such a degree of intensity that I thought my head, my heart, my entire body must burst. For in it resounded a reflection of eternal life, the world of creative Majesty, and this inner resounding reflection felt too large for my soul, too large for my body. It didn't fit into the limited size of my being. The same thing happened with poetry, which also accompanied me during my childhood with a force similar to that of music. This feeling, that the higher life in which I took part on earth was too large to fit into the physical body, was an experience which I will describe later in a different context, because it had to do with a decisive event in my later life.

For me, music was then the land of unlimited possibilities, of comfort, happiness – a piece of home to which I always had access. And through it I realized that there had been people who, with their existence in the earthly world of forgetting, had been in a similar situation to mine, for they had savoured and witnessed the eternal, true beauty of the World of Reality. I came across a letter in Mozart's biography which read: '*I have been chosen for suffering.*' (A statement which can perhaps only be correctly understood in the existential sense as described here.) And in a note by Beethoven: '*For you, poor Beethoven, there is no happiness from without, you must create everything in yourself, only in the ideal world do you find joy.*' This remark relates to a corresponding impression of my feeling as a growing child. I often asked myself: Where are 'my' people? Where?

As a child, I was by no means a 'crybaby'. But sometimes in the middle of the day, even in a calm and peaceful situation, I was suddenly overcome by a deep pain so that the tears streamed down my cheeks, and my mother in consternation asked what was wrong.

I couldn't give her an answer. I had none. Since my earthly awakening day I simply had carried around a heavy burden that I was not completely 'at home'. But how should I make that understood by the people around me who did not have such perceptions? So I buried this burden inside me in order to be happy in everyday life, which was how I was seen. But sometimes the heartache emerged forcefully.

Nevertheless, I was better off than Beethoven. I understood very well what he meant with finding 'no happiness from without' and having to 'create everything yourself'; but after all, I had found him and Mozart and Mendelssohn and all the others! There they were, my friends! They probably didn't know me. We didn't meet on earth. But I could turn to them anyway – they, who clearly were 'in heaven' and whose core of being I had perhaps associated with during my visit to the World of Reality, within which the wise selves lived. These, my true friends, were always accessible through their heavenly messengers, their musical compositions, an essential and faithful substitute for the spiritual communication lacking with contemporaries living on earth, and their music was also a delicious wellspring of imagination, from which I gladly and thankfully drank.

***

I don't remember exactly when it began, but it must have also been around the year I started school when I began to 'tell' about my life. I'll try to explain what that means. What I was offered as the usual children's and young people's literature, I read with little enthusiasm, or without much interest or not at all. The few exceptions proved the rule: books by Otfried Preussler, Erich Kästner, Michael Ende, Kenneth Grahame with his *Wind in the Willows* or Grimm's Fairy Tales. When I occasionally enjoyed a juvenile novel or detective story, it always left a slight aftertaste. Such books were good for 'diversion' and probably had the same effect that comic strips or television have for children today. But it is just this diversion – the exact word – that diverts the capacity of our human core for active concentration, and thereby inhibits the force of imagination. So they didn't nourish, but – although the expression may sound somewhat drastic – *hollowed out*.

Apparently my soul needed something more lively and exciting. And what can be more lively and exciting than life itself when one doesn't know what to expect from one moment to the other? Without having decided or planned to do so, I began to speak to myself silently or in a low voice – when no one was around, whom I might disturb or alienate – to tell about my life in formulated and, if possible, well-structured sentences, about what I had just seen, lived, did, thought and felt. I told it to myself in the third person, for example: *'She observed the tiny shivering bundle from a distance. Its brown-white striped fur was impeccably clean and must feel wonderfully fluffy. She felt the urge to run immediately to the kitten, but decided to stay still in order not to frighten it.'* In this way the prosaic nature of everyday life acquired a certain poetic note. Thus I had my own novel, which was not limited to a certain number of ages, but was truly a 'Never-ending Story'.

Through this entertaining ritual, something else intervened. I came, at a distance so to speak, to what I thought, felt and did. I observed myself like a stranger whose actions are seen by another, who has access to my secret thoughts and feelings. This led to my being more conscious of the outer world, especially when a person or an animal was involved, and to be more interested in others. It had to do with making the novel as precise and rich in details as possible, and also to examine the thoughts and feelings of others and to describe them. Furthermore, it resulted in my becoming conscious of my own thoughts and feelings and learning to observe them whilst having them. I had not intended this at the start, but soon realized that it was a way of having at my disposal a means of correcting my own actions, which offered the chance to act less impulsively and to give the inner and outer events a different direction than would have been the case when stumbling blindly through the various situations in life.

If these characteristics are not already given by nature, one could – insofar as one has a liking for poetry – make the described practice into a method in order to become a more observant and considerate person.

***

A few months before the beginning of secondary school, that is, shortly before or after my tenth birthday, something was given to

66

me which I consider to be the most precious gift of my life. It is more difficult for me to describe it than anything else that I have described and will describe in this book. It is not at all easy to describe this event, but I will try.

It wasn't a material gift, but an immaterial one, and most readers will probably agree with me that it is the immaterial gifts, as opposed to the material ones – however beautiful and expensive they may be – which possess an immeasurably greater worth. Such immaterial gifts are very individual. They are not available by their hundreds in department stores, cannot be ordered and given as gifts online, in thousands or even millions of identical copies. In every person's biography events occur which make this biography unique, for the events – of which we consider some to be 'gifts' – are just as unique as the individual persons. The conviction that most readers will also agree with this gives me occasion to hope that what I describe now can be accepted impartially, as an individual experience.

On the other hand, we have all surely had the experience that the impartiality of our fellow human beings (and above all of ourselves, although that is seldom and reluctantly admitted) leaves much to be desired. Thus we often painfully experience, by an honest observation of our own actions, that the criterion for the things we perceive around us is actually our own. The application of a personal criterion hinders an impartial perception, or, in other words, a fundamentally objective, scientific approach. For then, one is unable to really get to know the other, the new or the unknown, because one immediately introduces a *value*-criterion. And as a rule this turns out to be distressingly simple as well as silly. It goes like this: If *I* do not know and cannot confirm what the other says, then something is wrong with the story or with the person himself. Unfortunately, there are quite a few people who give so much value to their own opinions that they cannot rest until they have finally collected and pieced together from various sources more-or-less – apparently completely new – passable confirmation of their own opinions. But in the end this should only relieve them of the unreasonable demand to change their personal experiences, ideas and the resulting standards and perspectives – to correct them or, more appropriately, to expand them and thus gradually objectify them. We are lucky that we didn't behave like this in our childhood! Otherwise we could never have learned anything and would have known as adults exactly as much about the world as an infant. This unpleasant phenomenon seems therefore to be mostly an adult's affliction. This might be explained by the relatively well-known and often quoted words from the Gospel of Matthew: *'Unless you change and become like children, you will never enter the kingdom of heaven.'* (Mt. 18:3) It would certainly do us good if we as adults took as a basis for our encounters with the different and the new at least a small portion of what we as clear-headed adults call – perhaps hastily and arrogantly – 'naiveté' in children.

Despite our perception that our own biographical experiences are our own, we are extremely skeptical concerning other people's individual experiences. That's a remarkable disparity when we consider that we expect complete acceptance by others of our own experiences. One doesn't have to immediately accept as a generally valid fact something unknown when claimed by someone else as his or her own experience. However, one could learn not to judge something as impossible because one has not (yet) experienced something similar oneself. Certainly it's human nature to question things (one could also call it scientific interest) – that we can question whether material or immaterial perceptions are involved. But questioning nowadays – it was not always so in human history – has acquired a certain tendency. It seems to me that our questioning, born of an original, typically healthy human curiosity, has turned out to be a frantic search for proof of the impossibility of the phenomenon being investigated, especially when immaterial facts or questions are involved. Naturally it is not as easy to find objective evidential criteria for immaterial facts and phenomena as for material ones. But that is mostly because competence for healthy judgment, which depends not only on intellectual but also on intuitive ability, is lacking.

From birth on, we are endowed with a noble ability: We know what concerns the essential areas of existence without someone else having to tell us what is good – from a higher, impersonal viewpoint – and what is bad; what one may do and what one may not do; and what is ethical and what is unethical. And, more closely considered, it is our respective cultural socialization and education which changes this original, intuitive knowledge, so that we learn to do certain things that we would prefer not to do. Even a child who from birth on experiences the slaughter of animals in his or her home environment, which is a matter of course and of necessity for adults, must overcome that inborn barrier against taking another being's life the first time he must carry out the killing himself. At some point, man becomes accustomed to doing what he feels bad about, not only because his culture demands it, but also because he derives a personal gain, or because he too often emerges unscathed. The first falsehood might be an unpleasant memory because it wounds his inborn conscience. The second, third or three-hundredth, no longer. Nevertheless, he can still remember his inborn conscience and, by means of this remembrance, become conscious that perspectives and criteria for judgment exist that are completely different from his own corrupt personal ones. He can tell himself: I possess an intuitive gift! It may be buried by the ballast of my civilization's temporally conditioned values. But I can retrieve it from the depths of my self and thus accustom myself to being able to deal with all the unexpected situations in life. Thus, one could create a second support to stand on (one which has long existed) alongside the intellectual ability to think. This second support can be employed when one cannot advance by intellectual speculation. For example, using the intuitive heartfelt ability, one could ask: If what another tells me is a fact based on their individual experience but is for me, due to my own lack of experiences of this kind, not explicable or provable, can it seem otherwise legitimate? Does the person involved appear to be reasonable? Can I comprehend, thinking for myself, his or her thoughts about other things? Can I observe good intentions in his or her words and actions? In brief: Is this a good person, with healthy common sense, who is authentic and credible? Whoever has not buried all his inborn 'knowing' will soon come to a certain impression. And then, if he is also able to avoid undermining his impression by his old preferred ideas and value-criteria, he is not far from a truly impartial means of observation.

One can only hope for such an attitude on the part of the people whom I will trust with the special 'immaterial gift' about which I will now tell, and which decisively shaped my life.

But there is still another point which could potentially be an obstacle for understanding what I have to tell. The suggestion could arise that my account be construed in a religious sense, even a confessional religious sense. And I must confess that it is understandable, at least for those for whom it is not easy to comprehend what I have written here with the appropriate sensibility. However, it was not a religious-confessional experience which was given to me, but something which I would describe as a sublime as well as a simple fact. Facts are independent of ideas, opinions or belief systems and are not subject to the various religious faiths. It is also not true that I was inculcated with a confessional religious message, which in my childish impressionability I somehow psychically absorbed and processed. No! I first became religious (and not in a confessional sense) *because* of this *experience*.

When I describe this experience after that long introduction, it will perhaps be seen as not particularly uplifting and perhaps even something to smirk at. But over the years I have realized that in certain circumstances it's the apparently small, modest or simple things which veil the largest most profound things. And such things are simply too profound to describe accurately. Furthermore, the experience is a very intimate one, and until today only the people closest to me – whom I can count on the fingers of one hand – know about it. The fear of soliciting contemptuous or mocking reactions was too great. But when I come to consider it, the impulse to write this book came directly from that experience. Furthermore, it is a gift which was indeed given to *me* (in that it came to my consciousness as an experience), but it was given to me in order that I might understand in the fullest sense that every human being receives such a gift. Therefore, I will describe my experience as briefly and simply as possible, but not in a rhetorically exaggerated or pathetic way. For I consider myself incapable of describing it so that the reader will, even approximately, receive a truly authentic impression of it. For this reason the attempt to move my readers to tears would be completely out of place.

On that day – in reality it was at night between the state of going to sleep and a state that I can only describe as a conscious staying-awake, or even intensive wakefulness while falling asleep – I was taught what *love* is.

It was no dream. It was anything else but a dream. In my whole life I had never been so awake and so conscious of my self. Yes,

70

compared to the experience I have already described as having entered the World of Reality and Truthfulness in which I was an 'organ of perception' for the wonder of existence, it was a – what shall I say? – a more 'individual' consciousness. In this state of consciousness a spiritual presence emerged before me. And at the same moment that he emerged before my conscious inner actual core of being, I knew with irrefutable certainty: that is *Christ*.

This presence, this Entity, did not have to introduce Himself. He made clear who and what He was by just being how He was. There were no questions and no doubts. It was God Himself, but in a manifestation that made it possible for me consciously to experience Him, for I knew that no one in their present state of consciousness would be capable of a *total* perception or encounter with the creative primal Majesty. But that was neither the essential insight – which by the way had nothing to do with a feeling of inferiority or intimidation – nor the reason why the encounter was granted to me. It was more an aspect of the encounter, for in that state many aspects could be experienced and understood at the same time. Encounter, communication, question and answer were there, but also again not, for they dissolved in the timelessness, or rather the simultaneousness, of this state of being. There is nothing with which to compare it with here in this earthly consciousness and in the scope of earthly conditions of existence. And I experienced in Him all answers; in Him all desires and wishes are satisfied; in Him is my home; in Him, Christ. And His incomparable presence 'spoke' to my heart – it was a different form of communication though, rather like an insight of my consciousness – '*I am the Alpha and the Omega.*'

In case one considers this impossible, I must describe here a fact: Until then, I had never heard anything about any kind of higher messages from Christ. And until that moment I was never made aware of a Greek expression. Nevertheless, the words '*Alpha*' and '*omega*' were suddenly just as clear as the word '*Christ*' in my consciousness – in my heart – and at the same time I became aware of the meaning of this sentence: '*I am the beginning and the end.*' (This sentence has occupied me anew for many years, until today. In trying to comprehend it one realizes that the usual everyday way of thinking is mistaken. One can only achieve an inkling of the meaning of these words when one applies another way of thinking to them; that is, if one dares to forgo the reasoning which one

71

normally uses when pondering everyday things. One doesn't get far that way. But with time if one is able to consider them differently, one can achieve the same stilling of desires, have the same sense of home and of being in His immediate presence – although I must straightaway correct this formulation, for His presence is always immediately present, only we so seldom accomplish the kind of attention described here, the corresponding consciousness to perceive it.)

When I think about it, it was quite remarkable. For it never for one moment occurred to me that this was Jesus – the Jesus whom I had of course already heard and read about. For this Jesus – the Christian, Jewish, Islamic and Buddhist confessions essentially agree – is distinguished by being especially close to God, who performed various exceedingly remarkable deeds, and was a wise prophet and a compassionate, good man. Furthermore, the Christians were of the opinion that He was the 'Son of God'. What that was supposed to mean was never clear to me. I never understood how the Son of God – in spite of all the miracles He was supposed to have worked – could be so human; furthermore, how he could end dying a miserable death on the cross as a criminal, which the Christians could somehow depict as a victory. But now I understood it (within the confines of my limited knowledge). The Entity who stood before me then and enclosed me in its arms was not the Jesus about whom I had heard and read. It was so superhuman that I understood what I had not previously understood: This superhuman Entity, in which everything that exists took its beginning – the Entity of which we can say that it is Alpha *and* Omega, because in it there is no 'end' as we know it, and because in its Omega the Alpha again rises – was that Entity which had once lived in Jesus. I conceived of Jesus as His earthly body-garment, so to speak, in which God's actual core of being had lived approximately two thousand years ago, basically like us. I perceived our outer body-garment, visible to all, as a part of our self, but not the actual person, including consciousness and His self-knowledge. The outer visible and physically touchable body-garment was in a certain sense the instrument for working in the physical-sensory outer world, and hence also the holy domain of the actual human being's core. This was obviously also the case with Jesus, with the essential difference that in Him no *'human being*

72

core' lived, but a *'divine being* core'. And what was exceptional was not the death of this Jesus, but death's *overcoming* by the power of Christ.

So I had finally received the answer to my question, what comes 'afterward' – after earthly death. As I understood it then, the unique presence of God in the human being Jesus demonstrated that the actual human core is immortal! That although the body can disappear, as did the body of Jesus, the actual *core of the human being* does not. And this showed me that He was capable of full consciousness, which was clearly diminished by his descending into an earthly situation, into an earthly body. (I already had this impression on my awakening day on earth.) He, however, 'informed' me that it would not be so forever and therefore, in order that we humans can one day achieve complete union with our consciousness, HE, Christ, came to us on earth. The physical body, as the starting point for the return to our higher being, was made possible by Him.

After the death on the cross it was not Jesus who had risen, but His actual core of being, the Christ! (From that day on I have cringed when hearing someone say that Jesus is the 'Son of God', and has 'risen'. I often wonder why Christians call themselves Christians and not jokers or something similar.) It may seem like fussy faultfinding, but to me the difference is absolutely essential, without which the event of Golgotha, the actual core of Christianity, is meaningless.

What I am describing here may seem like the complicated theoretical consideration of a theological-philosophical question. That is not at all the case. It was manifested to me as a plain, uncomplicated fact, which is as short and comprehensible as the words: *'I am the Alpha and the Omega.'* The remarkable thing about it was the recapitulation of this experience through everyday earthly consciousness, that is, with my 'brain' understanding, for I myself was mystified in the encounter with that Entity which I only knew about from Christian confessional sources, that there really was a 'Son of God'. It was immaterial to me that the word 'son' could also be interpreted in the usual earthly human sense. It did not apply to the Entity which I had encountered. And yet at that moment no other word occurred to me to better describe the Entity I had perceived than 'Son of God'. I could understand the objections that only a person steeped in denominational Christianity could make such a claim. But that was not the case. As I have already affirmed: I was only affected by true religious feelings concerning this Son of God *after* having had this experience. And I could only comprehend something of this concept because of this experience. Such questions were not discussed in my surroundings then, and my age should be considered. So I can only repeat: the existence of the Son of God was revealed to me as a non-denominational fact! I understood Him as 'son' because God, the creative entity, had detached a part of Himself and sent it to earth, becoming a human being like all of us; and, through His life, death and Resurrection back into the unity of divine wholeness, gave us to understand the way to follow, back to that unity. Therefore, Christ was our older brother and in this sense Son of God, to whom we as children – beings created by the creative Majesty – look up to and strive towards as to a father. Thus, like Him we could return to the Father, following Him, Christ, if only we could learn to conceive of ourselves as immortal human beings. My experience had opened *my eyes* to the fact that there actually is a divine being who can be called 'Son of God' or 'Christ'. Therefore, this Entity was a fact. However, one thing invoked this fact, and that was Christianity. Nevertheless, during the following years I had the impression that this Christianity understood· something different by Christ. I have never heard a representative of the Christian religion, regardless of the denomination, speak of the same Entity of Christ which I experienced.

Of one thing I am certain: that whoever had or will have a similar encounter with this Being, regardless of their religious background or how deeply they are connected to a denomination, would confirm that it has no similarity at all to the general concept of a Jesus figure – just as little as a real 'angel' (a self that has developed higher than a human being) has no similarity with a full-breasted, rapturous angel with long wavy blond hair, a pretty flowing gown and feathered wings.

It was a powerful, sublime force in the sense of a beneficent ability – a 'light' that was actual life, the source from which inner and outer life feeds and from which all the colours of the earthly and over-earthly world originate. At the same time, it seemed to supply true higher *understanding* and also an intensity of *love* unknown to us here on earth, which streams out from the presence of this Entity, which was what the Christ-being represented. But I had heard no one coming from a Christian background describing such a Presence as a direct witness. I don't doubt that there are such people within Christian institutions. In the history of Christianity, and thus of the Church, they doubtless existed – something of which I was later convinced by means of the evidence that remains of such individuals. And they surely also exist today. But unfortunately, as a child and youth, I never met or heard of them. It would actually have pleased me very much. I always presumed that such people had to exist within circles where they outwardly dedicate their lives to Christianity, but I didn't meet them. Because of my experiences, personally I found it insurmountably difficult to join the system of institutionalized Christianity, because the features of such an institution absolutely contradicted the essential attributes of the Christ-being I had encountered, in particular, the thoroughly hierarchical organization of the Church, which delegates different functions to different people and thus effectively before God.

But perhaps, I thought later, the personalities who had similar experiences to mine, and nevertheless entered institutionalized Christianity, that is, the Church, are wise people because they know that the earth is not Paradise and that, as long as one lives on it, one must be satisfied with compromises. Although as a child for a time I wished to enter a community that was oriented towards contemplation, I later realized that I could never make a compromise of this kind, namely to recognize such differences in authority and in the positions of people and the sexes before God, because of my experience of the Son of God. And – I can't help making the following comment here – I consider the theological thinking about the pre-eminence of men over women, because a man is supposed to have existed before a woman and furthermore that she caused the offence that got them expelled from Paradise, to be a ridiculously narrow figment, even when the most prominent and learned heads defend it. And that was not because I was born a woman, but out of consideration of the reality of *Christ* and what He represented and was to me. For the actual 'human being core' is neither male nor female! And the 'kingdom of Heaven' has to do with the human being's higher development, which was the object of the Son of God's encounter with my core of being.

The core of my encounter with the Christ-Being had to do exactly with the above point, although considered from a completely different perspective from the all-too-human ideas and interpretations on prevailing reality. I have already mentioned that on that day I learned what *love* really is. That was *actually* the gift bestowed on me. (Everything described previously, and much that is not mentioned here, was already 'clarified' at the moment of my first encounter.)

But the high Entity turned to me, to my human-being-core, with a request. This request was not like a person's request in the everyday world. As an intention it was to a certain degree translucent, transparent, and was therefore also an answer, that is, the reason and simultaneous justification for its appearance. Certainly, the justification for the emergence of the request had its origin in the Entity of Christ, but not the appearance of the request itself, which was rather in my own actual inner being. It was as if, in my inner being, a connection to the request was hidden from my normal consciousness, so that it seemed to be a request from the Christ-Being that I could be attentive to. And this request was that I *learn* something special.

This learning also had completely other facets than a learning process in the everyday world. (Because of the need to use terms which cannot completely describe what is essential, certain circumlocutions are used in order to avoid giving an incorrect impression of the matter.) This learning included traits of remembrance. For some of the things I now learned were already 'known' by my human-being-core. Not by my earthly consciousness, but my actual self could connect in a special way with what I was shown. Nevertheless – in a seemingly paradoxical way – the newer things which were taught me constituted an overwhelming experience, as if they were experienced for the first time by my human-being-core. Later, as I realized through similar experiences, the living facts in the World of Reality are perceived in this way when they are 'entered into' – not intellectually understood, which is impossible, but directly experienced. That they are devoid of any contrived or unreal – that is, dead – elements, indicates the overwhelming authenticity of what they are: living truths which, due to their everlasting aliveness, are never routine.

And thus the Entity Christ became in that moment my best, noblest teacher and at the same time my first and most beloved friend.

I would hardly be able to express what happens in the soul when it consciously stands before its Creator! The grandeur of this Entity is so powerful that it is not possible to imagine that it would direct its attention to one individual among the billions of human beings, in order to teach her something in such a patient, warmhearted and compassionate way. But that's how it is! And I became a witness to what for our human understanding could only be seen as an absurdity or a miracle: that the world's Creator, humanity's Saviour, offers his undivided devotion and attention to each one of us.

He taught me something ineffably valuable already by His devotion as well as His very Being, which the actual request – the actual teaching offered to me – was not part of: I learned what a true friend is.

Although I will not attempt to describe the wide spectrum of what such friendship inspires inside a person, I will at least try, in a brief sentence, to outline what is essential about this true friendship, which as such does not exist on earth. It is true because it is *total*; because it is totally oriented towards the *other*, the friend, and contains *no* hint whatsoever of self-interest. It is wholly pure. Total dedication.

When one experiences this dedication to friendship, one experiences at the same time, and in one's own soul, what trust means. Unconditional, total, invulnerable trust – and therein the soul finds consummate peace.

As my core of consciousness found itself embedded in the indicated mood and sphere, the Entity of the Son of God turned to me and showed me something which I can best describe with an image: He arranged around Him a great throng of human-being-cores; they seemed like children. I was also among them. He lingered and presided over us, protecting us, being with us. I became aware – I didn't have to be 'told' – that I was to remain in this state and perceive it, down to the deepest layers of my consciousness.

This I did. Thus I could experience what humanity lacks on earth. But this insight, and the painful feeling for what is lacking, followed later from what was experienced in my everyday consciousness. At that moment, in that state of being, I did not perceive the privations of our earthly humanity, but in the conscious presence of God I perceived the blissful stilling of all human desires and privations. (I had the impression that a human being is only human because his higher spiritual nature, his actual being, has the capacity to develop what I sensed in my 'I-body' through the Christ entity.) What I could experience was that in all human beings, whether they realize it or not, is a steadfast primal need for true, living and total *love*.

The Son-God gave me the possibility of being within unconditional, total, purest love – a love after which there is nothing more one can wish for; a love which is without beginning and without end, though it is so sweet and full that it would burst the human heart if it filled the physical body. But such bursting would not be destructive, but rather an expansion of the human soul's space. Nothing about this love was violent, unfree, intrusive or too 'little'. It was more beautiful than anything the human heart can imagine. At the same time – and this is what I learned – being within it, one felt no longing to have more because it was so beautiful that everything about it was already perfect. Also, no demand arose to have more of it than someone else. This love, which penetrated me and the other human-being-cores, connected us with each other, because we all, in that we were blessed by it, shared the same heartfelt love with each other. There was no fear of being neglected because He paid more attention to another, for nothing detracted, for even a moment, from His total attention and warmth. There was no jealousy, no envy or resentment. In this state of being it was impossible and even unbearable for this love to be denied to any human being.

Thus my great, holy friend and teacher taught me that *all humans are equally loved by God*. No human-being-core was the same as another, and He treated each as an individual being. But His love was equally great for each, and it was an *all-embracing, total* love in which *there was room for all!* No one needed another love, and it was denied to none.

In this, the Saviour's love – I could consider Him as such because He freed me from the overwhelming desire for my spiritual home as well as certain selfish wishes – I found *complete peace*. And when I returned to my everyday life and remembered this love, I was astonished that in that state, in which all people were equally and intensively loved, I never felt the slightest hint of jealousy or fear that I could somehow receive too little, because so many others also received so much. I had learned that this love was so perfect because it was received *by all*. I was able to feel how all people, His creations, His children, are just as unconditionally and overwhelmingly loved as I. But while I was so unconditionally and overwhelmingly loved, there was not the least thing I had to do without or could wish for. *Only in this love*, given equally to all, did I find in my life the total fulfilment of the human primal need for real love: in *community* with *all* beings.

Through this precious gift I learned something fundamental about the essence and 'task' of my honoured, beloved, divine friend and teacher: I could experience this inexhaustible love and thus what true love is. I knew that not even the most caring and devoted mother's love can touch His love, because it cannot be as pure and comprehensive as His. However – and this was the most important insight granted to me, except for the pure feeling of God's love – every human heart, every human-being-core, is potentially able to bring this love forth. For if one can feel it, can *consciously* realize what it really is, can *accept* it, then one can bring it forth from one's own actual human-being-core. And what I understood was that my divine teacher, Christ the Son of God, as the source of that love, had given Himself the task of teaching us human beings how to feel and develop this perfect love. The first step was to 'show' us His love. He had already shown it to us once by becoming a man and by His sacrifice on Golgotha. How this was to be precisely understood, however, I only learned later. But – and this I was able to experience immediately – He shows us this love also today, two thousand years later! For we human beings of the present must find our own living relationship to Him, and that doesn't mean merely through knowledge of the historical events, and also not through belief alone. It is only possible through individual lived experience. Through the direct encounter with Him we might learn how to achieve true love, and what getting to know this love requires. By means of my experience, I learned that He teaches it to us in that He shows us *Himself*. For He is the source of this perfect, all-encompassing love. And this love was the spiritual life.

Thus I was witness, as already mentioned, for what is considered to be either 'absurd' or 'miraculous' by our human understanding

– that the Creator of the world, the Saviour of humanity, gives His undivided caring and attention to each and every one of us. Always and omnipresent. We may be certain of this. We need only accept it.

Thereby I could perceive that there was a difference between the creative Majesty ('God') and Christ (the 'Son of God'). It was as though the magical life-force, and everything that has ever been, comes from the creative Majesty. To me it seemed 'responsible' for the disposition and management of the cosmic world-plan, in which everything which had ever existed found its relevance. On the other hand, the Christ-Entity, whom I came to know then as a 'part' of the creative Majesty, and thus participating in the being and becoming of everything which has ever been and will ever be, was specifically entrusted to work with us humans – with the development of our 'higher human being'. The Son of God seemed to be occupied with our human existence and therewith also our 'housing' that is, our human corporeality, as well as the 'land' upon which this housing of our true selves has been built: the earth. And, I came to the conclusion that the development of the 'higher human' in us is only possible if we know the secret of His divine love. For then as a consequence, I felt, everything on earth will be different, because no one could any longer act in the way I observed, bewilderedly, as a child: the crudity and blindness of people concerning life and the divine land upon which it existed. Whoever once experienced this love would strive to regain it. Without question, He would dedicate His life to winning this love for the benefit of all humanity and all beings. He would know through His encounter with the source of true divine human love that this love is not experienceable today on earth, but that it can become experienceable. He would know, I thought, as I knew because it had been 'shown' to me, that perfect love will not be experienceable on earth as long as people do not beget it from within themselves. But as long as they know nothing of the source of this love, they would not be able to develop it and bring it forth into the earthly world. I realized that this perfect love does not simply stream onto the earth like rain. It takes a divine detour via us *human beings*! The human being must want a relationship to the source of this love in order to beget it from within himself. For he can only become a source of this love himself if he has absorbed the initial source. Others acquire sensitivity to this love in as much as those who have experienced it are witness to it – and this can lead to a higher mindfulness and some day to a similar, independent experience.

The consequence of this decisive experience was, among other things, that I now knew that the 'hunt for my consciousness' had a justified basis – one that was to a certain extent welcomed by a higher authority: I wanted to strive for the conscious union with the source of this love. I wanted it wholeheartedly and, I dare to say today, with a selfless urge. And I undertook to become worthy of receiving this source of perfect love. (It is hardly necessary to mention that I was not successful, but that did not affect my efforts to pursue that goal. It is, after all, the most essential reason for human existence. The effort to achieve this goal should only change once the goal has been reached.)

I would like to add that the idea that my experience is probably the psychological, compensatory result of emotional neglect in kindergarten is about as accurate as the assertion that I am a blonde, one-legged man! Even if it were the case that I felt emotionally neglected in childhood, it would have been impossible for me to imagine the experience described above. Because, as already explained, there is no such love on earth as that experienced in my state of consciousness and existence at that time. That's why I could have neither wished nor imagined it. Furthermore, a mental picture is, as a rule, as far from a living, real experience as a mirror image is from the reality. Nobody will deny that there is a difference between thinking of placing my hand on a glowing hot stove and really doing it. No less drastic is the difference between the experience I have described here and a psycho-pathological hallucination.

During this crucial experience I passed through a 'gate'. The reader might have done something similar. The question remains as to whether or not the reader was able to pass through this gate with me. Or, if my description went too far, leaving the reader confronted by a closed gate, and inducing him or her to turn back and lay this book aside.

For me, this experience was a kind of gate, because from that day on my relation to the World of Reality became significantly richer. I had met a Being who, although body-less, possessed a kind of 'corporeality' which was distinctly more real, consistent and substantial than our human mortal corporeality. Its corporeality was identical with its being's core, which led to the fact that the entire superhuman inner faculty of this Being also radiated out of its (super-material) 'corporeality'. Thus I met a tangible Being who spoke directly to me. And I recognized it as an essential part of the creative Majesty, as 'Son' of God, and by the encounter itself – not through a denominational religious interpretation or representation. Through this tangible encounter my view of earthly (and super-earthly) existence, and for the question of how I wanted to use my gift of life on earth, was made clearer.

My experience was also a gate in that, from then on, a more purposeful or conscious connection with the World of Reality resulted, from which the most varied experiences, discoveries and insights unfolded. Beyond this now opened gate, it was as if the actual world became open for exploration. I will speak of this subsequently.

For the reader, the description of this crucial experience may also constitute a kind of gate. I can well imagine that one or another reader could accompany me inwardly with what I have described previously, but that the journey breaks at this point because for them the whole thing has taken on the whiff of religion. That would be a pity, especially since I have taken pains to describe the relationship between my experience and the religious sentiments that resulted from it, and how little it had to do with a religious institution or with any kind of indoctrination. Nevertheless, I must reckon with a withdrawal on the part of some readers, because in my life I have observed that, when confronted with something 'religious' or 'spiritual', people are more likely to react in this way than with a neutral, open or even positive stance.

Describing this experience, or rather the event itself, is really perhaps comparable to a gate that opens onto a castle situated behind a moat. In order to gain entrance, one must intentionally open the gate and pass over the drawbridge into the castle. Each person decides whether he lets the drawbridge down or not. Back then, I went through the gate and over the bridge (it was not a question for me, it was so evident what I would experience and had already experienced), but I have also gone through that gate now – although in a different sense – because, with this description of my experience, I have dared to give my readers an inkling of the fact that, behind the gate, there really is a castle full of things even more amazing than that which one encounters at the castle's entrance. And when I continue telling my story I have in fact, together with my reader who accompanies me through the gate, left the gate and the bridge behind me. For when one passes through the door once, the description of what is behind it, in respect to its existence and reality, is no longer justified. This book would be too long if I provided the following narratives with so much voluble 'assurance' as thus far. You can be sure that the contents of the following narrative originates from the 'castle' *beyond* the gate, and that one only has access to it by passing through the gate. It boils down to this question: Do I consider it (at least) *not impossible* that what the author relates is more than her vivid imagination? Or, in other words, whoever considers entrance to the castle possible will also be able to consider what is contained within it as possible, as well as participating in it. On the other hand, whoever does not consider entrance possible, or sees the gate as a delusion, will not see the castle and the rooms within, and will most likely consider the person who relates her entrance to it and describes the rooms within as either not serious or simply crazy. In this respect the reader is standing here at a crossroads.

When, in the course of this writing, I was thinking about whether in our world of permanent and ingrained distrust of a 'spiritual reality' it is sensible or useful to describe my own experiences of this reality, the testators of our cultural and spiritual heritage occurred to me, such as Herder, Goethe, Schiller or Hegel. And for a moment I thought that if one takes seriously what they said about nature, humanity and human consciousness and the spirit, and if one honours them as spiritual greats, then one should have no problem with the sort of reports I am providing in this book. But, is it so? I mean, is it really so that those greats are taken seriously? Of course! Every reasonably educated citizen will affirm this. But let us look around in our contemporary cultural landscape. Has it not become somewhat – pardon the expression – snooty? Today, everywhere people have an almost schizophrenic attitude toward our spiritual testators and their work. We gladly help ourselves to them and to their work for the invention of, as well as support for, new theories. By itself that would be legitimate and even gratifying. But all too often what isn't understood is swept under the rug. And that mostly has to do with the spirit, or, expressed differently, the super-sensory world. It is simply ignored, as though it weren't there. One can certainly ask what benefit is gained by reading a *Wilhelm Meister* or by attending a performance of *Faust* if one questions the existence of a spiritual world. Nevertheless, Goethe's work still attracts people as if by magic. We seem to unconsciously *cherish* what we outwardly, in everyday circumstances, *deny*. But we deny the whole work when we deny the source from which it comes.

And so it goes cheerfully on; for example a piano concerto by Mozart is performed in such a way that one has the impression one is taking part in a circus programme; or when chorus parts and arias of the Christmas Oratorium are sung in such a hurry that one thinks the director and ensemble members must have an urgent meeting at home. Bach, however, is not more up-to-date (or 'better') if played rapidly. It's similar with the opera. For example, during the past several years people attending the German Opera Berlin must have had the feeling that they had not attended a real opera performance if there weren't at least one naked woman and 20 uniformed soldiers of the North Korean Army or the German Wehrmacht on the stage. Or, as in the last act of the memorable performance of Mozart's *Die Entführung aus dem Serail* (The Abduction from the Seraglio) at the Komishe Oper Berlin a few years ago, when the Turkish ruler did not, in the manner of Nathan the Wise – and as intended in the original and sung about on the stage – seek revenge for the wrong done to him and gives his prisoners their freedom, but together with his servants proceeds to a wild mass copulation and finally spectacularly executes the two lovers from the distant Occident using plenty of 'ketchup'. And take theatrical stagings where the directors find that they are more likely to be successful and achieve recognition by helping 'old' plays by injecting 'modern' elements into them. For example, when Iphigenia is supplied with a mobile phone with which she frantically tries to reach her father Agamemnon on the Greek mainland – unsuccessfully of course, because the satellite reception in Tauris is so bad – which can lead one to wonder why the battery hasn't run down after her years-long involuntary stay on the island. Or, when a director suddenly cuts whole scenes from Part One of *Faust* (ones he doesn't think it absolutely necessary to show the public, whilst Part Two is sacrificed *in toto*), and when he interlaces a number of 'topical' references without realizing that the play *is* already super-topical…

Although such escapades and blunders cannot much harm the genius and worthiness of such creations as those mentioned above, on one hand it reflects the tragic loss of a higher understanding and corresponding sensitivity for the profundity of such creative masterpieces drawn from 'other' sources, and on the other hand betrays a tremendous hubris. The director thinks he is on an equal footing with the master himself. In that sense the question is justified: Do we really take the great masters seriously? In considering this state of affairs, the fear grew in me that even these noble gentlemen might not be able to offer me any support.

Nevertheless, as a steadfast realistic idealist, I have dared to reveal my experience here as a gateway to what follows. The reader's 'intuitive gift' for testing its veracity remains firmly in view.

***

Since that day in 1982, my objective has always been to become more familiar with the source of love. I wanted to look after 'Him', for He looked after me in a very dedicated way – something that I had experienced directly. But I couldn't even find what I was seeking for in the Christian denominational high school I attended, for which I had passed an entrance test. The Entity, as it was revealed to me, was not discussed – not even when the subject was 'Jesus Christ'.

Instead, I found something else in that school: the Ancient world. During the fifth year, when studying Latin, we entered into that Ancient world as part of an intensive course focused on antiquity. To claim that Latin is a 'dead' language does not acknowledge that its spirit wafted through the Ancient Roman Empire, which is evident when one reads the legends of classical antiquity, such as Ovid's *Metamorphosis*, in the original language and in verse – that is, in Latin and in hexameters. In the first year we had begun to read short, simple texts, from authentic clay tablets, with tales for the children of those times, or about everyday life at home, on the street, in the senate or in the Roman army – which constituted an ideal means for deciphering the somewhat dry, prosaic language. The Ancient world provided an inexhaustible, exciting field of study. The Roman world of antiquity was, however, mainly a burning lens through which I found entrance to the noble *Greek* world of antiquity. As a child, I could well understand what the Romans found so fascinating about Greek mythology, for I myself was thoroughly captivated by it. In that world, people were more open to the super-sensory forces than in ours – and to the connection with the 'invisible selves' of the gods and the powerful spiritual forces in nature's household – through Heracles and Theseus, Orpheus and Eurydice, Icarus and Daedalus, Achilles, Menelaus, Paris and the beautiful Helen, Odysseus (not to be forgotten), Aeneas and all the rest.

I felt much closer to that world which once existed on earth – evidence of which stands as ruins in historical places, as well as wonderful artistic sculptures in museums – than to the contemporary world. At first, I didn't wonder why. I just absorbed everything about the Ancient world that it was possible for a ten- or eleven-year-old child to find and understand. But that resulted in a larger picture as well as insights which I had not expected. What especially fascinated me were the Greek gods. For in reading their history, it soon became clear that each god had its own quirky character. For example, the jovial father-god Zeus, who, although holding the fate of the world in his hands, was often angered and succumbed to his passions, including risky escapades of adultery, not only with goddesses but also with mortal women – which shook up the world's structure and caused unpleasantness to the direct and indirect participants up till the second, third and fourth generations. Not least because his betrayed and always complaining wife Hera, eaten up by jealousy, forged intrigues against the illegitimate mortal descendants of Zeus and their families, but who on the other hand also seemed genuinely anxious to maintain a minimum of discipline and order on Olympus.

Eventually, I realized that in the gods of Olympus the various highs and lows of human nature had been given a kind of face by being assigned to other higher selves, or spiritual beings. Often, within one god, two 'mirror-natures' were represented, just as in the soul of man the well-known, 'two souls, alas, are dwelling in my breast'* – or two different gods stood for such mirror-natures, such as Athene and Ares, Zeus and Hades, and so forth. In any event, the world of the gods and the world of men were always directly related to each other. The gods didn't just sit on their Olympus – as is generally disseminated about Greek mythology – without concerning themselves with the fate of humanity. In truth, they were closely intertwined with humanity.

This 'humanity' – in the sense of the 'all too human' behaviour – of the Olympian gods was what made it hard for me to draw a parallel to what I had experienced of the creative Majesty and the Son of God. The Greek gods seemed to be a kind of personification of the different soul-forces-bodies of people, or – the further I went back in the godly genealogy, to the pre-Olympian gods – personifications of the magical life-force in the various aspects of creative life, such as man, animal, plant and earth (albeit in the macrocosmic and microcosmic sense), sun and moon or air (in the sense of a super-material sphere of existence penetrated by divine light).

I presumed that Greek mythology was a long narration about the genesis of the world. (It describes events reported in other sources, such as the 'great flood', which is also described in the biblical Genesis and in the epic of Gilgamesh.) Also, that the description of the genesis of the world is especially concerned with the development of our humanity. Or, rather, the progress of our earthly consciousness as well as that of our 'actual' spiritual self. I found that the myths could and must be understood literally, but not with the same spirit we are equipped with today as everyday awareness, and with which we consider the events and conditions of the purely material world. It was evident on one hand from what the myths revealed, and on the other hand from what I had experienced internally, that what was 'seen' spiritually was as much a part of the narrative as what one saw with the senses. Both had their place in the narrative. Both were also directly related. They weren't two separate worlds – as a large part of my contemporary culture wanted me to believe – in which all religious convictions were so neatly separate from the vision of the material world – as though only the material world existed and anything above and beyond it was no more than a kind of personal opinion or belief of certain people who were believed to be unable to get on well

---

* Goethe, from *Faust*, Part One.

in the material world and must therefore engage in an unworldly 'hobby'. *That* was the reason the world of antiquity and its core – Greek mythology – so attracted me! It was where I found understanding for what I had inwardly experienced myself, namely that both worlds, the super-sensory and the sensory are, in reality, *one*.

One day I experienced a mental breakthrough. It was as if scales had dropped from my eyes. A poem by Goethe, which we studied in German literature, gave me the hint. While studying the poem 'Prometheus' I also read the Prometheus myth, which captivated me for reasons I could not identify. It was by being occupied over months, perhaps even a year, with the Prometheus myth as well as Goethe's poem that the real meaning of the Prometheus myth became accessible to me through Goethe's moving words, which previously I had not completely understood.

The tears streamed down my cheeks. Here was written down nothing less than the historical development of human consciousness in its relation to the Godhead where man was created, and to the earth on which he could truly become human! The human being had once undergone the Fall from Paradise, as it is called in Genesis. Then came the eating of the fruit of the Tree of Knowledge, that is, the receiving of earthly understanding, a certain human self-knowledge (what I called the everyday consciousness in which I felt so 'naked' on the day of my earthly awakening) – or, expressed in non-spiritual scientific terms: he appeared as homo sapiens on the earth. The more experienced he became on earth, the more intelligent and self-conscious he was, the more disenchanted of him became the spiritual world, with its forces and beings, of which he had once been a part. This was expressed in the heroic myths, for example Theseus who defeated the Minotaur, an untamed soul-nature inhabited by unconscious primitive people; or in the myth of Hercules and the Hydra. During his earliest times, man was trying to really become a human being in a higher sense. For this, he must first learn to assert himself on the earth and distance himself from the instincts he could also observe in animals. He wanted to become his own master.

Prometheus, the son of Titans, an offspring of the gods who, by his consistent support of the human race and his support for the prophesy that a 'twilight of the gods' was approaching, had made himself unloved by his peers. He wanted man to recognize and overcome his dependence on the gods, to become master over his natural instincts.

At that moment I considered Prometheus as *the* representative of Greek mythology, as the key figure in the development of human consciousness. He embodied humanity's *struggle* for freedom from the old gods and also from the hitherto *unconscious soul-forces*. How should man ever become conscious of his *human-being-core* if he didn't first become conscious of the forces within him which over-ran that human-being-core? According to Prometheus' will, man should no longer offer sacrifices to *those* forces!

In Goethe's consummate words, Prometheus spoke through humans. It was the voice of the higher consciousness of the human being who was still unconsciously but gradually striving for earthly intelligence. He directs his justified anger at the representa-tive of the Olympian gods with a beautiful and triumphal self-con-sciousness, against which the might of the gods suddenly seemed to weaken:

> *Bedeck your heaven, Zeus,*
> *With clouds of mist,*
> *And like the boy who lops*
> *The thistles' heads,*
> *Disport with oaks and mountain-peaks;*
> *Yet you must leave*
> *My earth still standing;*
> *And cottage, not built by you,*
> *And my hearth,*
> *Whose glow*
> *By you is envied.*

Later I understood that the cottage probably meant the earthly cor-poreality of humanity, and the hearth's glow meant the human-be-ing-core's knowledge-fire.

> *I know nothing poorer*
> *Under the sun than you, gods!*
> *You nourish meagerly,*
> *With victims' taxes*
> *And whiff of prayer,*

Your majesty,
And would starve, were
children and beggars not
Fools full of hope.

'Children', 'Fools full of hope', were the humans who were dependent on the gods – who were subject to them in respect to their conscious-ness. They would remain fools, could never be gods themselves if they did not free themselves. Goethe's Prometheus called this dependence on the gods, who themselves were consciously asleep, 'slavery'.

Who helped me
Against the Titans' insolence?
Who rescued me from death,
From slavery?
Did you not do it all yourself,
venerable glowing heart?
And glowed young and good,
Deceived, salvation thanks
To the sleeper over there?

'Did you not do it all yourself, venerable glowing heart?' – 'Salvation thanks to the sleeper over there?' – Oh no, certainly not!

I honour you? What for?
Have you ever soothed the pain
Of the heavily burdened?
Have you ever dried the tears
Of the anguished?

No! The *soul-forces-bodies*, whose representatives were the Olympic gods, could not do that! Unrestrained soul-forces, unconscious feel-ings and desires, *they* created the pain and the angst! To soothe the pain of the burdened, to dry the tears of the anguished could only be done by entities who had awoken their *core-of-being* and brought it to accomplished development, which enabled them to practice *altruistic* love, compassion, mercy – beings who kept account of the eternal plan of destiny of every immortal human-being-core, that is, every individual. Entities who were even Lords of 'Time' and Lords of 'Destiny'.

> *Was I not fashioned as a man*
> *By omnipotent Time*
> *And eternal destiny,*
> *My masters and yours?*

These highest entities of which Prometheus speaks here were the true lords of men and the (lower) gods, of the soul-forces! For they were complete divine beings, the healers of afflictions and ulcerations of the soul, the saviours of the human soul, the promoters of the development of human fools to true divine, self-aware people capable of love!

> *That was the 'creative Majesty', that was the Son of God, the Christ!*

Christ was the personification of those highest beings, who could tame and still the excesses of the soul-force-body and make it gracious and untainted.

I sensed that it was Prometheus who enabled human beings to become independent of the ancient world of gods and no longer instinctively animal-like. He advanced man's battle to free himself from unconsciousness. And it was Christ who could enable us to rise to such an independent Prometheus-man or earth-man, to higher, full consciousness, to divine humanity. He was to advance the unification of the human being with the creative Majesty, independent of the 'lower gods', and with full human consciousness.

I realized for the first time the importance of Christ being the actual core-being of Jesus, who brought Himself to accept 'the cup'. It contained something exceedingly bitter, which we would rather not drink. In reality it was an image for the courageous and consistent conquering of the soul-forces overrunning the core of being, defeated by means of the core-being's power. That was on a large scale what I observed on a small scale: that whoever was conscious of being dependent on feelings, possessions and desires (smoking, for example), would be able to dominate them. If he was then able to convert this will into concrete actions, he would become a true master – one of the few people I had admired from a distance. If it had perhaps been bitter to give up the comfortable and superficially pleasant vices he had become fond of (the small man's 'cup'), in return he had gained invaluable goods: peace of heart, clear vision and the capacity for compassion. Jesus Christ was our shining example, the wise guide! God Himself had shown humanity this mystery of metamorphosis. Now I knew what to do; a hard path, becoming master of one's self. But it was the only one leading to the goal, and the only really beautiful one! How shaken and moved I was when, several years later, I came across Goethe's poem-fragment 'The Secrets', in which he wrote:

> For when a man excels by gifts of nature,
> It is no wonder if his life is blessed;
> In him we worship the Creator's power,
> Through feeble human clay made manifest;
> But he who overcomes himself has gained
> The greatest triumph, stood the hardest test,
> And well may he to all the world be shown:
>
> Yea, this is he, this deed is his alone!
>
> With all our strength we strive to live and labour,
> Wherever by fate our twisting paths be wended;
> Whereas the world oppresses, ever impeding,
> And seeks to tear us from the way intended;
> Within this inner storm and outer struggle
> Our spirit hears a word scarce comprehended:
> The power that holds constrained all humankind
> The victor over himself no more can bind.

In this way antiquity (together with the German classics) helped me more to find answers about God and Christ and our human relationship with them than any class on Christian religion.

* * *

Acquaintance with the world of antiquity allowed me also to be attentive to something which became ever more important as I grew older, and eventually became a necessity. This was the presence and the appreciation of *beauty* in the world and its importance for the human soul, and consequently for the human spirit.

Painting and the other fine arts didn't give me as much soul-food as music, but almost as much. I also had some practical talent here, probably because of paternal genes. My father was an interior architect of the old school, and in fact an exceptionally talented one – something confirmed as fact by the critical consideration of neutral third parties. One should not confuse an interior architect of the old school with an interior decorator who provides some aesthetic wall-paper and furniture to a clueless client. My father, who possessed a strong aesthetic sense, had also trained as a carpenter, which honed his practical talent for details. But he also intervened in the building's structure, so that a house designed by him only retained its original outer shell. What I mean by an interior architect of the old school will be clear to anyone who has seen drawings by Karl Friedrich Schinkel, that go from the broad view down to the smallest detail, thus forming a comprehensive concept. In fact, much of what my father designed and carried through in the construction phase showed a stylistic relation to the work of Schinkel, that great builder and painter of Prussian classicism, whom we both admired. Much of his work in my immediate surroundings, namely in and around Berlin, had been preserved, repaired or reconstructed after the war. Until his death, I saw my father in one of two positions. Every day and until deep in the night – even during vacations (in which all the necessary tools were taken along) – he was bent over his drawing-board, for everything was done by hand, from the details of a window's profile to the elevation of walls and complicated spatial outlines and perspective. (There were no computers as yet, and when they came they were never used for the supreme discipline, the spatial representations.) Or, he was consumed in tireless work at the construction site with a yardstick, pocket calculator, goniometer and drawing board. I often accompanied him in order to help – because it was a genuine challenge for me to be of real help – for example by calculating an exact measurement, which caused me great joy. Because my father worked in his office in the same building where our apartment was situated, his occupation was very present for me, from childhood on. Although he didn't have enough time and leisure to teach me certain skills, and thus never systematically instructed me, I copied a lot from him, and from early on developed an eye and a heartfelt affinity for the fine arts.

My parents recognized early on that I showed a certain talent for spatial drawing and painting, so they encouraged this indirectly by providing me with many picture books about painting from the time between the Middle Ages and modernity. Just as with music, I carefully studied painting and, to a lesser degree, the biographies of the artists. I invented a kind of game, trying to find out in individual paintings what told of the zeitgeist and the painter's biography and what was, so to speak, eternally valid, truly beautiful, and if so, what it actually consisted of. That couldn't be so easily determined because it always appeared in individual form. There was often a bridge between the musical and the painted compositions of a certain epoch, so that the impressions gained from various artistic activities complemented each other to give a more complete picture of the respective epoch. But it wasn't the stylistic methods alone that determined whether something was a true work of art or merely a pleasingly good work. It was something which lay between the lines, or between the brush strokes.

What the musical and pictorial arts had in common, and what I also found in poetry a few years later, was the possibility of adding something out of 'nothing' to the existing natural world that could be just as nourishing for the soul as the beauty of God's work, nature. The human being could succeed – and he had already succeeded – in making what is truly beautiful in the *World of Reality* visible, audible and knowable in the world of external appearances. And sometimes whilst enjoying a work of art I found that here the higher spiritual potency in man had found the instrument with which to show and nourish humanity. I saw the truly talented artist as the bearer of a brilliant divine spark, which worked through his individual human-being-core so the divine could use it. Thus the artist – at least for the hours of his creativity – became a kind of divine entity himself, who had created something for others which was of consummate and lasting quality.

Such earthly things delighted me. I saw them as tangible evidence of the divine spirit acting behind them, even when I could

94

not say exactly what each one had to do with the great cosmic plan. A special magic surrounded them, which stimulated the imagination and filled the heart with wonderful thoughts. I felt that everything artistic, everything created by human beings, was an expression of their invisible, that is, super-sensory, inner life. — GREAT!

But when this inner life was fragmented and without awareness of the existence of an overriding whole, then ugliness or 'squalor' was created, as I often observed in modern art. When I saw people in museums apparently fascinated by looking at a monochrome painting or by one divided into two different coloured halves, I had little or no understanding of it. Their expression was meant to demonstrate artistic comprehension. It was a puzzle for me that they stood for so long before this 'nothing'.

Perhaps I was simply not mature enough to realize the deeper meaning of such a painting and therefore to feel the clearly resulting pleasure. But I must admit that not much has changed today. Of course, one can talk about the meaningfulness of monochromatic or the so-called Action painting. One can also discuss the meaningfulness of a randomly created sculpture, like a melted-down bronze meatball. Certainly, Action painting has a specific background, and one can quickly see that it reflects the artist's momentary attitude on political or social ideas. But aren't these all aspects that require an intellectual examination of the work in order to be able to really appreciate it?

When I asked some people why they were so fascinated by such works, to my great surprise they assured me that they felt the piece spoke to them because they could see the soul of the artist in it. I observed the scene again and wondered if those people weren't deceiving themselves a little. Or did the souls of a Jackson Pollock or a Barnett Newman really look as empty and desolate as their pictures?

In an exhibition I read a quotation by Newman, which I found again during research and seemed to confirm my fear. It read: *'I believe that here in America, some of us, free from the weight of European culture, are finding the answer, by completely denying that art has any concern with the problem of beauty and where to find it. The question that now arises is how, if we are living in a time without a legend or mythos that can be called sublime, if we refuse to admit any exaltation in pure relations, if we refuse to live in the abstract, how can we be creating a sublime art? ... Instead of making cathedrals out of Christ, man, or "life", we are making it out of ourselves, out of our own feelings. The image we produce is the self-evident one of revelation, real and concrete, that can be understood by anyone who will look at it without the nostalgic glasses of history.'*

Well, obviously I viewed his pictures through the 'nostalgic glasses of [art] history'. Certainly, as a child I was no art historian or expert of any kind, able to defend an opinion formed by long years of study. I tried hard to acquire a taste, to 'understand' such pictures through feeling, and stood before them with unreserved neutrality, because I wished to learn everything new and to let it affect me – to try it out, so to speak. After all, many grown-ups stood spellbound before such pictures and crowded into exhibitions where they were willing to pay high entrance fees. Astronomical sums were offered for the works themselves. Even if I was spoiled by the art of the past, why did these pictures not speak to me in their own way? Why was there nothing alive in them? Why did I feel as dragged through treacle and exhausted after looking at such pictures in a gallery?

In the final analysis, the artist himself gave the answer to how such a picture could even be made, and why it had this effect on my inner life: he considered beauty to be a 'problem' by definition, that we should consistently ignore. Furthermore, he proclaimed: *'Instead of making cathedrals out of Christ, man, or "life", we are making it out of ourselves, out of our own feelings.'* Yes, but isn't the self of the person a cathedral of life, a cathedral of himself or of the divinity living within him? And when this self becomes creative, does not the spirit of 'Christ', 'man', or 'life' also live in the artistic 'structure' which originated through him?

Obviously, Mr Newman did not mean the *higher self*, but the largely unconscious one, in which the remaining unconscious feelings are manifested. If the great number of only monochromatic pictures painted over many years really reflect his 'own feelings', as he says, then that must mean that he consistently, that is, with extreme brutality against himself, ripped out of his heart every sensibility and appreciation for the life-forces within him. But why? How can it happen that people only understand 'beauty' as the reflection of a personal inclination, a petty sentimentality? Why were there

---

* Newman 1948, In: Harrison/Wood 2003, p. 701.

people who recoiled from 'legends and myths' like the proverbial devil from holy water? The only answer I found was that they obviously were afraid of being unable to find themselves amidst all the 'weight' of their thousand-year-old culture. It seemed to me, though, that the possibility to truly find oneself is given through a relationship to the cultural history of humankind. I saw clearly what happened when all that had already been accomplished was rejected: a picture which reflected precisely the artist's inner life. And this picture showed a simple-minded, sclerotic, empty life of feeling, which one can barely call life; rather, a rigidity of feeling unable to touch the beholder's soul and inspire his spirit. In short, the ability to achieve a loving gesture to the other human being through art.

But that was just what I had experienced during my encounter with Christ as the uppermost concern of the healthy human spirit. Therefore, it was comprehensible why the art of artists like Mr Newman could not be 'revelation' for me, as he had hoped. After all, he had spoken out in favour of the opposite of what I had chosen. Namely, he wanted to make no 'cathedrals out of Christ'.

But we can safely leave the concept of Christ aside and simply say that if, when observing an artwork, the soul does not feel inspired to go searching for the source of life – and such a search for the source of life can also result in the encounter with a dark subject – then the person stands before an artwork only with his intellect. Nothing stands before his soul – or, worse still, he stands before a devastating vortex. On the other hand, if the artistic object in question was filled to the brim with longing and love for the whole – to which the history and the super-sensory aesthetic 'biography' of humankind belongs – then the artist would have created something beautiful, with a beauty beyond temporal duration. And this beauty has a healing effect on the spiritual and physical organism. I could observe this everywhere.

But above all one could observe, even outwardly, the destructive effect that ugliness has on the human soul. For man is not only capable of creating the eternally beautiful, but also ugliness. Gradually, I began to ask myself which spiritual force was expressed in man as creator of ugliness, which in itself is pernicious for human life-forces. It must have been a powerful being, for, as far as I could observe in my surroundings, people of the present produced far more ugliness than beauty. An *Autobahn* [freeway] was undoubtedly a practical thing. But it bisected the land through which it ran, and brought with it acoustic, olfactory and visual pollution. Such unquestionably practical inventions for the comfort of people like the Autobahn were evident to me. But why wasn't it possible to counter this perhaps necessary evil with something that alleviated its laming effect on the soul?

The older I grew the more I felt – and I still feel that way today – that there is no longer any magic in our world, no fantasy. We have lost the sensitivity for beauty, although we need it no less urgently than water and air, because we get more and more sick from its absence. Art, music, architecture, speech, even clothing, hardly show beauty anymore; beauty in which the eternal, which is edifying for the soul, can unfold. And our souls become poor through what we surround ourselves with, through our works; and our works become poor through our poor souls.

How wonderfully the architecture of antiquity fitted into the natural surroundings in which it was embedded! Where once wild and beautiful nature ruled alone, nature was placed within the scene, emphasized, venerated, and at the same time softened and ennobled. But the builders of the Renaissance, or Classicism, also had a noble goal in mind – although with a touch of the romantic – which the people of antiquity didn't need to work at, because they had a certain intuitive understanding of the *beautification of the earthly world.*

Do we still have an understanding for what truly beautifies the world? Do we still feel the need to make it 'beautiful'? Or, by inserting ever more ugliness into the world, *'by completely denying that art has any concern with the problem of beauty and where to find it'*, and being educated in this way, do we not notice either its presence or its absence? If this were so, we would be on the way to depriving ourselves of the chance to ennoble our own selves. We would be denying ourselves spiritual nourishment, the life-forces, if we trained ourselves to no longer recognize ugliness for what it is: something which corrupts the whole person, but instead come to feel disgust for beauty to the extent of rejecting it. Then we would be about to turn the world upside down, to live entirely in a lie, in an illusion that one day would turn into an earthly reality. This kind of 'soul-death' terrified me as a child, for in so many places I discovered a total lack of interest in the true source of spiritual nourishment, and the crudeness with which the venerable, unifying totality was treated.

I experienced what today is even more drastically evident: together with the sense of eternal beauty, we have also lost the love of timelessness. Instead, we have a haste that rushes us past what is beautiful. Have we not almost forgotten how to be mindful of the world's nuances? With our ears stopped up with an MP3-player whilst jogging, we cannot hear the birds' enchanting song which can, without the help of the other senses, tell us so much – such as the time of the year, whether morning has just arrived or whether the evening is sinking into night, whether it's a song of courtship, or the merry question-and-answer game of two neighbours in different territories. On a furiously racing trekking bike, one cannot observe the procession of clouds and their continuous changing forms, as if designed by an invisible hand. With sunglasses on one's nose and roller-skates on one's feet it is not possible to study a blossom – let alone encounter its essence – for in this condition you wouldn't even notice the flower. To put on a dress surely takes longer than hot-pants with a zipper. But are the hot-pants thus more beautiful? Would the aesthetic-feeling heart really like to see every feminine figure in skintight leggings and every masculine upper-body in a 'muscle shirt'? Which maleficent spirit could have inspired the people who invented the parka, or later the hooded anorak, with drawstring and over-sized pockets, with loud-coloured artificial fur trimming for women, in which the noble Prometheus would not even recognize the human beings created according to his image? Of course, from a soul-spiritual perspective it is not important how the exterior form of the body is wrapped. However, the way we are wrapping it today indicates that we no longer even possess a soul-spiritual perspective.

In my schoolbooks I looked wistfully at the pictures of antique clothing in Greece, where through artistic draping of the material the currents of force were visible, which constantly flowed from the earth through the people to the invisible World of Reality – and from the invisible World of Reality through the people to the earth.

In Roman clothing, an even more differentiated allegory of the invisible human body seemed to appear before my eyes: I saw the inconspicuous tunic covering the physical body as a material reflection of the magical life-force form. And in the often vibrantly-coloured toga covering the tunic, I saw the image of the soul-force-body which, with its shimmering colour-filled undulating emotions, was like the magical life-force actively covering the organs. When in a museum of antiquity I stood before that kind of clothing and imagined them coming to life, something inside me said: Yes! That is man, that is the human being! That is man as a soul-spiritual being who is incorporated in a physical body on earth. That is the form of his physical body, the play of his muscles when he carries the shield and the sword; there the magical life-force, the tunic; here the soul-force-body, the toga; and by his bearing and by his expression, the human-being-core, the actual higher self, the spirit, is revealed. Yes, this is how the human being as earthly man 'rightfully' looks!

But then in my surroundings…? At the time I found little that made me feel certain that I could observe the totality of the human being. Either we disappeared under sack-like over-largeness, which made the last broken gem of our individuality practically undiscoverable in today's bodies. Or, we dressed in such a way that only the physical covering was shown to advantage – which is ever more the case in today's fashion – to the extent that clothing barely fulfilled its function of covering the body and offering it a certain protection, or warmth. I rather had the impression that the person observed looked less naked without clothing than with it. By contrast, in the world of antiquity there was sheer gauze-like silk material, which did not conceal the body beneath but on the contrary made the entire body visible – but nevertheless it conveyed a completely different aesthetic impression. It was easy to discover how that was. In both cases, the physical body was emphasized. In the first case, a vulgar sex-appeal was reflected, which arose from an unconscious soul-life and thereby could and should make the person just as addicted to such a sight as the urge to smoke a cigarette. In the second case, however, in which the transparent silk fabric flows around and over the body, elegance and 'Eros' is reflected, in the sense of the Greek god. Here, like with antique architecture and landscaping, the earthly body, as the highest created form, becomes further ennobled by an artistic rendering of its garments.

Already as a ten- or eleven-year-old child I found this exclusive emphasis on the body – the transitory element of earthly mankind – somewhat obscene, but not because I considered the body itself as impure or obscene! Neither I nor my family were prudes. I found it obscene because this trend revealed people's blindness to the World of Reality – yes, even to their own higher immortal selves, and to the beauty of the physical and soul-spiritual totality. They seemed just as bare in respect to the awareness of their inner life and the forces of a higher nature flowing around and through them, as the scantiness of their clothing. That is what I considered obscene: the mind directed exclusively to the earthly world, to the outward aspect of material practicality, or the indifferent carelessness in which other dimensions are barely given space. In this respect the clothes, matching the prevailing trend in painting, music or architecture, fitted very well our current (in the truest sense of the word) squalid zeitgeist.

We knew all of this very well. And yet we can no longer compete against the empty and ugly aesthetics of the prevailing zeitgeist. The spirits we called upon are no longer so easily captured.

At that time I was convinced that a remedy existed. In the end, it always came down to this – even with sensitivity to the aesthetic and the unaesthetic – whether or not one was able to bring things and conditions to one's consciousness. Thus I experienced especially in a screaming, violent person, whose facial expression not only betrayed his – in the truest sense of the word – blind rage, but whose voice also took on an unaesthetic timbre and whose words became ugly, how much the feelings and surges of will whipping up in the unconscious could distort the (eternally) beautiful, the divine in man, to a never-ending ugliness. Ugly could distort. I was convinced that mindfulness of beauty in the world could provide relief to the plagued and sickened soul, which must constantly digest ugliness; if the soul-force-body received wholesome nourishment, the human-being-core would also become active – one's 'actual self' would come a step closer, and the magical life-force would flow in a wonderful way, smoothly and more rich within one's inner being. I observed this direct connection on many occasions, also in myself. It was a tried and true remedy.

So I helped myself to a bit of the 'beautiful' among the rampant 'unbeautiful' with a trick. When I was eleven years old, our family grew. Although it was not a little sister or brother – to my great regret I remained an only child – a dog, a little fox terrier puppy, moved in with us. That exuberant being needed extensive exercise – so from then on I often took it for walks. On these walks, during which I thought about my life, I often immersed myself in a different time. I would have liked to translate myself back to the times of antiquity. But the places where my walks took me had nothing at all to do with antique customs – neither architectural nor topographical. But I very much wished to be back in a time when the sense of the beautiful was not so completely lost as in our own. Therefore a different time had to be discovered, vestiges of which could be found in my surroundings. At that time I lived in a beautiful section of West Berlin in which there were many grand old stately homes between carefully tendered parks. Those mansions, built during the nineteenth and early twentieth centuries, were, in part, lovingly maintained in the traditional manner. Many had stately central staircases and servants' entrances on the side, whilst others – of which I felt most attracted – had many small bay windows, with glassed-in, winter gardens supported by thin metal frames; exterior spiral staircases leading up to small towers with look-outs, or a pergola in the garden entwined by wild vines, in the shade of which cast-iron benches invited you to linger outdoors. On my walks I thus imagined myself living at the turn of the century. When I came across something ugly, such as the modern two-storey apartment house in which we lived, or a flat-roofed bungalow from the fifties or sixties with a punctuated facade, ungainly large flower windows in the upper area or with mushroom-shaped garden-path lanterns made of yellow plastic, I closed my eyes and let my dog lead me along the path past the house. As soon as a house with character appeared, I opened my eyes, knowing exactly where on my route that house stood. I slowed down when passing these beautiful mansions. I enjoyed every moment and included them in my 'story'. I most enjoyed walking through the streets from the time of the Kaiser, paved with old cobblestones. In summer, between these cobblestones, so much moss grew that from a distance they looked completely green. Then I imagined the clapping beat of horses' hooves and the clatter of coach wheels.

I thought of the people who once lived and worked here, what they felt and thought. I tried to live into the corresponding time so that I also experienced the dreams and concerns of the inhabitants of that time. The noble oaks and sycamore trees that gracefully bowed over the bumpy street must have witnessed the activities of those times. When I looked at or touched them, I was also touching those times from long ago that were suddenly alive within me. Thus the trees were also a vivid part of my story.

In this way I filled many hours of the otherwise busy and prosaic everyday life with as much 'beauty' as possible – be it through the conscious perception of nature (created from a higher place), of the urban environment (designed by people with an aesthetic sense) or through the countless stories (born in my imagination) from past epochs. These experiences nourished me. Because of them, I became happy and satisfied. Conscious living with 'the beautiful' became the indispensable compensation for the lack of interchange with the people I knew about the World of Reality.

* * *

The incisive event which I described earlier, and which I designate as my 'Christ experience', subsequently brought – as already mentioned, but not yet explained in detail – changes to my relationship with the World of Reality, with the World of Spirit. For this reason, my Christ experience was *incisive*: my relationship with the World of Spirit became more intense and tangible. The change probably began when I experienced more consciously 'remaining awake' during the process of falling asleep. I had resolved to strive towards the World of Consciousness in order to recall the love bestowed upon me by the high Entity, by the Son of God. Due to that Christ-experience and also because of my getting older, my rational thinking had become more focused than before, and with that the ability to clarify certain goals or ideals and to consider how I could achieve them. So I decided to behave in such a way that one day I might at least sporadically become a 'domicile' of the high Entity, in order to let something of that love, that I had been allowed to feel, flow into my earthly environment. At first that was of course 'only' an ideal. But achieving that goal began by spiritually understanding it – although

103

the path to the goal seemed to become longer and harder the more I learned and the longer I was on that journey. But I had the great luck to have once encountered my 'ideal' before setting off on the path, so that I never lost the impulse to be true to this ideal, no matter how arduous the path later became. I had only to think back to my Christ experience, to His presence – and the divine, unbreakable human brotherhood made by His love – and my heart was again in flames. Thus, I finally overcame the lethargy and despondency caused by the everyday sensory-material temptations of the all-too-worldly influences surging in the foreground.

Perhaps the specific reflection on my immaterial, higher goals was the trigger for the progressive differentiation of my inner life. Perhaps it was also induced by the high Entity – by Christ Himself – whom I had recognized as my divine teacher and who intended to prepare His little pupil for encountering the multiple realities of the World of Reality. Perhaps it was both. One of these realities was to know my own being – and not only my higher, actual self as a large radiant light of consciousness, but also to descend, with a torch of this light, into the depths of the subconscious. In fact, the first could only be achieved by means of the second. This was made understandable to me in an impressive way by my *staying awake when falling asleep.*

I lay in my bed and closed my eyes. Soon sleep would spread its dark, soft blanket over me and silence all earthly perceptions, until the world would completely disappear. But this time it was different, although exterior perceptions gradually levelled off and the few noises I heard were muffled as usual. But suddenly it became clear to me that I was observing it all – that sleep did not rob me of the ability to observe that I was falling asleep. I pondered it, but my astonishment about this odd situation didn't bother me. It was as though I grew out of the usual place of residence within my body; as though I withdrew from it – for example from the fingers, which now, whilst sleeping, had no need to feel anything material; or from the ears, which during sleep did not need to be attentive to the sounds of the sensory world. I understood why at night one forgets one's surroundings; why one is dead to the outer world. It was due to oneself withdrawing from the sensory organs. It wasn't something ominous that came over you from without and took away your daytime consciousness. You did it yourself in that you no longer resided in your body as you did during the day. You were no longer stuck so fast within the individual organs. Fascinated, but at the same time totally relaxed, I observed what was happening so softly, so naturally.

Suddenly, something blood-curdling sprang at me! It was like a hideous, contorted face, followed by many small, ghastly creatures. They all hurtled at me like furies.* Then, in a split second, the face bloated into a gigantic, menacing apparition. I was so frightened that I fell back into my day-consciousness and all the apparitions burst asunder. I pulled myself together. My heart beat fast. What *was* that? I was not a child who imagined ghosts. I had never gone to bed afraid because I pictured something evil lurking in a corner of the room. But what I now saw had been so real as only some physical-material phenomenon could be! What in the world was that? I couldn't explain it. I walked up and down in my room until I lay down again in bed and, finally – in the usual way – fell asleep.

In the following days or weeks the experience was repeated three of four times. I worried what the dreadful apparition was that frightened me terribly every time, and why it disturbed the process of peaceful observation.

One night – it was probably the fourth time – I again observed the going-to-sleep process and thought that perhaps this time I would emerge unscathed, but suddenly the dreadful creature sprang at me again. It was extremely abrupt and unexpected, and it seemed to spring directly up to my face (although, in that state of consciousness, I wasn't really 'inside' my physical face). It seemed to be aiming at me for some reason. It was the same kind of horrid, strange phenomenon. As far as I had been able to survey previously – because I had always been so violently frightened that I had been startled back into my daytime consciousness, for which of course the entity did not become visible – the ugly thing actually consisted of many equally ugly creatures bound up in a kind of swarm that took on a shape, the main part of which formed a huge fearsome face, which grew in front of me, eye-to-eye, so to speak.

---

* Furies, Greek Erinyes, also called Eumenides, in Greco-Roman mythology, the chthonic goddesses of vengeance.

This time, however, I reacted differently. Not that the dreadful thing was less scary. No, the violence with which it approached me was no less forbidding and, because of its abrupt springing up, was just as frightening. Also, I hadn't intended to react in a certain way in the case that it appeared again. But this time I made a spontaneous decision to endure the presence of that ominous creature. I didn't want to give in to it. The decision was not made under the conditions which are present in day-consciousness, that is, in a calm, unhurried way; it was made just as lightning fast as the appearance of the fury. There were only two options: to wake up from fright or to persevere.

The decision to resist fear led to my *not* falling back into my day-consciousness. I succeeded in being able to keep observing. What I learned in this longer state of observation about the fury was to some extent, however, disturbing. By standing up to that being, I was no longer prevented from 'expanding' even more. I now experienced myself as expanding over the limits of my body's outreaching self-awareness. I became very *large*, comparable to a balloon that is inflating. But it was not my *body* that was inflating, but my self, that is, my *consciousness*. One could imagine the self-awareness of day-consciousness as being within the confines of a crumpled-up balloon, whereas in the state I was now, my awareness was like the inflated skin of the balloon as well as the particles of air inside it.

I was in a state in which my consciousness had extended quite a distance beyond the limits of my physical body. And from this 'perspective', the reason for the encounter with the ghastly fury became evident: the being composed of many different ghastly creatures was a part of myself! The tiny little beasts sat in my own psychic components, or sheaths – above all, in my soul-force-body, but many also nested in my magical life-force-form. It was no less than the imaginative appearance of my own – until now unconscious or unresolved – 'quirks'. These are detrimental to the eternal connection of all created creatures and the brotherhood founded on selfless love: stubbornness, gossip, lying, jealousy, vanity, superiority, feelings of resentment and revenge, cowardice and complacency – much of which can, sometimes more or sometimes less, romp about within the human soul and, in the worst of cases, become habits that are difficult to overcome .

What happened? I – that is, my consciousness – by continuing to expand, had passed beyond the natural limits of my sheaths. I had passed through them, 'loosened' by the transition to sleep, and by doing so I ran into something I hadn't really been aware of until then, which, largely unnoticed by me, could cause hurt to those around me.

This, then, was me!

I had of course already felt that the image I had of myself was more flattering than what reality would indicate. (It was a vague image, because at that age I still had not really thought about it much.) I had not expected that it would be so severe, though. In the state I was in, however, strangely enough this knowledge didn't bother me. It was simply a fact, just as other facts which one has nothing directly to do with can be accepted without much ado. I was by no means indifferent, but there was no personal reference which, because of disappointment or vanity, would have led me to deny or gloss over what I was seeing. It was simply a fact that part of me was that way. And it was a fact that this part had a detrimental effect on the welfare of the world as a whole, and thus also contradicted my goals and ideals. To 'see' this made me a little sad, but it was not the sadness we know from the usual conditions of life. It was as if I felt compassion for another poor person. I no longer felt that I was on the earth. I felt just as expansive as, now, my consciousness expansively perceived and thought. This meant that I felt 'with' the facts, objectively; I felt, from the perspective of a greater harmony, the effects of my feelings, misdeeds and attributes that remained largely unconscious in everyday life – within areas which are not usually considered to be related to one's private, inner life.

I was aware that I had vividly observed my whole self for the first time, just as I had often observed the turmoil in other people's soul-force bodies and their effect on their environment, except that now I had experienced my self as a whole; not just certain aspects, as when I sometimes observed people during the day. I had directly 'seen' my being, experiencing it as it had developed since the beginning of my existence. And a portion of it consisted of those bad aspects which appeared as grotesque figures during the process.

These figures had a striking similarity to the fantastic creatures in Hieronymus Bosch's paintings. When I first came across copies of some of his work a few years later, I was overcome by the similarity. Everyone I showed the paintings to in the books attributed them to his vivid imagination, or remarked laconically that, 'in the Middle Ages people still believed in such things'. Someone who was considered knowledgeable in this subject explained to me that the artist was completely under the influence of the Church and his paintings followed pedagogic, but above all economic, interests, namely to threaten people with the torments of an alleged Hell so they would pay indulgences to the church. That did not convince me at all; neither did most of the explanatory texts under the paintings, which were highly speculative and terribly clever. They all agreed on one thing though: the ugly creatures in Bosch's paintings did not exist. I, however, was certain that Bosch really saw these beings, representing the excesses of human characteristics in pictures. And yes, by painting them he wanted to warn his fellow human beings about continuing to deny the self-concealed aspects of themselves. But by so doing, he certainly wanted to help them and not push them into the clutches of a money-grubbing clergy. For nobody who had ever experienced something like this could be indifferent to his fellow human beings' fate, because through such an experience he inevitably must have recognized what he was doing to them by his own selfishness, and indeed how much the whole world suffered because of it.

I found this to be true in his painting 'The Seven Deadly Sins', which depicted the seven main vices of the human soul painted on a tabletop and arranged in a circle so that they could be perceived equally as one went around the table. And one of the seven sins was named by the Greek word *acedia*, which could be translated as 'antipathy', 'cold-hearted' or 'indifference'. So Bosch couldn't have been indifferent to what became of his neighbour who observed his pictures if he called one of the seven deadly sins 'indifference'! In the centre of the picture, as though it were the pupil within the coloured iris consisting of the seven vices, was the resurrected Christ, showing the stigmata of His left hand and pointing with His right to His side wound, as if these were the sluices through which the vices of men had flowed out with His blood. Underneath were the words: *'cave cave deus videt'* – 'Careful, Beware, God sees'. It was clear to me that someone who wanted to be with God would also want to behave in such a way as to be able to experience His presence. No one who pursued this ideal would want to present himself to his beloved, revered friend and supreme teacher with such misconduct! And such a vice would not be called a 'deadly sin' because it would be punished with death by God; rather, that one is preparing one's own death in the World of Reality by being addicted to such bad habits as envy, pride or greed instead of transforming them to goodwill, modesty or willingness to sacrifice. This experience made it clear to me that from then on I could only enter the World of Reality, or see clearly in it, if my vices were left outside, before the 'gate'. But for this to happen at all, I had first to recognize them.

One could perhaps think about all this: What could a girl of ten or eleven years of age have done which is so terrible that it attracted such horrible apparitions from the super-sensory world? But one must bear in mind that these apparitions are individual and therefore relative. It is always only about the individual human being in respect to his or her personal deeds. And the transgressions of a child appear to the child just as drastic as those of an adult to adults, aside from the fact that in the World of Reality it is irrelevant if one is a child or an adult on earth, because what is experienced and recognized is a function of the human-being-core, which is neither child nor adult. It is not about two different people here, of whom one is better and the other worse. To judge that would probably be reserved for the divine Entity, for nothing that I experienced indicates that 'the good are kept and the bad are expelled'. In any case, in this preparatory trial one person never comes off well or badly in relation to others, because in relation to his faults he faces only himself. He must face the truth about himself in order for the 'gate' to open for him.

Thus, by touching upon my inner debasements, I had actually passed a barrier. I had left the bad side of my soul-force-body behind by recognizing it; but I kept the good side, because I realized that it would be needed in the sphere or world in which I now moved, in order to keep *feeling* (a property of the soul-force-body). I hardly need mention that this feeling was also different than in the sensory world, because although in a certain sense one still felt subjectively or independently, it was no longer felt selfishly.

And if that crept in again, one fell back, that is, one no longer saw the essence clearly – one obscured oneself.

In this almost 'purified' state I was able to expand further. I became ever 'lighter' and 'larger' (my consciousness, that is), but my consciousness was clear and bright and, furthermore, 'with me'. I perceived the *presence of a spiritual Being*. I had the sensation that it had already been there before I discovered it, and was waiting for me to recognize it. It's hard for me to describe what this sensation conveyed to me. For I have now reached the point in my narrative where the words normally used in the sensory-material world are no longer adequate to describe the relationships and events in the non-material world. It is necessary mostly to use metaphors or paraphrasing. I had the impression that the spiritual Entity had already been waiting for me. It didn't tell me this in words, but by the way it was. It radiated patience, loving forbearance and solicitude. And I entered directly into this radiance by expanding. In this way I participated in what the Presence was, thought and felt. But this thinking and feeling was not comparable to our everyday way of thinking and feeling. The spiritual Entity *thought* feeling and *felt* thinking, but in a completely sincere, refined way. In our day-consciousness our thoughts, feelings and desires are mixed together like motley colours. We are barely able to think a thought not influenced, or even undermined by, some sympathetic or antipathetic feeling or personal wish. This makes the thought 'corrupt', as long as we are not aware of the impulses influencing it. The difference in the way of thinking in the World of Reality, which was also practiced by the Entity whom I perceived, was that our everyday thinking is determined by our feelings, whereas the thinking of the spiritual Entity was consciously pervaded and warmed by feeling. Its thinking could quite rightly be pervaded by feeling because its feelings were completely conscious and it ennobled its own thinking, which was thus full of wisdom. They were all loving, altruistic thoughts which radiated from the Presence and in which I consciously participated, because my consciousness was within them.

In this way the means of communication emerged, for the Entity also participated in my thoughts and feelings – in my whole being in fact – in that I expanded into its circle of activity. It seemed to know all that ever mattered to me, what I experienced, thought, felt, did or wanted, but there was nothing in any way disagreeable or compromising about it. I did not have the feeling that my privacy was infringed upon. After all, I no longer felt myself to be earthly-personal, and I had 'opened up' myself. But it was also the case that absolutely nothing proceeded from this Entity which tempted me to hide anything, for its intention was completely selfless and 'noble'.

Gradually, the impulse which proceeded directly to me from the Entity became clearer. I had first to learn to orient myself in this world and at least begin to learn the new means of thinking and feeling and also the new way to communicate. By means of an inner turning to myself, which as a child I called 'heart language', the Entity made me understand that it wanted to teach me something, that it would be my teacher in that world. And as I perceived this, I realized that I wanted the same, and that is why I could even become attentive to the Entity. By my orientation towards it, I recognized its orientation towards me. If one wished to translate into earthly words what the Entity communicated to me and what my consciousness communicated to the Entity – and if you considered the loving forbearance of that Entity, its patience and helpfulness, which on earth can only come from the region of the heart – you could do it with the words: *'You have entered this realm. Therefore follow me and learn!'* And my soul asked and at once answered in the same breath full of admiration, hope gratitude and joy: *'Please, teach me!'*

And that is what the high spiritual Entity did from then on. Whenever I 'awoke' whilst falling asleep in the way described, my consciousness brightened for the World of Reality and the same high Entity appeared and instructed me. Sometimes other Entities joined in, but only to help me to better understand something by playing a certain 'role' in one of my classes, but never trying to convince me of something. Rather, did they benevolently and generously reveal one of their activities or wisdom in order that I could obtain an insight appropriate to my present level of consciousness. To my wonder and joy, I later experienced occasionally that such Entities – sometimes higher standing than my dear teacher-Entity (at least apparently) – greeted me as if they knew me from the times before I had forgotten everything. They answered with a spiritual 'gesture', by appearing to bow before me, or by benevolently allowing me to continue the path I was to follow by stepping aside. And when I left their presence again, it was – in a dreamlike notion – as if I had in a wonderful way once been with them in other times. (All these attempts at description are merely images of an inner happening.)

I learned to develop an understanding of what were often totally different aspects. I also learned things which I had never known existed, or about which I had not seriously thought. The Entity introduced me to the complex mystery of the human being, to the history and almost inexhaustible connections of the world, to the relationship of man to the earth and to the spiritual world, and directed me always back to my own self, which I thus learned to better understand. The Entity always accompanied me patiently. Sometimes, though, I was left to investigate freely, that is, I experienced something in which my attention was totally directed to the teaching content and the Entity remained in the background. Then it appeared to me again and asked me what this or that learning experience meant to me, so that alongside the 'factual knowledge' there was always a new 'self-consciousness'. Often what was conveyed to me was clarified by inner picture-like parables, which ultimately made the revelations recognizable as a parable of their reality; sometimes, however, certain contents were taught directly to my feeling-thinking 'heart' as living knowledge. In passing, I also learned at the side of the high Entity the inner principle of the World of Reality, its structure so to speak as a living spiritual organism. This was baffling for a long time because it was so utterly multilayered. For my limited awareness it would have seemed chaotic if everything I encountered in it – I was a part of it – had not existed in a mysterious but unsurpassed order and 'hygiene'.

Over the months and years the Entity took on – together with me and for me – ever new 'perspectives', so that I soon realized that everything that I learned, however great and sublime, was only a part of the whole, an extract of the whole perspective. To partake of the whole perspective permanently was obviously only possible for the high, divine Selves. One could only 'nibble' at it, and even that was no real perception of it all, but only the achieving of a certain overview. This led me to understand that I only entered a certain 'sphere' of the spiritual world. And I also learned that the World of

Reality was divided for me into higher and lower spheres, because I was not yet able to perceive that world in its entirety. Thus, here the concept 'sphere' actually indicates the stage of development of consciousness reached in this or that domain. The less I was conscious of the World of Reality, the lower the sphere in which I found myself. But the more I became conscious of it, the more clearly I saw how many spheres still lay ahead of me. This ascent and descent, or narrowing and widening, could also occur during a lesson, for the lessons were always duties I had to cope with. I used to call them 'trials'. And when, during such a trial – which of course had nothing of arbitrariness or harassment against my person, but was rather sent to me from the high spiritual world for my inner development and maturity – an inappropriate impulse or thought for the World of Reality and Truth slipped in, in a sense I fell back into a lower 'sphere', which simply meant that my consciousness had darkened and I 'saw' and understood less clearly. In such a case, I had to get a grip on myself and freely seek the high Entity, which in such moments of unsuccessful trials had disappeared because my spiritual gaze had deviated from it. But then, when intentionally I again sought it out, it attended to me with undiminished patience and indulgence. Or, my possibilities were exhausted for that time and I slipped back into the normal state of sleep, or awoke in 'blind' day-consciousness. Otherwise, it was usual that the exercise was ended by the spiritual Entity itself and I returned willingly to the everyday world.

It is hardly possible to describe the appearance of the spiritual Entity in earthly words. It had absolutely nothing corporeal about it, but at the same time possessed a kind of spiritual corporeality which occupied a certain 'super-spatial' space – a corporeality that was filled with its consciousness. In comparison to mine, this consciousness was so highly developed that, to me, it so to speak 'radiated'. When I was at my wit's end, it shone on the path of knowledge for me. But the idea of normal light, even consciousness-light, is not sufficient to have an impression of this Entity. One must imagine this light being full of warmest goodness and devotion which – together with the wisdom and experience that must have been acquired during enormously distant times – the Entity bestowed its majesty. I called it 'the majestic light'.

What was so special about such experiences, which since then have continued with new non-material teaching, is that during the day I did not forget what I had learned. Perhaps now and then I forgot some details, but it was not a problem because it had been inscribed in my whole being, as a part of me. What I experienced since my Christ-experience beyond the portal of the sensory world, however, was clearly different from my fantasies whilst listening to music, looking at and painting pictures, strolling or writing stories. I experienced then the reality of the existing – with or without me – (Holy) Spirit! There are few things that are more drastically different from each other than moving around within a self-generated fantasy world and learning within the World of Reality and Truth under the loving but stern and watchful 'eyes' of a spiritual majesty – which doesn't mean that one cannot commit errors or have difficulty understanding within that world. In order to commit fewer such errors, there were the above-mentioned trials. But everyday creative activity had a favourable effect on consciousness in the spiritual world, because it led to a specific flexibility beyond the 'threshold' – beyond the 'portal'.

***

Shortly before my tenth birthday I began to write down some of my inner experiences. I didn't keep a diary – that seemed too dull. I tried it a few times, but found that not every day of my life was full of existential discoveries that needed to be recorded in writing. I found the 'tell-me-about-my-life' concept more diversified, because I could spontaneously respond to the unexpected. Instead of a diary, therefore, I sporadically wrote down things that seemed of value. I had nobody to converse with – at least nobody living on earth – so I replaced the missing conversation with the writing down of an experience or a question which occupied me. Mostly, I directed my writing to God – or also *Adonai,* Hebrew for *Lord,* as God is called in a certain edition of the Bible I owned; for the name 'God' seemed too pantheistic or impersonal – as though I were telling him about my experiences and concerns. I knew, of course, that God (the creative, benevolent Majesty), whose wisdom was limitless, accompanied my meagre thoughts and worries, as well as my experiences beyond the 'portal', and knew them very well

114

without needing my notes. But it was easier for me to express the experiences when I had the feeling that I was telling them to an actual being. Furthermore, I realized that I was given more precise answers to my questions or concerns when I expressed them in writing. It must have been because the questions were clearer when they were expressed in that way, and were therefore more amenable to solutions and clarifications. The subconscious worked more effectively on them, so the 'other side' – the divine Self – noticed that I was trying to understand and could therefore more easily 'accommodate' me.

I began making my notes – mostly in vocabulary booklets, sometimes in large format notebooks – from when I was ten years old and continued until I was about fourteen. After that, I seldom noted anything down, and if I did it was mostly in lyrical form. In time a considerable quantity of notebooks accumulated. I guess there were about thirty until… yes, one day I destroyed them in order to protect their content from curious eyes and prohibited access. At that time, I thought that it wouldn't be so bad if I destroyed them because they only contained my own experiences. Nothing would be lost, for the contents were preserved in remembrances and in my head, for no one could pry into my heart from without.

But it is unfortunately not always so. We forget much that cannot be brought up with difficulty – sometimes not at all – from our overloaded storage of memory. I realized this a decade later – when I looked into four little notebooks that had survived my destructive action, because I had hidden them in a place where not even I could have found them – the day I moved out of my parents' home. But even then, when I found them whilst clearing out my things, I put them hastily into some bag or box without opening them. From then on, they moved with me from one home to another without being noticed. The first time I began to read them again, I was twenty-five years old and had become close to a person whose openness to the World of Reality was greater than anyone I had ever known. This person – he later became my husband – was one of the few to whom I entrusted the contents of my notebooks. At that time, I was amazed at what I had written as a child. The remembrances arose again in me and even the circumstances, motives and feelings that had existed at the time I wrote them, appeared before me. Without these little notebooks I probably would never have remembered what was written in them.

I have decided to include some of these childish notes here and there in my narrative, because all that I have written until now about my inner life is in the words of an adult. Although the thoughts and experiences are precisely described, I was of course not able to formulate them as I have here. For that reason, the reader will have a more authentic impression of that time and of my experiences if I include and share some of my notes. (It is really sharing, for I have always considered these notes to be my most private treasure. During my childhood and youth, and until today with few exceptions, I have kept them secret from other people – always fearing that derision or criticism could offend the spiritual world and the entities to whom they are dedicated. And even though they are perhaps only the somewhat laughable writings of a naive child – I was really a 'child' for longer than the grown-ups I compare myself with today – I ask my reader to treat them with the discretion that he or she would like his or her own psychical-spiritual treasures to be treated by others.)

Unfortunately, only a very small number of the notebooks have been retained, so that the sample that I give here does not draw on the full amount, but only on the four notebooks which I still possess. The earliest entry is from 1982, when I was ten years old; the latest from 1985. One of the notebooks is undated, but the handwriting indicates that it is also from 1982. Several of the notes in these four books describe inner experiences in the way I have just explained. At that time, I did not describe much of the technical or methodical aspects – for example the levels of consciousness that changed upon falling asleep and waking up, and other such things, because I considered them to be self-evident and 'settled'. Instead, I have given the contents of the trials and lessons. Of course, I had no idea that someday another person would study these notes. (One of the notebooks is adorned on the first page with the worlds: 'Judith's secret book. It's nobody else's business. Whoever reads it, it's their own fault!') Had they been written for the eyes and understanding of others, I probably would have been more detailed and would surely have been less careless and paid more attention to form and orthography. Also, to this point (details, form and orthography, as they are to be seen in the unadorned facsimiles), may the esteemed reader practice indulgence and try to glimpse the inner world of a fellow human being without the aspiration to deduce the original meaning of every detail of this unknown world.

1984 (about 12 years old):
Many people don't notice how they look when they are angry or sad. Sometimes I can see the colours of their husk, how they loop into each other like cold warm character smoke. When one of them thinks about something bad the colours curl and ripple more within and become an ugly dark-red-brown-grey, and if one is aggressive, the colours shoot out dark-red from each other and come close to the one being insulted. If people could see themselves this way, they would think twice before blowing their top like that.

1982/83 (about 10–11 years old):
Something remarkable happened to me in bio[logy]. We're examining the human body. Mostly all the organs, and I think that many organs (maybe all?) are like frozen husk movements of the human soul. As though they were frozen, forming a stiff material. The soul-husk-colours keep moving along. As though all the movements at each time were formed solid, so that many organs were formed. You can see that mostly, I find, in the inner-ear and the fallopian tubes and ovaries. I don't know where the soul-movements-freezing in men came from. They have no fallopian tubes or ovaries. A pity that I can't ask Frau T.[...]

From when I was about six years old until I was sixteen, we travelled regularly during summer vacation time and sometimes during Easter vacation to Salzkammergut in Austria. I spent the happiest days of my childhood and youth there, and I am to this day deeply thankful to my parents that at that age they did not drag me to a Balearic or Canary Island, where the burning southern sun, the smell of suntan lotion and the inevitable view of masses of people populating hotel pools would probably have eliminated any substantial inner activity. The natural diversity and beauty of Austria's lakes and mountains were the 'magic realism' of my childhood soul. I was completely absorbed there, with the external perception of nature as well as the discoveries in the supernatural weaving of the spiritual forces.

I could kneel for hours at a mountain stream and listen to the murmur and soft gurgle of the caressing and sparkling water on the moss-cloaked stones and pebbles, inhaling the wonderfully refreshing scent of flowered riverside meadows, the flight of bees, bumblebees, butterflies and dragonflies, their wings glittering in the sunlight in all the colours of the rainbow, like the copper veins in the rocky outcrops of the majestic mountains. How enjoyable it was closely to observe a small section of a rock face, covered with moss and fern, that a multitude of tiny creatures called their home! I possessed a small rubber figure, a so called Smurf with white wings, to which I projected myself and took on the perspective of an insect or tiny bird, for which the section of rock face was a whole mountain on which the ferns and lichen growing on it appeared to be forests. I imagined myself to be a resident of this microcosm, and I discovered everything that formed and thrived on the small section of this rock wall – from the tiny trickle – which from my new perspective looked like a rushing waterfall – and the countless narrow crevices and depressions in the rock, which now became the entrances to mysterious caves and tunnels.

But I could also experience what is hidden to sensory eyes in nature's history, and nowhere as much as there did I feel myself to be a part of this spiritually immersed earthly world.

Each time at the end of the vacation, when the city child had to be wrenched away from its beloved adopted home, it became ill. The pain at the loss of an environment that gave me so much to be able to endure life on earth was so overwhelming that I developed a high fever and terrible stomach ache every time we left, which saddened my mother greatly.

The following note shows my inner relationship to my adopted home on earth:

1984 (about 12 years old):
As we left Salzburg I cried my eyes out. I was so sad that I must wait 100,000 years until we return. In Austria it is always very different from here! It smells different and sounds different and looks different. I always feel much more real there than in Berlin. It's because nature grows as it wants to, and is also able to. The Austrians are also very considerate. A mountain is much older than people can remember. They were already

there when people were not yet even on the earth. I always have to think about that when I look at a mountain, and I am awestruck. Not because they are so big, but because they are so old. And I can hear them. They resound only because they have enclosed the sound inside that they got from somewhere else. I think the sound existed before the mountains had not yet become solid, and the rest, what we now hear, sounds like an echo, when the voice has long stopped calling. Nevertheless, we hear it quite loud!

I like best being alone with nature. With grown-ups I have to act as if everything leaves me cold, or that I find everything simply beautiful. They take photos but they show nothing about them. In the pictures there is absolutely NOTHING about what the mountains really are. They are the most ancient things that exist in the world, and then comes the sea, that is the second oldest. When I am allowed to be alone, I am always on the way up to the P. alp. In one place a little stream ripples over the rocks. That's the most beautiful place. As if the water caresses the rocks and sings in doing so. The moss has pushed itself between them. It takes something from both. When the sun is shining everything sings the most beautiful song for me, and shows me that it loves me. But the very most beautiful is the place where you hear almost nothing from outside, but only from within. Unfortunately we were only up there twice. And once I sneaked away while both [mother and father] were sunbathing. The grass was warmly moist and the air smelled of it and the cows further down.

When you climb on the rocks, you get away from all the bother. That was the highest point of the alp. Of course not as high as the Huhberg across from it [There was a mountain there that had the shape of a hunchback and for my amusement my father liked to imitate it with extended arms and a hunched back and a bloodcurdling 'Hooo' cry], *but the highest peak of the P. alp.*

Nobody saw me, because nobody climbed there anyway. Actually strange that the highest highest points are not all occupied! Then I took my clothes off so they wouldn't be in between. Then I stood with my feet on the rocks and heart in the sun and my own head stretched toward the sun, like the mountain. And dearest God, it was soooo beautiful!!!!!!

I was the part that belonged in between, I mean between the mountain and the sky. And they both accepted me and were glad. So the song of nature was also within me. And I got it from the mountain and sang it to the sky. I was so happy that I had to cry. As I came down a lady spoke to me. She wanted to help me find my parents. She thought I was crying because I was lost. If she only knew...

The enormous contrast to these soul-enriching impressions was found in the inner city of Berlin – an impression, however, that stimulated other thoughts.

1985 (about 13 years old):
Today we drove along the autobahn, and as I looked out the window and the city flew by, my gaze focused on the many, many roof tiles on a house, hundreds of roof tiles, perhaps thousands. All of them are man-made. And I realized that everything to be seen in this city was man-made. There is hardly anything left of what can be seen at the sea or in the mountains. You don't notice it in everyday life. Nevertheless, people accept it like an unplanted, self-grown tree in the countryside.

Then I thought that everything created by man seems so much like it is God-made to man that he can't tell the difference between divine nature and the divine that man shows in his works. Man creates like God himself. But I think that they forget that they could never create anything without what God has put in them.

But so much is also indescribably ugly in this city. Which force is here in man? When something is destroyed by human hands which had been produced by others, are you involved in that too, God? It can only be the evil, bad in us. But is it an attribute inherent in people?

I think a lot about it, and I believe that it simply cannot be! If what is good in people comes from you, then what remains would be inherently bad.

But that can't be. In reli [religion class] it's called original sin. But a baby is pure and untouched by evil, I think. I don't understand all that about original sin. It sounds so much like superstition. When you are talked into this original sin you immediately feel so bad that you can't be bothered to do something good. Why does Herr F. [a teacher] pull Stefan's ear? He can't help disturbing the class, it's the original sin in him! When does evil come into people? And why does it cause unrest in us? One thing I know for sure like nothing else: When I die I lose the evil, just like when I come to you, when you let me enter in your heaven. Then I see the good and the bad in me and what hasn't yet been completely decided. I look at it like clockwork inside a glass case. I see inside myself through the glass case. And you take me in your hands and make me only all good and leave the dry shell lying outside.

120

At the end of this entry a question is touched upon which occupied me for years into adulthood: the possibility of human ennoblement or, expressed differently, our inner *development*.

Did God allow original sin? Or was he not powerful enough to prevent the 'tempter's' actions? That would mean that there is a spiritual force that is even greater than the creative Majesty – not benevolent, however, but wicked, evil, debilitating or even destructive! But I had never noticed a force which was stronger and wiser than the creative Majesty. And furthermore, hadn't the Son of God, the Saviour from all non-benevolence, been revealed to me as the Alpha and the Omega? But the Alpha and the Omega encompassed *all* creation, *all* being. So during the origin or the amplification of creation a 'fluke' must have occurred. But how? I could only explain it by God having insured that we would be able to decide for ourselves what we wanted to do and what we did not want to do. He never interfered in this decision. It could also have been so with other beings, things or forces created before us, who for some reason had decided *against* God, against the whole. How would it be if they had increased and developed over millions of years without changing their ways and interpretations? Because they are older, wouldn't they be more experienced compared to us, but terrible, evil beings? And maybe they tried to outsmart human beings and win them over to their side?

But how were we humans ever to contend with their cunning if they were always ahead of us because of their age and experience? Was it possible that we could ever become wiser? Of course it was. We could learn what was vital from the *Majestic Light*. We could also recognize by observation of the good or bad acts of human beings whether they developed more or less well. But life was so short! Could one come so far in life to be able to compete with such forces?

It seemed virtually impossible. When I looked at the many grown-ups around me, their behaviour indicated that they had not advanced much further in their inner development than we children. And between them and us there was an age difference of several decades! One lived, had a few experiences, perhaps very important ones – for most people obviously related to earthly-material existence – and then died; and yes, what then? Then one 'went to heaven'. And there it was again: the cold horror that always gripped me at the thought of 'eternal life'. This futile 'existence'! Why did God need a bunch of human beings who had learned more or, likely, less in their short lives and then peopled His heaven? Or did one continue learning in heaven? But then one could no longer change things on earth. Or could we? Did one become a wise, capable spiritual being who could intervene in the earthly world's fate? Somehow I couldn't avoid the feeling that one needed this earth in order 'to prove' oneself, to succeed, to find one's actual self again – and for that one could not simply wait for life in heaven. Because if it was indifferent as to whether one did it here or there, then why did life on earth exist at all?

Such questions occupied me over and over, and with assurances like 'don't worry, in heaven it's very beautiful', they became ever more urgent. Unfortunately I did not come closer to solving these questions for a long time, but they festered in me.

***

Perhaps, however, I should interpose here some comments about the unusual world in which, at that time, I moved during the day: my school. The process and experiences at school which I underwent certainly had only indirectly to do with my 'inner world', as described in this book. But this inner world belonged to a human being who lived within a very specific environment that was so strikingly different from it. The conditions in which I lived may have had less influence on my inner experiences than the way I learned to deal with them, with myself and with my surroundings. So the following remarks about my schooling may cast some light upon the exterior relationships I had at the time my childhood notes were written.

I will say at the outset that, in view of the narratives that are yet to follow, one need not be surprised at this world if one knows that it was a school that, judging by its whole structure and practices at the time, one would rather expect to be in the nineteenth century than the present one. The dismayed reader of my childhood notes may have asked where, in the eighties of the twentieth century, a teacher was permitted to inflict corporal punishment on a pupil. It was not permitted anywhere, but was not – to a certain extent – an unusual aspect of the place I wish to describe. Thus, the episode of the teacher pulling the unruly pupil's ear was not a sensational event in my school's everyday life. I once heard of a parent who dared to protest at a parents' evening about the treatment of his offspring by the teachers. They were told in a terse manner that this school was one of the most sought-after elite grammar schools in Germany and that many parents were standing at the gates waiting for a place for their offspring. This was supposed to mean that no tears would be shed for those who took their children out of the school – although there was certainly a bit of sabre-rattling involved here, because of course they would not have liked to see a press release to that effect.

Nevertheless, that world did make it into the news, although not because of this book. The discussion about abuse in religious schools, and within the Catholic Church in general, has only recently become widely known, as some ex-pupils of my school made their experiences public. I hadn't known about all that at the time. For one thing, the abuses might have diminished somewhat during the time I was at the school, as was recently reported. Also, I was a girl, and it seems that girls were not as attractive to the persons involved as were the boys. Although at the time I had no clue about this, I do have a general idea about why nobody dared to speak about their experiences. It was simply impossible! I think one cannot make such things believable to someone who was not directly involved, as we were. The word 'authority' would have to be understood differently than it is today in respect to schools and teachers in Germany. And in addition, one would have to try to drill a kind of peephole into the past, so that one could get a glimpse of the characteristic atmosphere and the everyday rituals and regulations within this singular world.

My first memory of that school was the interview which took place with the principal as part of my admission test. He was a priest and monk of small wiry stature with roguish, sparkling eyes. In order to advance into his chambers, one had to pass through an imposing building complex built by the Krupp company in the 1930s. I felt that there ruled within it a strangely severe and, despite its stature, somewhat gloomy and oppressive atmosphere. In the building's first floor, behind a kind of portico, there was the study and reception room of Father Zawacki. Two large double doors opened and accompanied by a secretary, we passed, through three high rooms panelled with oak parquet and preserved in their original style. At the very back, behind a massive desk, sat Father Zawacki in his black habit. He bade my parents and me to be seated in large leather upholstered armchairs. Toward the end of the interview he asked my parents to leave the room and I stayed behind, alone, with him. I remember that he asked me what I wanted to be when I grew up. My answer was probably the same as that of many nine- to ten-year-old girls, namely a pediatrician. He seemed to interpret this as something that my parents had told me to say in order to make a good impression. But it was not. He nodded and whispered, winking: 'I always wanted to become a Formula 1 racing driver!' Although it was obvious that he wanted to gain my trust in this way, nevertheless I liked it, for the surprise worked. Who would have thought that this dignified priestly figure, who lived behind such heavy stone walls, would have said such a thing?

It wasn't always so much fun on schooldays though. In a class of 36 children and two more parallel classes, we received strictly-imposed instruction, partly carried out by the priests. Because of the presence of and direction by the priests, there was a completely different atmosphere than in a non-confessional school, and this atmosphere was always tangible, even on days when we had no classes with the priests themselves. If you happened to go by the teachers' room with its creepy, high folding-doors, you could sometimes hear murmuring in Latin – which was spoken by some of the older monks – on subjects not meant for the students' ears. If you ran into a priest, you were automatically silent and well-behaved, even more so than usual.

In the sexta (fifth class) we sat at desks from pre-war times, with a notch for the pen-tray and a hole in the middle for the inkwell. When the old heating system broke down during harsh winters, classes nevertheless continued. The teacher was a person of such respect that, in addition to the blackboard monitor, we had a designated door-scout who, at the end of a break when the teacher's menacing approach was heard – his steps resounding along the stone-paved hallway – would announce in panic: *'He's coming!, He's coming!'* That was the signal to finish the last corrections to our homework and get everything in order. When the teacher entered the classroom we had to be at our places, in order and silent. At his greeting we stood up. If it was the first or the last class of the day, we turned to the cross – one hung on every classroom wall – and prayed, sometimes also in other classes in order to practice prayer in a foreign language. Then the attendance list was checked. Even today I can recite most of the alphabetic list of names because, during years of repetition, they became embedded within me. When the break was announced by the bell, there was no jumping-up, as happens in many schools, where the teacher's words are drowned out by the tumult. With us, it was the teacher who decided when the break would begin – not the bell. When school was over for the day, we were to leave *demurely* and in pairs, walking *silently* on the right. We marched in rank and file to the bus-stop, about a half a kilometre from the school, where we got into the bus in order, always under the observation of Father Glorius, who was capable of terrifying the poor driver and the passengers as well. And as the doors of the bus closed, he would pipe up – each and every day, as long as he carried out his guard-duty at the bus-stop: 'And greetings to the loved ones at home!' Whoever, however, made the mistake of not behaving correctly at the traffic light, immediately got a bad mark – the third bad mark meant expulsion – about which the 'loved ones at home' were already informed before their child arrived there. One could, however, be certain of Father Glorius's approval by paying, from one's pocket money, for the *Misereor* magazine, which he sold during his monthly rounds through the classrooms in his capacity as a kind of pious representative, and which he touted with exuberant enthusiasm and a disarming torrent of speech. If someone had been mischievous during class or within the school building, they'd have to stand in the corner with their face to the wall, leave the room or, in more serious cases, have to attend detention or help Brother Friday with maintenance or garden work. Also, the teacher would have it in for him during the upcoming classes. For disturbing class by talking or making faces, a painful knuckle to the head was forthcoming, or a blow on the hands with a key ring, which was often no less uncomfortable.

I had the impression that many a teacher – seldom actually the priests – considered the pupils to be their enemy. In that school, instead of praise and encouragement to motivate the pupils to do better, the discouraging shaking of heads – or even the principle of public humiliation – was practiced. There were teachers who, instead of encouraging, kept questioning you for so long that you felt small. An example was Latin class, feared by all, with the teacher mentioned in my notes as Herr F. The class began when a candidate – we never knew who beforehand – was called to 'the front'. That meant that one had to stand next to the teacher's desk before the whole class and be interrogated about the vocabulary words due for that day, in their various conjugations and declinations. Getting stuck, even just a little, resulted in a barrage of unexpected, quite difficult questions – often having to do with grammatical exceptions or translating a short but meaningful text with some kind of built-in trap. That was a stressful situation, because most of us had high expectations of ourselves and were afraid of failing in front of the teacher and the whole class. One left the battlefield bathed in sweat, as a humiliated loser. Furthermore, you could never let yourself be lulled into a feeling of safety, even if it went relatively well (or perhaps even to enjoy the lessons), because the teacher would call you up to the front again the next day. And you could be sure that, for weeks or months, you would be reminded of your disgrace by little sarcastic remarks, until finally nobody even remembered the original offence. But by means of this repeated derogatory allusion, all were convinced that you were a failure, or at least not particularly bright, in the respective subject. You could only escape from this vicious cycle by a great effort, mostly accompanied by words of 'appreciation' such as: 'Oh well, a blind chicken also sometimes finds a seed', or at best: 'Well, look at that! XY isn't as dumb as she looks.'

This kind of education was not for everyone. I knew children who were broken – most probably for a long time – by this method and therefore left the school early. For the rest of us, Nietzsche's motto was applicable: 'What doesn't kill us makes us stronger'. And I must admit that, looking back, this 'smiling in the face of adversity and holding your ground' was the basis for being able to cope with thoroughly existential impositions.

There were other experiences, for example with the German teacher, Herr Bengsch, whom I much appreciated – a dignified gentleman of advanced age who always wore a suit, vest and tie and never had to utter a loud word to ensure that his instructions were followed.

After the usual entrance procedures, we heard his usual words: 'I am looking at the homework.' Yes, he really did see the homework, for no one dared not to hand it in! The homework books had to be placed on the upper right side or the left corner of his desk, open to the appropriate page; the title was to be underlined with a ruler and the date written clearly in the right margin. He went through each one with a green ballpoint pen, marking that the work had been done, before inviting someone to present theirs. He was one of the teachers whom we respected, not because of threats of punishment, but because we sensed that he seriously wanted to teach us – and also because he was a highly educated and disciplined man who did not apply lesser standards to himself than to his pupils. In the quinta (sixth class) I had the privilege of enjoying his attention because I won the school's internal public speaking competition and was then prepared for the district championship. He called me once or twice a week into his small office, and together we looked for suitable texts for the 'free style' option. I not only have to thank him for a broad basic education in German literature, but also for awakening and deepening my love for the German classics.

During the first two years (in the fifth and sixth classes) we had to attend a morning Mass once a week, before the regular classes began, in the school's own chapel. Rehearsing canons or other songs was compensation for having to wake up so early. After all, most of the children came from all over West Berlin, including me – it took me about an hour and a half by foot and public transportation to get to school.

The chapel was the scene of an episode with which I will end my review of this bygone history. One day we went with Father T. to the chapel during religion class. We brought our fountain pens (the only ones we wrote with) as he had instructed. As we sat in the pews, he handed out slips of paper. Then he instructed us to write our cares and worries – which might well include dissatisfaction with a particular teacher – on the slips of paper. We were then to fold the pieces of paper and place them on the altar so God could read them after we had gone. He, Father T., would put them all in the 'shredder' afterwards. That was the first time I'd heard the word 'shredder', by the way. Of course, we should not forget to write our names on the slips of paper, so that God would know which problems belonged to whom. Although we all felt queasy at that, and were certain that God did not need to read slips of paper with our names on them in order to be informed about our individual cares and problems, no one dared to complain. Under the category 'difficulties with a teacher', I recall having written that these instructions given by Father T. seemed to lack seriousness. I expected sanctions, but fortunately there were none. The reason for this should be obvious.

There is an entry about Father T. in my preserved childhood notes. I'm quite sure that I did not do complete justice to Father T. in my opinions of the time. Seen from a distance now, I can see that he was a serious person, as far as faith and theology were concerned, as well as the salvation of our souls, but who perhaps could not find an ideal contact with children and teenagers.

1984 (Quarta, 7th class, 12 years old):
There is one thing I don't understand: why Father T. became a priest. He is afraid of people. And especially of us. We are not, I think, the right people for him. You [God] did not mean for him to be a teacher, or did you? What makes him do that when he could select his profession? Maybe he does it to overcome his fear. When he prays in front of us, it is only for us to see. I never pray to you when we pray in school. I can only do it when nobody is watching. I think that you understand that, Adonai. I feel sorry for Father T. I can see how he struggles every day. Unfortunately, he usually loses.

Even if one did oppose 'the system', in practice there was nothing one could do about it. We were integrated into a committed (suffering) community in which different laws prevailed than in the world outside the 'cloistered' walls of grey stone; laws of which the parents – at least as far as the psychological mechanisms were concerned – had no idea. The system had created a situation in which one would have felt ashamed to criticize it openly. One would have felt a traitor to the community, to be fouling one's own nest. For the prevailing feeling was that one was much too unimportant and powerless to even question the authority of the highly educated, patriarchal priestly community. The priests and teachers were feared and at the same time revered persons of authority and, in everyday life, untouchable. And whoever received even a spark of

128

recognition or praise from them, even if it was for fleeting moments – which is how long such moments usually lasted – felt like they were in seventh heaven.

Despite all the drills and lack of empathy I still owe that school something, as do most of my schoolmates. In addition to a good general education and the development of discursive thinking, we were taught a skill that without a certain amount of rigour and discipline could hardly be achieved: the ability to motivate oneself to perseverance and not throwing-in-the-towel because of minor or major setbacks. And in retrospect, I would even say that it did none of us any harm to recognize and accept our momentary place within a hierarchically structured order as children and adolescents – a hierarchy that, however, had a certain justification because, for the most part, these were teachers who were not only extraordinarily competent in their subject area, but who also put into practice themselves what they demanded of their students: discipline, diligence, reliability and conscientiousness in relation to the tasks assigned to them. We didn't mutate into cowards and hypocrites because of that. Rather, it has helped us to keep an overview in confusing life situations or to find the right position in life, and to presume that the probability exists that there is someone in the world who is a bit more able than oneself. We also learned to finish what we started, that is, to develop the stamina, or to undertake and master tasks which one would prefer to leave alone because of laziness or egoistical reasons. Through all this, the soul was encouraged to develop apparently different aspects, namely in relation to higher feelings – like appreciation, respect and veneration – towards higher contexts, facts and beings.

This is what my life at school was like when I was writing about the experiences and observations described in my notebooks.

***

It was – as indicated in the above notes – mostly psychical-spiritual observations which I made and which were partially related to the super-sensory evolution of man and the world. For by means of my nightly 'instructions', it became increasingly possible for me to 'investigate' super-sensory conditions and relationships during the day. So that whereas I had an outwardly undisturbed and open disposition, I also experienced something like a 'tone' belonging to certain 'objects'. This tone, however, was as little audible to the physical ears as the magical life-force was visible to the physical eyes, but no less real and intense. On the contrary. It was the impelling force, so to speak, which we otherwise send through our ears in order to hear something in the sensory world, which had to be activated in order to perceive this 'tone'. There was a direct connection between the heart and this force, which otherwise travelled through the ears, so that the 'tone' began to resonate in the centre of my own being. One was spread out with one's centre in the super-sensible outer world, as if turned inside out, so that the 'tone' could be caught as if with a fishing net. But at the same time I brought this outer world into my inner being, because during the day I was more strongly connected with my own bodily structure than at night, during the outer state of sleep. I realized that every object and being had its own tone, which was more or less complex and always unique and therefore unmistakable. The tones of the various things and beings were in a kind of communication with each other, which moved forward and backward in time, because the tones came from the World of Reality's enduring facts about these things and beings, which of course accumulated during the course of their development. One could learn a lot about their origin and purpose by the way they 'intoned'. There was a great difference between the tone of 'soul-less' things or beings, such as minerals and plants, and ensouled beings such as animals, humans and, strangely enough, planets and stars. I noticed that the strongest and most complex tones or tone-groups, like chords, came from the planets and especially from our central star – the sun – as well as from other stars. For this reason, I didn't see the heavenly bodies primarily as clumps of rock or gas-balls, as astronomy teaches, but I always had the impression that there was another side to the stars, just as the heavens seemed to have two different forms of existence – the one which astronauts could approach or even visit, and the one that is, as a part of the World of Reality, the actual selves of the dead, or what my awakening higher consciousness absorbed during sleep. The stars and planets seemed to me to be like representatives of powerful spiritual beings, for only souls and spirits could 'intone' with such complexity.

1985 (about 13 years old):
Dear God, Your world is unique, like a beautiful picture which also intones! Everything vibrates with tones and the most beautiful, powerful and majestic tone is the sun's! It is as though it breathed on all the other things. That's why the other things also intone.

A sycamore tree intones differently than a poplar! And my piece of quartz buzzes as unearthly as it looks. It is next to the slate, which intones a little like clay but sounds quite different. Nevertheless, they all intone harmoniously. But I'm not so sure about stones, if they only get their tone from the sun or if there is something else in them, something very old.

When a drop of water falls on a stone it intones differently again, because water by its very nature intones like the moon. When the sun also shines on the wet stone, its true properties appear radiantly. Then the past and the future, hidden in the sunbeams, appear and wake me up to being able to see the vitality in them.

1982 (about ten years old):
Good evening Adonai, King of the world! [...] You know, I learned something else. It was like a trial in the night, but in the daytime. It is the following. Many flowers and plants like to suck up the disorderly, ungodly soul colours of the people around them. One can observe it. This afternoon we were in a florist shop where I watched people and then I observed the lively colours of the customers. Each one looked different, because they were different. What happens is that the impure soul colours are sucked up by many plants. Like in a dream the people moved to 'their' plants without knowing why. And the disorderly, impure in them went to particular plants.
These plants became hot... well... at least somewhat warmer than their normal temperature. The disorderly, impure soul colours feel especially comfortable in the warmth! At the moment when they are sucked up by the warm plants they make the plants poisonous. In most plants (especially flowers) the poison comes from human feelings. When they are full of them they become colder and their leaves darker. That's a neat feature of nature! Like when a glass of water is spilled and one can soak it up with a sponge. It may not be completely gone, but it's mostly in the sponge and doesn't cause any more puddles. It's also the case with the ungodly in people that is soaked up by the plants.

Where people quarrel a lot such plants should be set up. Geraniums are apparently especially good. In the south, in Austria and Italy, the people fill up their balcony window-boxes with geraniums. And it's said that the people there are more temperamental. But they are nevertheless friendlier than Germans and somehow happier. Maybe this has something to do with it.

> *Adonai, please protect all*
> *the people in the world and*
> *don't let it burn up*
> *and don't let an atomic bomb*
> *fall tonight!*
> *Yours, Judith*

What I had observed here was a super-sensory relationship of forces relating to certain plants. Two basically different streams of action: the 'feeling-will-force-body' or 'soul-forces-body' of the people met the magical life-force of the plants – somewhat individualized in the specific plants – which did not have their own soul-forces-body. This meeting or penetration of the various streams of force was, as a rule, without consequences, because they were two parallel, non-disturbing processes. But according to my observation, something unusual was happening in some mostly non-European plants: namely a super-sensory interaction between human and plant, or rather between plant and human. I seem to remember that when I spoke of 'poisonous' plants in the flower shop I meant not only geraniums but also petunias, although I didn't know their names.

The prayer-like closing remarks of my notes might cause people to smirk today. Because of my age I was still naive and knew little about politics. Nevertheless, I grew up in a city which I heard called 'an island in a red sea'. Whenever we wanted to leave the city by car to go for a vacation we – like thousands of other West-Berliners – had to wait at one of three transit stations on one of the ten to thirteen queues for what seemed an eternity, until we were checked at the GDR* border. Our identity cards were taken from us for the duration of the transit, and unless you were stupid enough to accidentally forget the *Tagesspiegel* on the dashboard, or owned a

---

* German Democratic Republic, i.e. the once Communist East Germany.

132

dog – as we did – which, after further endless waiting in a special parking lot, received an alleged health check in exchange for 50 West German marks, you were allowed to drive through the GDR, provided that you did not leave the autobahn and did not make contact with any resident of the 'zone'. After about three to four hours, depending on which route you took – and quite shaken up because of the poorly maintained autobahn (built by the 'Führer') – we reached the West German border and breathed out, in the truest sense of the word, because the desolate villages and grey cities visible from the motorway were mostly covered in a blue haze caused by brown-coal, Trabi two-stroke engines mixed with industrial exhaust gases. I always found my stay in the GDR depressing, not just because of the ailing infrastructure, but also because of the political situation. I knew something about this from my father, who happened to be visiting his mother in West Berlin on the day the wall was built and therefore escaped the inhuman GDR system. He never saw his father – who lived in Leipzig – because, until the Berlin Agreement of 1972, my father could only leave the city by air, for otherwise he could count on being immediately arrested in the GDR. And even after that, he felt uneasy until we crossed the border. Although it was everyday life for us children in West Berlin to grow up in a city surrounded by a wall with a death strip, I never got used to the fact that the superpowers were in an arms race during the so-called Cold War. Even though I couldn't know and understand the actual political developments in detail, since the beginning of the 1980s I perceived ever more strongly the 'invisible' tension between the countries. This tension vibrated like an electrical storm, and I, with my super-sensory feeling, stood between them, like a psychical-spiritual electrode. I have no proof, of course, but I am quite sure that – more than once during the early 1980s – the world came within a hair's breadth of an atomic catastrophe. For years I had sleepless nights at the thought that the world, as the arena for human development created by the creative Majesty, might have to cease to exist due to the boundless stupidity of some power-obsessed individuals.

The end of that note contains another unusual plea to God – a request to 'not let it burn up'. For many years, until late in puberty, I said that prayer before going to sleep at night. Why, I didn't know.

I had never witnessed a blaze or experienced damages caused by fire, whether to my relatives or acquaintances. Nor did fire bother me in the least. I liked to gaze at the light of a burning candle – and on a bet with my parents I passed my index finger quickly through the flame. I also liked to help my grandfather light the barbecue fire, and I greatly enjoyed watching the cheerful dance of the blaze when we were invited to my pediatrician's family's house, who liked to light their open fireplace for us in the appropriate seasons. Furthermore, since my sixth year we lived in a ground-floor apartment. My room had direct access to a terrace at the level of a garden. There was no reason at all to fear a fire, which I never did on an intellectual level. But the anxiety had been planted in my heart like a primeval instinct. I feared only and specifically an indeterminable great fire, which could break out during the night. But for what reason could not be determined.

***

My inner experiences of the World of Reality during the nights were almost always accompanied with a trial that gave me the opportunity of gaining a new insight. Of course, one should not confuse these trials with the usual examinations in school. After all, what I have already said about these trials has perhaps made it clear that they occurred under completely different circumstances. They were given to me with inner orientation by the Teacher-Entity – the 'venerable Light' – and served exclusively to increase and enrich my field of vision. But they also differed from earthly examinations by not being given in one of our earthly languages. The soul had to listen and learn in order to understand. That meant, however, that all the means and perspectives of human reason, that is, the intellect, could not be applied! They simply don't exist beyond the 'gate'. Nevertheless, the World of Reality is not one bit less 'logical'. It just isn't limited to the earthly intellect, but has the almost unlimited possibilities of an intuitive, higher thinking. This higher thinking can help the 'newcomer' to better understand the prevailing facts in the World of Reality when it reveals its mysteries to the newcomer's soul through metaphorical images, with which the soul is in a tentative relationship until the spirit reveals the content of the trial and the mystery is deciphered step by step.

1982 (about 10 years old):

Adonai, I had the eagle experience again. This time I was quicker onto its back in the air. [This relates to an earlier note in which the 'eagle' emerged as the higher spirit of myself, which lived hidden in my blood vessels during day-consciousness and could seldom soar freely in the spirit-air.] *It showed me all the countries of the earth. But what was strange was that each country was of a different time. We'd fly over a country covered in snow. I had to find out which time applied to each country. That was the eagle's task who, like the venerable Light, presented me with questions and tests. But I couldn't determine which time it was because I couldn't see the land's surface through the snow. The eagle spoke: 'You can see nothing because the snow covers the past. The snow is now. If you want to see the past under the snow, you must look through the snow.' Thus was the mystery of the stars revealed to me: 'Only if you look at the future can you examine the past', said the venerable Light. Yes! That was the solution! The advice came from the venerable Light. And the Light that shines in the darkness is the future! Where does the* [spiritual] *light come from? The place from where the Light comes is far distant, is the future! No* [spiritual] *Light come from the past! Otherwise it would be extinct light, un-intoning light.*

So my task was to guide the venerable Light's loving sun-beamed light of the future onto the snow. And look! The snow melted and I could see the country's past.

One should never think like the daytime-theatre-world in respect to such trials. That wouldn't work at all. You have to think backwards or, better still, not at all.

1982/83 (about 10-12 years old), see page 256ff:

Last night a light-night-dream came again. First I slipped out of my body and became wide. An ugly face came through me, that stuck in my head. At first I was afraid that it wouldn't let me go. I looked around for the venerable Light, but couldn't find it. I heard its thundering voice though. It heart-spoke: 'Judith, you are still Judith. As long as it stays bright around you with the wrong brightness! But in brightness you cannot see me shine.' I had to get rid of the ugly face, and it became blackly dark and suddenly I saw the venerable Light, that showed me the way. I was certain that I was really outside of my body. Then your venerable Light led me directly into an old man. Suddenly I was an old man who wore a heavy cloak of thick material. I felt all the man's feelings. They were my own. And then words came from the man's mouth in a language I didn't know. It sounded quite full and at the same time delicate. Overall much truer and unaffected than our language. That man lived a long time ago. His speech was like a living picture. Like a moving painting. Sometimes Latin was also there, but I had the impression that he didn't much like to speak it.

The man, that is I, was on the way to a cellar-vault. Many more men had already entered and gathered in the great hall. They showed something at the gate entitling them to enter. The hall was jam-packed. There were beautiful stained-glass windows in which I would have liked to immerse myself. I knew that it was something special, otherwise there were no window-panes.

The men all spoke excitedly to each other, like hens. I (in the man) heard their voices from without. I walked across a courtyard and into a hallway with short stone columns. In each column there was a wise saying. They all stood at the same distance from each other. In that way harmony could arise. Each one was differently shaped and gave its own tone. The distance was the rhythm for the tone, which they all intoned together when one walked by them. They were reading columns for the world. Not merely some kind of construction. But that they held up the roof also had an important meaning. The roof covered the head or the head-force of the people, who were to think about God beneath it, so that their head-force didn't simply fly up and around heaven, but remained well within them. The I in the man went up some stairs (or down, I don't know which anymore) to the hall. A young man followed me. He was like a grown-up pupil to a teacher. Very deferential. It was like a dream, but much MORE real.

Then we stood in the hall. I didn't go through the entrance that all the others used, but through a small door at the head of the hall. As soon as I walked through the arched door suddenly everything fell silent. I found that amusing, as did the man, I think. The hall was so full that they all had to stand, but they *stood calmly and listened anxiously to what the old man would say.*

In front of me was a small table on which there were three bowls made of thin metal. One bowl with grain kernels, one with water, and an empty one. The old man then gave a talk, like a class, which I cannot remember rightly. It was quite complicated. He wanted to show that the water, and even the kernels, came from the contents of the third bowl, which was empty. That was how one should imagine the divinity in heaven, like the empty bowl out of which everything which man needs for his life comes. If God's heaven is in a bowl, which is empty, then the human being also comes out of it.

It was much more detailed, but I couldn't understand all of it. A little bit like the grown-up pupil in the hall. In that part, I was in the old man's thoughts.

At the end I, in the old man, said that it would be better not to have your nose in books all the time, but rather to walk along the great river and observe the stones washed up on the shore, and wonder where they come from, which path they travelled, how they had changed their form and where they will still go. They were all very surprised to hear the old man speak like that, because the old man was known to know all the books in the world.

I was only visiting the man though, and when I flew out again I looked at him with the eyes of heaven's emotion and saw how he wanted to go to his teacher where he received answers to his questions. He went into an old church and then out again and also out of the city's traffic to the river. There he cried and lay flat on the ground and kind of embraced it. But then he came to his teacher and was very much smaller before him than his pupils were to him. So I was glad, because everything was fine.

> *Tomorrow or the day after I'll write about how the test from the venerable Light brought me back. It's enough for today.*

1984 (about 12 years old), see page 261ff.:
Last night there was another test. It was quite difficult. At first I am above again, having slipped out and then [became] enormous and happy hovering in the real world. Every time it's the

137

nicest, tenderest, most loving heartfelt feeling. It is a thousand times nicer than the anticipation of a party!!! The beginning of the test was quite hard. I was really tiny, squashed into a dim point of light. And I waited again for the great venerable Light to show me the way. And it soon came and spoke to my heart: 'Come to me, if you can.'

Then everything was like a deep, dark valley, hollow and endless. And I, little dim light, had to get over to the venerable Light on the other side! But there was no bridge or anything. That was the test! Suddenly I got it! I had to go over the abyss without there being a bridge.

But I, silly little person, had to deal first with fear, and because of that the abyss became darker and more evil. An ugly blood-red horror also came. I thought: That just wants to gobble me up. It was strange, because I always think of red as fiery and hot. But the dirty-red was cold and dead. It was a hideous face.

Then I noticed that my light had become weaker.

Then I thought of you, my dear Jesus Christ, and that you always love me, even when I do something wrong. And at once my light became a little larger and brighter, and the ugly abyss became only dark again, but the awful face disappeared. The venerable Light was very patient and still shone.

It waited for me. And when I saw it again, it shone more splendidly than before in order to give me courage. It gave me the trial's task: 'You must dare to take the step. I can only lead you if you trust me,' it said.

And just when I decided to step over the abyss, although there was no bridge, the venerable Light gave me an idea. I should speak in my light-heart:

> *In the name of the Father,*
> *and of the Son,*
> *and of the Holy Spirit.*

I spoke those words in my heart, and when I trusted myself to take the first step it went easily. I had my eyes closed before the abyss, but I could see that the venerable Light had held out his light-arms and was glad that I had passed the test.

It was a little like when you must close your eyes and let yourself fall backwards, trusting that someone behind you will catch you. Only in the test you have to catch yourself.

When I was beyond, I was to look back and compare the first thing behind the entrance. I could see that in front it was no longer dark like at the beginning.

And I could see everything as it really looked. So I realized that the bridge was actually the shining rainbow dome through which I floated over and that touches the other side. I hadn't noticed that. Only when you penetrate through to the other side of the colourful dome can you reach the light and become light yourself. Then all becomes bright.

My altar-root grows from a deep warmth. The swan wings need no eyes, but feel and touch the heartbeat-light of the world, and my wind-sword, rises up between these two.

I experienced the actual being of man as threefold. I didn't have to explain what I meant by that to anyone, because I knew no one who would have taken my observations and experiences seriously. And, because I didn't have to explain what I meant by the threefold human being, I made no note about it. (Or, I forgot about it and it's in one of the destroyed notebooks.) However, in the remaining notebooks there are many insinuations of this threefold inner human form. I used three concepts, which seemed more or less appropriate, to describe what these three spiritual members were to me: *altar-root*, *swan wings* and *wind-sword*.

I will try to describe this threefold inner entity as I perceived it then:

The *altar-root* expressed my inner connection to the earth, which I experienced especially when I returned from my 'trips' with consciousness, having re-entered my physical body – the members of which I then had to grasp and pervade in order for it again to become the instrument of daily life. Then I felt the full weight of the material body that I lived in during the day, a weight that one is usually hardly aware of. I had the sensation: It is exactly this feeling of weight that allows me to know that I belong to the earth with my body. But it was not only because of the weight that I felt united with the earth. It was also due to all the life existing on the earth about which one is usually not aware of. By this I don't only mean subterranean flora and fauna, but also those forces that, from the earth's interior, inspire the material existence of the three kingdoms of nature (mineral, vegetable, animal). These forces – which, for example, stimulated the growth of the plant together with the forces of the sun, as I had once observed with the cress seeds – also permeate the mineral substances of the earth's body. What appears blunt and dead to the sensory eye – the minerals – I 'saw' strengthened by God's will, the presence of which I felt disseminated in the spiritual sphere as well as in the smallest, densest interior of earthly substances. Only a *will* can *form*. For me, God's will was the form-giver of the earthly – and the form-holder, the form-keeper. Only in this way could life exist in and on the material earth, and that's how I felt myself – as a materially existing inhabitant of the earth – as part of the super-sensory life of the form-giver.

Everything existing on the earth was invigorated by a super-earthly will, which streamed into human corporeality from the densest substances and maintained it in earthly life – such as a root secures a visible plant – as was my physical body and its members of my human core, grasped every day as though on a divine foundation built on a consecrated site – an altar rooted in the earth, or a root pulsating on the earth by the paternal primal forces as an altar for the service of life: an 'altar-root'.

The 'wind-sword' forms the pole to it. Like the wind that blows in the heights and does not let itself be stopped or constrained – free and unbound – thus I felt my spirit. No thoughts, no idea which comes from an understanding 'heart', alive in the highest sense and a part of the World of Reality, had necessarily to be *thought* in an earthly body. This spirit needed no heavy head, which with great effort had to be balanced on the trunk, day in and day out. The real spirit lifted itself beyond the bodily limits to the sphere of ideas, and from these created forces for life, which itself was, as Holy Spirit, inspiring human heads to high and lofty aims, which it leads to the Kingdom of Reality.

It was *reason* in the very highest measure and sense, sharp like a sword and brave like the knight who wields it and fights against his own weakness: the wind-sword.

And in the centre, between these two poles, forming a living bridge to both, were the *swan wings*. The swan in its elegance and power, a snow-white bird flying between the waters of the earth and the clouds of the sky, flapping its wings up and down. Its wings, which touch both below and above in a rhythmic pendulum-swing, so as not to let the opposing forces of will and thought drift apart, were to me the pure heart beating in the centre of the human being. The heart as seat of my *soul*, of the fountain of feelings, compassion and love. It didn't only connect above and below, it also impregnated something of itself there. What would the thoughts in my head be without the empathy for what they relate to? What would my limbs' volition be were it not be filled with love for the deed that it accomplished? Only when *altar-root* and *wind-sword* are connected in harmonious rhythm through the centre of the heart by the *swan wings* does the full *earth-spirit-man* – the real, divine human being, arise.

1985 (about 13 years old)
Last night I sat on a stone at first, and then I flew to my test. This time the test was similar: It wanted me to look back before I look ahead. And when I looked down I saw myself sitting on the stone. Completely false and distorted, as though I had a stomach ache, twisted like a worm. It only seemed so, though, from the place where I was being tested. I thought, if I pass the test I'll be free [from the distortion and twisting]. *But that was an illusion.*

Dear Light, I understood what you mean, that's why you always show me my comfort zone! My Altar-root, my two Swan wings and my Wind-sword.

With my Altar-root I stand firmly on your gripping-root-earth. Firmly anchored so I can see myself. The Swan wings flap up and down in my heart, like a pulse-beat, like my heartbeat, and it beats to the rhythm of the whole world and all of heaven. Below the wings touch the Altar-root, and above they touch the Wind-sword. It sprouts high from my heart and frees itself to fly higher than the Swan wings, because it freed itself from their beat. The sword seems unleashed when it is erect, and I admire my own Wind-sword, Lord! It gives me more courage and I wished that someday I could take it with me [into everyday consciousness].

It was a good test. Because I could go where the sun goes when it isn't shining on us. When I fly back I squeeze myself

into my little uncomfortable body and have to find peace
with the circumstances at home. I am especially bad at this.
Normally at least.

***

'To find peace with the circumstances at home.' Yes, that was what I most
desired then.

The chapter which should be written here, and in fact has
already been written, would have opened a completely different
world to the reader, the world of 'circumstances at home'. If the
story of my inner self is to be told with even approximate complete-
ness, then those domestic circumstances – which were acted out
behind a fastidiously maintained facade and within which these
inner experiences took place – should not be completely excluded.
Nevertheless, for various reasons I must dispense with this chapter. It would be too burdensome or unsuitable for some readers if
my childish notes were included which describe my despairing,
nearly hopeless situation, resulting from not being 'recognized' as
an individual by my own parents, and by not finding an 'ear' for
my inner being, who would have so gladly expressed all thoughts,
experiences, questions and hardships. It would be too disturbing
to read about a childhood where one had no confidence in one's
parents; about a continuous pendulum-swing between loving
attention and material care on one hand and unpredictable and
baseless withdrawal of attention on the other – a situation much
more difficult to withstand than the years' long, regular palpable
reprimands to an always obedient and studious child. The childish
complaints about the complete lack of privacy and the feeling of
oppressive assertiveness by constant suspicions, insinuations and
controls, probably because of exaggerated care – perhaps also as a
reaction to the necessity-driven concealing of my inner being and
life – would be too depressing. Another reason not to write about
it is to avoid wounding anyone and to avoid the misinterpreta-
tion that my intention is retaliation and not, rather, an attempt to
provide the reader with a deeper insight into the child's psychical
world of experience.

The cornerstones of this non-existent chapter were nevertheless
to be mentioned, or at least indicated, because they belong to my

biography, and much of what follows can probably only be understood and sympathized with when one knows that there was also another chapter in this story which starkly contrasted with the sublime and solemn experiences with the 'World of Reality'. This taught me early on that paradise is not to be found on earth (but is all the more to be striven for as an eternal ideal). And, I might add, constant seeking for this ideal does bear productive fruit – even if only decades later.

***

1985 (about 12–13 years old):
Last night I dreamed that Mama and Papa were sinking in a swamp. Something told me: You can only save one of them! That was terrible! They both held up their arms waiting for me to help them. But I couldn't decide which of the two to save. They are both equally dear to me. I thought, if I decide for Papa, then Mama will see it and think that I love her less than Papa. And the reverse if I choose Mama. I thought, what am I doing to the one I let sink? As soon as I decide, I am condemning the other one to die. And because I couldn't decide and found no solution, they both sank. And I had to cry because I was responsible for the death of them both. Then I thought, it would be better if I also sank in the swamp, then I'd be with them again. But something held me back and I woke up.

1983 (about 12 years old):
My dear God,

Something has occurred to me: Mama is sometimes missing her left half and Papa the right. I can't explain that better, but you know what I mean. Isn't it strange that they don't complement each other in a good way, but complement each other badly! Somehow, it is mostly not the left hand of Papa and the right hand of Mama that come together, but the two empty halves. When the empty parts are united, my parents disappear and an ugly Violence jumps at me. It comes whenever the two empty halves collapse. It only comes when it happens at the same time to both Mama and Papa. As though it were waiting for that to attack me. It is a cold thing that I can't even ask why it hates me so. I did nothing to it. One cannot speak from the

heart to Violence. I think it hates me so because I love your ven-
erable Light so much and speak with him from the heart.

This Violence has no heart-feeling. I must admit, Lord, that
sometimes I am afraid of it and hope that the hours pass quickly
when all three of us are together [in this condition]. *I am so*
afraid because the Violence seems overpowering, whereas I am
completely alone. But then I have to be brave, for that's not
actually true. Rather, what happens is that when I think now
it's over and the ugly Violence will jump into me, it can't. It
bounces off in front of me like off a wall. That seems to make it
even more furious.

I have thought about trying to prevent both filled out halves
from breaking apart. You must give me a sign by the venerable
Light, Lord, about what I should do, or if I can help. Sometimes
I feel that my parents need help much more than I do, but I
love them both very much. But I'm sad that everything is so
complicated. Do you know, Lord, my dear God, that sometimes
I am without hope and feel so endlessly lonely. It seems that I
knocked at the wrong door when I was born. Where are my peo-
ple????? Perhaps my people are not on the earth at all. Why did
you then make me so that you always show me my stars-home?
It hurts so much, sooo much, that sometimes I would rather not
wake up in the morning. I know that it's a sin to even think in
this way. One should not wish that something perish that is
your divine creation. I'm sorry, Adonai!

***

My experiences with the World of Reality led to deep religious feelings which, however, had nothing to do with confessional institutions, my family circle or any theological teachings, but to my own
encounters with those exalted spiritual entities for which my soul
felt the most holy esteem. But just as little as I found a community
of people in my presence whose hearts beat like mine for the veneration of God, so much more did I sometimes experience wonderful
things, which led me internally to olden times in which I felt oddly
at home, for there the spiritual world was still a certainty. But these
experiences were made more painful due to the fact that my intimate spiritual feelings and visions were obviously not shared by

others. My inner self felt lonely amongst all the people who did not experience such things.

When I was in the *quarta* or *quinta* (the sixth or seventh grade), we went on a school trip to the Harz mountains. There I experienced an impression which made me shake with emotion for its authenticity. As far as I can remember, it was in Goslar where we toured the old city and entered the Neuwerk church. Suddenly the breath of history became alive to me, as the old ruins indicated how people once lived in sincere devotion to the spiritual world, and how these emotions found their expression in the building of the church. Suddenly it was as though I heard the clear voices of a convent's choir; as though the old holy sages were again filling the empty, gloomy walls with sweet nostalgic reverence for the Salvator Mundi. My soul turned around – there was the *Light*! It was another kind of light which came through the windows. It was more colourful, yet also severe, more serious. It must be so, for thus one's own soul becomes more earnest, more receptive for the colourful vibrations of the light that permeates it. The walls became broader, larger than the church – a *cathedral*! What a different spirit! What an ambiance! The Lord, He was there!

Go! Follow your Lord and God! The heavy cloak that weighs down the body with earthly gravity – the soul ready to fly to heaven, tearing itself away and into the infinite seeming heights of the narrow cross vault. Go! Follow the procession! Your Lord and God will be carried forward in the holy vestments of the sacrament. Yes, my soul follows You. And it is right that the soul is so heavy; in it is implanted what seems so humbling to it that it only wants to watch the Corpus Sanctus on its knees and with its face turned to the ground. Raise your dusty feet, you disgraceful soul which longs for His loving, forgiving omnipresence. And don't be offended, my heart, at the faded finery of those who dare to present the elements of His Highness! Rather, beg His forgiveness for their silly pride. They are also your brothers, loved by Him no less than you. So love them you also, my heart, and join the long procession, for your Lord and God will be brought forth!

How you yearn, my heart, to receive Him! My short earthly life is dedicated to You, my Lord and God! Take it and lead me always to your truth! It is right, there, where I am, for you have placed me there. The warmth of your love streams through my spirit, warming my soul, by You, my life! My body glows.

*'Judith! Where is Judith?' – 'She is still inside. There she is over there'
– 'Then go get her! We're going on.' – 'Judith. Come on! The others are
outside at the ice cream stand.'*

Oh no! Don't take me away from here! What a barbaric intrusion by
a world that hardly bothers to orient its soul to the creator's spiritual force – that prowls blindly through these halls mocking with
loud, clumsy disrespect every blemish, every honest inclination of
the hearts of those times, whose movements are still a part of this
place. This world, in which the spirit is alive in the upward striving pillars, in their curving capital ornaments which unfold like the
buds in springtime; this world, in which the spirit is alive in the illuminated tracery, whose centre seems to be in the infinite expanse of
heaven, in the stone floor made smooth by the pilgrims' footsteps,
in the innumerably touched and kissed shrines containing the holy
bones of those who followed Him to death. Do not the hot tears of
the believers – bowed down by hard lives and pleading for mercy
and help, who found comfort and hope here – burn under your feet?
Do you not see it? Do you not feel it all? Why does no one stop?
Does no one hear the whispering and murmuring, the soft chants
that waft through the times which were only meant for One? Do
you not see it? Do you not feel it all?

*'The caramel sticks in my teeth!' – 'Yes, really! Which flavour do you
have?' – 'Lemon.' – 'Ugh, that's icky!' – What do you mean! Caramel is
totally icky!' – No, lemon!' – No, caramel!'*

Where am I? Lord, where did you send me to? Did the world
forget everything? Did it forget YOU? What should I do here? What
should I do here!? Have mercy on me!

The Lord speaks in me and lets my soul say: It is right where I
am, for You have placed me here. The warmth of your love streams
through my spirit, my soul warms on You, my life. My body is
aglow. So I must have complete trust that it was You who wants to
see me in this barbaric world, and I have hope that you will soon
show me why you want this and what it is I should do here.

*'They are also your brothers, no less loved by me than you. So love them
also, my heart! They are the colour of my light, which warms your soul so
covertly and magically. So love them also, my heart, as I love you.'*

146

Yes, Lord, I follow You.

'Hey, Judith! You didn't get any ice cream! Which flavour would you like?'
'I'll have chocolate then.'

> 1984 (about 12 years old):
> *This you gave me:*
> *One day you will return,*
> *when all have been prepared.*
> *In darkness do you shine*
> *full of grace, and all the*
> *people will recognize your*
> *Light and they will themselves*
> *become ablaze with light.*
> *Just as the true world*
> *of love and life throws an image*
> *upon the earth, so will You*
> *be the sun which the*
> *moon's visage shines*
> *on people and they will*
> *reflect it back. Amen*

> 1985 (about 13 years old):
> *I thank you for my life's force,*
> *my Light.*
> *You shine in me,*
> *warm me, without*
> *ever questioning me.*
> *You are my support*
> *in the darkness.*
> *You stand by me,*
> *forgive me,*
> *grant me consolation*
> *when I don't deserve it.*
> *You shine within me,*
> *You embed clarity*
> *in my reason when my heart*
> *is deluded to put it in chains.*

147

You give me the impulse,
the force for my doing.
In your name
I will lead my life,
always be witness to your light,
never deny you,
just as You never deny me
and bear on your shoulder
for me, what I put on the other
day after day.
Hallowed be you, saviour,
Jesus Christ!

***

In my most difficult times, there was always one dependable and absolutely trustworthy being who was an indispensable support: my fox terrier, Cerry. She was always there, and could listen. I could lie down alongside her. She was always nice to me. But she was also full of character and stubborn, which I liked.

Cerry prompted me to study all I could about the essence of animals. It became clear to me that as far as her self or consciousness was concerned, as an animal species she stood, so to speak, between plant being and human being. Because she almost took the place of a sister, for a long time I tended to see her as close to a human being in respect to her super-sensory being, for she had such a characterful temperament with diverse mannerisms, which clearly differed from those of other dogs. Nevertheless, I had to admit that she lacked one thing which identifies us humans as humans: the actual human core, the spirit, which is able to recognize itself, to be conscious of itself. We humans were thus gifted with a definitive additional 'component of being': self-consciousness, the creative spirit. But, I felt, this spirit was for us – when one really thinks about it – an obligation to accept responsibility. It wasn't enough for us to use our spirit in order to make our earthly life more comfortable. For it was just this which was achieved at the cost of the beings for which the human spirit is obliged to be responsible: animals, plant life, the earth-organism. Whoever possessed a human spirit had to accomplish more than animals could. By means of his spirit, he must become master of his animal instincts and transform them into intuitions. It was possible. But it seemed to no longer be an option. What I saw everywhere was the opposite of improvement. Brutality and deceit, greed and hedonism, jealousy and envy – all traits which no animal could develop. For when there exists no individual will, but only an instinct to assure one's own survival and that of one's kind; when, instead of an egocentric self-will, there is only a general will to follow the higher plan, there can be no wrongdoing, no guilt. Man became capable of egoism by acquiring self-consciousness, whereas the animal remained immune. And this egoism was the seducer of his higher spiritual nature, his noble and actual human-being-core.

It seemed as if the spiritual principle of humanity, which was additionally given to his soul-force-body and which differentiated him from the animals, was divided in two: on one side self-consciousness, in which egoism was adopted and could make him blind and apathetic in respect to his environment, and on the other side the actual human-being-core, which enabled him to rise to greater things – which let him grow out of his ego-self and freed him from the dictates of his driven self: his divine self, the seat of his conscience. Or, expressed differently and in accordance with my first thoughts on my day of earthly awakening: the human-being-core was a singular thing which, however, was not yet complete in one part. The everyday consciousness of the corporeal human, in the state of forgetting his own actual being, could nevertheless strive for his complete state of being in which he could regain the consciousness state that he had forgotten – that he had lost by entering his earthly body.

In order to recover this state, one must subdue the egoism embedded in everyday consciousness. For this caused the human being to be brought down below the level of animals, in that he betrayed his higher, divine principle and his desires and threw it to the dogs. Thus what happened was that man could no longer even hold on to his animal instincts, which worked to preserve his own kind and the environment so important for life. So, through self-consciousness came egoism, and with egoism came culpability for the neglected, mistreated whole.

Such thoughts about the difference between humans and animals prompted me to seek a concrete way – which included my being human and my self-consciousness – to live up to that responsibility. What the venerable Light taught me must be applicable and bear fruit on *earth* so that I could be equal to what was placed in me as a divine seed.

Such a path must already have been sought and found by others before me. For those who have been recognized as culturally great in history, could only have come to their insights by ennobling themselves – at least to a certain degree. So, I thought, there must be a way to root out the grotesque-face images of my unpurified thoughts and feelings! The path must have been trodden by all those elevated, cultural individuals whose soul-force-body was so pure that it was no longer merely a component but an impeccable, life-giving home. This way must lead to the creation of the all-encompassing *mandorla* – the complete agreement of our inner being with our exterior appearance. Then, perhaps, one would become a *venerable Light* oneself. The ever-quarrelling and fallible human being could develop into a *venerable Light*! If he only wanted to! Through his spirit. *Every one* of us human beings. What was I waiting for then?

But it wasn't so easy to find the way, although I wanted to look for it!

The goal I was to aim for, and the plan to achieve it, had again become a little more concrete.

The way must have to do with *self-control*, something I noticed about myself. Namely, I experienced how every time I lost control of myself the force of insight was lost. And it must also have to do with knowledge – but not a lifeless knowledge learned by heart, but rather a wisdom-filled one that one *made one's own*.

I tried to approach the problem in a systematically planned way. First, I wanted to enter the world of thought and wisdom of the *great* ones. That meant, however, that I had to find out a lot about them. And that took time, because my parents' library – mostly popular fiction and political non-fiction – contained no *Symposium*, no *Divine Comedy*, not even enough classical German philosophy and literary history worth mentioning. So, I had to find an indirect connection to the masters' world of thought. In this respect, I had to thank my high school.

The second thing I wanted to do immediately was the consistent and practical work on my soul-force-body. I had very ambitious ideas about this. For example, I decided one morning to have not even one single bad thought throughout the day – that is, a thought that could cause harm in the World of Reality. Despite many attempts, I always failed miserably. It wasn't possible. If I had succeeded, I'd have instantly reached the status of a Buddha, that is, a totally purified higher being. The intention not to think any bad thoughts included, by exact analysis, eliminating all possible defective emotions, such as resentment about an injustice, or the latent disgust at the smell of urine around a drunken tramp in a subway station. I realized that it was unrealistic to attempt to open this whole package all at once! But these experiences also showed me how much still lay before me, and how long the way would be. I resorted to a reduced version of self-education. I intended to not make even a white lie for three straight days. That was a real challenge, for without that kind of help, peaceful coexistence at home was barely possible during those years. (I had to explain everything I did, no matter how unimportant – and besides, if I admitted the whole truth I would be scolded or punished. It was a 'question of survival' whether I dared to reveal all, or resorted to verbal tricks.) And strictly speaking, a white lie included leaving something out of my story that was decisive for what the other person imagined. It was also a lie to say something that differed from my real thoughts and feelings in order to not hurt the other person. This also related to lies within one's head, for I noticed that the *unsaid* words (thoughts) also had an effect on my counterpart.

But when I took stock and tried to review the day's activities in the evening, I was disappointed to realize that I had often simply forgotten to avoid a particular bad habit within a certain situation. During the day, when I was in the middle of the turmoil of my own emotional and mental confusion, how could I think about improving? I had the idea of drawing dots on the tips of my fingernails with ink: a dot for every bad habit that came to mind. But that didn't prove to be particularly useful, because mostly I saw the points when it was already too late. Furthermore, I was asked why I was defacing my fingernails. A white lie in this case made the whole idea of the dots absurd. So the matter seemed to require a longer-term effort.

Nevertheless, these often-failed attempts caused me to be more attentive to everyday events. Perhaps a benevolent being in the higher worlds took pity on my good intentions.

This first change showed itself in my dream life. By this I don't mean the experiences I had during the night which I described previously, in which the *venerable Light* helped my consciousness by 'trials' or tests, but the normal dreams that one has during sleep and which do not provide the same clarity of consciousness that one achieves when one leaves the 'seeing eye of the body', so to speak, and enters the Kingdom of Reality. Such 'normal' dreams were fewer than during the previous years.

I had always had a rich dream life – which, according to the applicable science, means nothing else than that one can remember dreams well. I remembered an average of three or four dreams a night, in all their details. But that was not new. What was new was that over time I noticed that I could influence my dreams. So I had 'flight-dreams', those wonderful dreams in which one can fly on one's own power. I liked these dreams the most, because the flying was so enormously realistic. Of course, it was not realistic that one could fly through the air like a bird. But it was most curious that the flying dreams conveyed an amazingly authentic impression, if only because a human being could not do such a thing and could never experience it. I had to exert considerable effort to rise from the ground and reach the (relatively low) altitude of ten to thirty metres. I could recognize the streets in the neighbourhood in all their details – and from a bird's-eye view. I saw what the streets looked like from above, which I had only known from below, of course – the roofs of the houses, the crowns of the trees, the backyards into which I had never seen and in some cases didn't even know existed. Or I flew over unknown landscapes, over fields and woods, and followed the topography over gently rising hills and areas descending into valleys. I could only explain such authenticity to myself if indeed my soul really did make such flights when it left my body at night, before it said farewell to this earth vista and passed over into the spiritual world. However, during such a dream my soul was not as awake or as conscious as during my 'initiation' experiences.

In any case, I greatly enjoyed this kind of dream and wanted to have them often. So I decided to have a flying dream just before going to sleep and, surprisingly, that is mostly what actually happened. I could also lengthen a nice or exciting dream and revise it somewhat when I noticed that it was approaching its 'natural' end.

And it was even possible consistently to continue a dream that had been interrupted in the night by some noise or other. My dream life developed further in this way. Due to a detail during one dream, I remembered a different dream which I had had a few days or weeks or even many years earlier, in which a similar situation or detail appeared, and I compared the earlier dream with the current one. It was especially odd that, while I was remembering a past dream during a current one, I could even often remember exactly when I had had the past dream, that is, in which month and year, in which situation and which mood I was in, and what I thought about the meaning of the dream when I woke up. I was able to go back into the old dream and look around. It was as if, when I was in such a state, I was able to access many remembrances that were otherwise in archives locked behind many locks, which even contained the remembrances of my dreams. Soon I also realized that upon going to bed, shortly before falling asleep, I remembered the previous night's dream – including the feelings I had had then. It was like a lightning-quick repetition of the previous night's dream. I could not explain how that was possible.

After my parents decided to turn their backs on Austria and had chosen Spain as our next destination for a vacation, my holidays were different. Life took place mostly around hotel pools and the nearby beach. In order to adhere as closely as possible to the cosmetic-aesthetic modes of the times, my mother ordered me to spend at least one to two hours a day on a sunbed that wasn't in the shade. That took a lot of effort, considering the temperatures, which threatened to cook my brain. As I had to lie still on the bed, in order that all the areas be equally exposed to the sun, I began some inner experiments to dispel the desolation. I observed what happened to my awareness, in relation to the perception of my body, when I remained totally immobile for minutes at a time. All of my limbs remained in exactly the same position as when the experiment began. I could then feel the following: After a few minutes – actually after a few seconds, once I had practiced sufficiently – a state was reached in which I could no longer determine where my arm lay. Did the right lie over the left? Or the left over the right? Was it behind the head? In a very short time, 'I' was so separated from my limbs that they lay somewhere in the sunbed whereas 'I' seemed to drift further and further into the warming rays of the sun. Soon I no longer noticed the physical warmth. Nevertheless, I felt something at the place to which my consciousness was drifting, which I can only compare to a kind of torrid but beguilingly pleasant heat. This state of being was, however, drastically different from the already described experiences. I neither had to pass through my soul-force-body, nor did the *venerable Light* meet me. It was all so easy. Too easy. But where after all was I exactly drifting to? During my inner trials with the *venerable Light* I also didn't know where it was leading to, but that was because I only gradually learned to recognize the facts by which I was surrounded – namely by means of the venerable Light's teaching – illuminated by my consciousness's ray of light. But they had always been just as clearly present before as *after* my having been successfully taught, because the world that the *venerable Light* revealed to me was the World of Truth and Reality, which never concealed itself. It was all only a question of my consciousness. Now I was being *drawn* to something in a remarkable way. That was also a completely different experience. During my trials I was invited, so to speak, to follow the *venerable Light*, and this was at the same time – as strange as it may sound – my own will. But it involved no exertion of will to lead me to an unknown destination. It simply happened. And the closer I drifted in its direction, the easier and faster it was.

The strangely pleasant (super-sensory) warmth enfolded me. I began to feel something veil-like in its emanations, amoeba-like, constantly moving beckoning hands, or like long hairs moving under water from one direction to another, forming a curiously meandering, softly flowing carpet. It was enchantingly beautiful. It was not an optical perception, but the perception of a psychical-spiritual impression or impulse. And this impulse guided me in a certain direction. I followed this impulse and let myself drift. The deeper I drifted into that world, the more I had the feeling of dissolving. I barely noticed how unimportant the clarity of consciousness was, which I had been seeking and striving for since my earthly awakening day. Now the pleasantly warm, mild, flowing inertia determined everything, and I felt the faint urge to stay longer in it. Just a little longer. Just a little longer. There was nothing difficult about it. On the contrary – it went on by itself. I didn't have to do anything in order to maintain or intensify that state.

I drifted on unchecked. Eventually a thought came to me. It was like a spoil-sport, and I tried to stop it. But it bored further and further, like a relentless thorn into the world of warmth in which I floated. That thought 'spoke' to me as if it had come from outside into my dim consciousness: 'Go back!' I kept trying to push it away. But the effort that I had to make disturbed the blissful state almost as much as the thought itself. But I had to deal with it. And something in the depth of my consciousness answered its call; something was made to vibrate like a sounding box and returned an echo, so that a weak impulse of will began to form – the will to turn back. So although it was with a certain reluctance, I finally began to give in to the relentless thought-voice and slowly 'stemmed' the continued floating ahead. It didn't want to surrender so easily, though. So I strengthened my stemming impulse a little. But I kept floating on. Now the thing became scary. I tried to accomplish a proper turnaround – a return to the psychical-spiritual direction. Then I sensed a strong force working against my will and not allowing it. This force came partially from myself, from my self-will, but also from a dynamic outside myself, which seemed to come from the pleasant warmth I was drifting in. I tried to overcome this force, but to no avail. As soon as I gained a little, I was thrown far back beyond what had been achieved, as if by a rubber-band. Suddenly the bubble of warmth I was in burst apart. It had been torn by a thought which hit me like a cold shower; the thought of my higher will, the will to strive for the complete consciousness of my actual self in the World of Reality. It was the sharpness of the thought that had penetrated within me that I felt like a cold shard of ice. But it was my salvation. I literally attached myself to this thought and finally reached my clear consciousness – the total control of my consciousness. I opened my eyes and squinted at the refreshing, sobering material world. I looked down at my lotion-oiled body, which lay there, just as before… but when, actually? Hours must have passed. I stood up and retrieved my watch from under the sunbed where it had been placed as protection from the midday sun. Barely ten minutes had passed since I lay down on the sunbed.

I considered what I had experienced. It seemed as if I had taken an Odyssean voyage to the sirens, only that no one had bound me to a mast, or my consciousness to my body lying on the sunbed, or to my core of being. I was in a highly pleasant state, floating through an enchanting world, revelling in its blissfulness. And it had been a fantastic experience, which I would have enjoyed extending; a wonderful state – until I, myself, wanted something different. What I finally wanted that was different was something that had proven to be the most beautiful and at the same time the most truthful in my other experiences. But in the world into which I had floated, the most beautiful and truthful was disruptive, an unpleasant intruder which instilled a bitter, ugly poison into the beguilingly comfortable state.

What kind of world was that for which the beautiful and true is unpleasant? In that world free will was a disturbance! As long as one worshipped self-will, surrendered to the magnetic indulgence, everything stayed pleasant. But woe if not! Into what kind of strange world had I entered? Did a super-sensory kingdom exist apart from the World of Reality and Truth known to me? Or had something else occupied the World of Reality and Truth? And which beings were the invaders of the World of Truth, or were the inhabitants of that *other* world, in which the *venerable Light* didn't illuminate – in which one did not perceive the actual permeating presence of my holiest and highest master, the Son of God?

Which beings could accomplish that? Was there a force more powerful than that of the creative Majesty, of God the Father? I asked myself that and rejected it.

No, stop! Perhaps it was otherwise! I had left my body completely without purification, without meeting the deplorable creatures of my soul. Might this not mean that I had entered the World of Reality together with all my psychical immorality? Could it be that I *did* really find myself in the World of Reality but it was not possible for me to perceive what it really was – because I could only see what the grotesque creatures of my own soul had deluded me into thinking it was? That could be. Therefore a clear vision of the World of Reality was distorted for me. In this way I had entered *their* kingdom: the kingdom of grotesque soul-creatures, the kingdom of fallacy. It seemed that this kingdom of fallacy lay like a barrier between me and the World of Reality, like a veil before the gaze of my spiritual eyes. And whoever suddenly advances into the spiritual world with veiled vision can get lost. The effect which

I had just felt was enormous. A steady, relentless, merciless pull. Didn't all those who reached the Isle of the Sirens forfeit their lives? They never found their way back. The way to the spiritual world must then have a branch, or perhaps even more branches: seductive byways.

The term 'tempter' came to mind, for I could clearly perceive an impulse of will outside of myself that was asserting itself. It seemed to be struggling to dominate my inner being. And I began to consider how the biblical tempter could relate to my own experience. I remembered some psychical-spiritual experiences I had already had and which should possibly be seen as having a connection. A description of one of those experiences is found in one of my salvaged notebooks.

1984 (12 years old):

Last night I learned that sometimes I no longer need to move something. It's enough to want to move it. (Now try it!), heart-speak it.

So I took the cap off Mama's hairspray and tried it. But it didn't work. It didn't move. But you have to practice everything, I thought.

Now I think, though, that I must turn the task into a holy feeling, then it can work.

Probably I simply approached it from the wrong side, and everything needs preparation from within before it can be translated into an act.

Sometimes I'm afraid that it may be something like when the devil tempted Jesus. 'Jump! You are the Son of God.' Even Jesus was tested, because he was also a man. Of course a most unique man. But if he had jumped and not died because the guardian angels had saved him from a false death, he would surely have had big problems with the venerable Light about the precipice test.

And when I am sometimes unsure if perhaps the ugly darkness has disguised itself as light, I think of the fortitude of Jesus and compare the Jesus-Christ-Light with the disguised light, and then I can recognize it! If the light shines because it loves you, then you can trust it.

*Actually I only doubt in the earthly world, in the real world I
am mostly surer and can judge everything better.
Thanks, that you are with me!! Yours, Judith*

In fact, there was confusion here. I was shown by the *venerable Light*
that it is actually the will-impulse that moves things and which must
be permeated in the limbs in order to be able to move something,
because the limbs are in themselves only an inert organic mass.
In the super-sensory instructions, which will not be more exactly
described here, but which I later recalled when reading the newly
found notebooks, I was 'told' that, with the condition that the will
was pure – that is, that there was no personal interest involved, but
only intense interest in the great divine cosmic plan – then it could
be strong enough to move a lifeless object, which was only a dead
piece of the World of Reality. If, however, one only used the will
to move a plastic bottle-cap around, then it did not have the realization of the great, good cosmic plan as objective. Something had
interfered which did not belong to what the *venerable Light* wanted
to make clear to me about the higher nature of the human being and
divine workings. In implementing the teaching material, a mishap
had occurred. In this case, I had followed a branch in the earthly
world rather than in the spiritual world (as I had felt it to be when
I written that I could 'better judge' in the 'real world' than in the
'earthly world'). On the basis of this experience, I intuit where such
a 'temptation' could easily lead: namely to psychical hypertrophy,
delusion, hubris.

Either way, that 'telekinetic' experiment failed. And the reason was
obviously that I could not develop a purified will, because in the
earthly world I was gifted with my soul-force-body, which – like
a psychical soup – was mixed with all the possible good and bad
ingredients of my being, meaning that the will remained interpene-
trated with selfishness. So, my unpurified soul-force-body had taken
the wrong path in my sunbed experience – not only in the 'earth-
world', but beyond, namely in the 'real' world, for I had entered the
spiritual world with it. I was thus protected, in a wondrous way,
during my early years.

However, on the sunbed I had begun the experiment with the
spiritual world out of sheer boredom. The motive was decisive.

The motive seemed to be crucial as to whether, on passing through the gate, one viewed the true aspect of being and thereby purified her soul-force-body, or not. And so, without realizing it, I had entered a sphere that could have a fatal effect. I had enjoyed having a veil over my eyes! The saving thought, which in that sphere I sensed as a penetrating, sharp instrument cutting through the flattering, placid veil, could only have come from the *venerable Light*, or even from Christ. That thought had sparked my will to turn back and sharpened my vision. Thankfulness and shame now filled my heart.

But Odysseus was right. It was important to at least sail close to the sirens in order to assess the danger which emitted from them. How else could one protect oneself from their tempting arts? I wanted to test how deep the sirens' power went into my own interior. I wanted to challenge those forces. For this, more-or-less risky experiments were necessary. At that time, between my fourteenth and fifteenth year of age, I looked for situations in which I deliberately exposed myself to the temptations of these forces, in order to resist them. It was a kind of trial of the will. For example, I sat in the Philharmonic at a concert, either in a prominent row with my parents or alone in the choir block directly behind the orchestra that was reserved for the relatives and friends of the musicians. When a slow piece was played – which also contained a long pianissimo passage – I felt that the moment had come. I realized that it was solely up to my will to act as befits a concert-goer. But what if I opened a door in the closet behind which the seductive forces lurked within me and were usually held in check? I could now choose, at this moment, to let loose a loud cry! I could break open the rapt stillness and scream! The audience would be shocked, the musicians would lose their thread, and the possibility for the music to pour its healing blessing into the hearts of those present would be nullified. It was a terrible idea! But nothing and nobody could stop me! Only myself. I carefully opened the door a little more. I could do it now!! I felt the seductive multitudes trying to force their way through with all their might and open the door. The gang could hardly be stopped. I let them through to the extreme limit. Just before I took a breath and opened my mouth, I grabbed the handle and slammed the metaphorical door shut with the final strength at my command. Done! As though from afar, from the depths of my soul, I heard the muffled growling of the angry gang.

***

In respect to the confessional religious conceptions and interpretations about God, Christ, the human being, heaven, hell, earth, life, death, sense and meaning of existence and so forth, I wasn't doing very well. Confessional religion didn't offer enough to give me the feeling that my experiences with the World of Reality could be in agreement with the Church's teaching. Most aspects of my inner experiences – at least as a child and youth – did not appear within it. And even when the terminology sometimes awakened some hope, that something was referred to that agreed with my experiences, it always turned out to be the usual interpretation of the scriptures, according to a simplistically constructed moral formula. I found the spiritual world – and also the human being, as an essentially spiritual being on a material earth – much more complicated. When one thought about it, man was actually a being consisting mostly of *spiritual* 'matter'. In the first place, there was the actual human core, the spirit; then the soul-force-body; and finally, the wonderful magical life-force permeating all indwelling matter, which was also a super-sensibly perceptible figure. Only the human body was essentially of a material substance. As far as I could see, the relationship was three to one. Nevertheless, the three spiritual members of man were essentially ignored in daily life. Rather, people acted as if the visible physical person was the actual human being. And when I turned to the Church, all I heard was something about the body on one side and the soul on the other side. I felt what they preached to be an imposition for the mature human spirit. No wonder, as it was almost never about what really constitutes the human spirit. The word 'spirit' mostly appeared in connection with the divine being – and, when it appeared in connection with the human being, I could never determine what was meant, for it seemed to be used as a synonym for the concept, 'soul'. In my understanding, though, soul was distinctly different from spirit, the actual self or spiritual core of the human being. And if one considered generously that, in the Church's terms, when the word 'soul' was used, the spirit was

160

actually meant, then where was the soul, with all its subtle feelings and unconscious desires? When soul and spirit were thrown together, however, it was impossible to bring any kind of substantial clarity to inner life! What was incomprehensible to me was that the Gospels and the Acts of the Apostles (think of the Outpouring of the Holy Spirit, for instance) contain all the relevant help and warnings about what can happen if one mixed up these two aspects of the human being. Only, these indications weren't discerned and addressed.

Furthermore, in such confessional circles they always spoke only of *faith*. One always had to have faith in something. I had no problem with faith as such. During my instructions with the *venerable Light* it became clear to me that faith – in the sense of impartiality, in the sense of 'believing things to be possible' – was the indispensable gateway to the World of Reality. It was no less – but also no more – than the gate to the World of Reality. It was the gate to heavenly knowledge or the world of wisdom. But why was it never about knowledge of the spiritual world? One could experience it oneself! You didn't merely have to assume it. And, in order to recognize its existence, you didn't have to discard your enlightened thinking or exchange it for a blind or naive faith. Only through its prevailing legitimacy and facts can many essential questions about existence be resolved or illuminated. Only through it does the earthly existence of the human race make sense! Of course, God had to remain a subject of faith if he was imagined as an old man with a long white beard who sat on a golden throne, somewhere far up there in heaven. And, without giving up the – pardon Goethe and pardon me for the use of this expression – 'total shitty temporal glory'. But God was constantly active within every person – also and especially in everyday life.

From whom had man the strength to generate true ethical impulses (in addition to what made self-consciousness possible for him)? On its own, his self-consciousness, which raised him above the consciousness level of animals, was not enough. Self-consciousness alone was not 'good' – also not 'bad'. An unethical, bad deed was quickly perpetrated because *self*-consciousness had brought along the focus on *oneself*, on egoism. But what raised man *above* egoism? It was *not* his self-consciousness. That was only the prerequisite for something else, something higher. What enabled man to set aside the egoism of his self was a 'divine' seed, a core that was more important than his self-consciousness, than mere earthly reason. A seed was planted in our deepest self which enabled us to achieve truly great things. (These great things did not have to be spectacular and noisy to be truly great, namely ethically and aesthetically.) The seed had only to be awakened, rescued and dusted off from under all the ballast and lowly needs under which it lay buried. Look at it, your divine seed, man! And use it! That's what my heart felt and called out for at that time.

***

I met so few people then who were attentive to these mysteries of existence, and life burdened me increasingly in the following years. The situation at home was the greatest challenge. Furthermore, my friends and co-pupils at school began to develop interests which I could not share. I suffered for a time with a single by a so-called German New Wave band named UKW. I listened to the record for several days, ten to twenty times in a row, because I hoped to get used to it – like I did with Rachmaninoff's piano concertos, for example. Without success. A school friend once dragged me to get the German singer Udo Linderberg's autograph, whom we met in a tiny, smoke-filled room in a Berlin high-rise, situated in a side-street off the Kurfürstendamm. But nothing helped. What my friends called 'music', I found to be almost blasphemy compared to what I had always called music. Neither the practiced listening to the 'music' favoured by my friends, nor bothering with the lyrics could bring me to develop sympathy for that genre. Nothing helped. This world of others – who would wait feverishly for weeks to attend a pop concert and afterwards talk for hours about the band – was closed for me. It was not worth it for me to attend such concerts simply to have been there. It bored me terribly – this kind of 'music' made me downright physically ill. Once, when I was seventeen, a boy invited me to a Rolling Stones concert in the Olympia Stadium. His father, who worked for a private television company, gave him two tickets for the VIP box. I couldn't refuse him. Everyone said as much. It was a unique chance. So we went. I found it to be atrocious. Two hours at a military shooting gallery or in a metal factory without hearing protection would have had a similar effect. On the other hand,

I found no one of my age who would have exchanged it for the idiosyncratic interpretation of a Schumann piece by the aged Vladimir Horowitz, which I heard in the Philharmonic. (We had only one ticket, which my father shared with me during the intermission, whereas my mother gracefully did without.)

I felt ever more lonely, ever more misplaced, ever more misunderstood. A year-long trial, worthy of Job, began. Actually everything was given to me – and at the same time taken away. Sometimes I was so deeply desperate that, if I hadn't carried the Christ-experience in my soul, I might have done something serious to myself. The discrepancy between my inner world and the outer world tore me apart, almost physically. I hunched myself on the floor in a corner of my room and cried without stopping – more than once, knife in hand. I cried whole nights through, until at dawn I staggered exhausted to the bathroom and dipped my face, minutes long, in an ice-cold water bath so my swollen face would not be noticed at school. Why had God opened my eyes to the beauty and reality of the world if there was no one else to see and treasure it? Why had he given me a beating and feeling heart if I was forced to witness the contempt for this world and its destruction? Why had he given me a spirit, which longed for its kind, but found none? My thinking wanted nutrition, creativity, interchange – but hardly got it. My heart was so full of joy, compassion, devotion and love that it threatened to burst – but nobody wanted to receive the gifts which I had to give in abundance. What had I done to deserve this cruelty? What escape was there, what relief? There was none in sight. I only wanted to go home. To my true home. Every day. Every night.

I developed a terrible, painful neurodermatitis. In the crook of my arms, knees, armpits and throat area, palm-sized red blotches appeared that looked like and felt like burns. I stopped using the prescribed cortisone cream after a while because the condition returned stronger than it was originally. I tried creams, powders, covering the affected areas, pressing and pinching alongside them in order to distract me from the irritation... Every nerve-cell ending in my skin seemed to be under martial law. Because the doctors' advice didn't help, my mother turned to offbeat methods. Once my mother took me to a sourceress. I found the magical formula that she mumbled as she waved her hands back and forth over my head extremely obscure, rather like the whole experience, including the furniture and stuff in the room, which looked like a film set. In fact, though, along with bathing in the Dead Sea, it was the only treatment that really helped for a few days. But the torment returned. I developed psycho-allergic asthma. My mother took me to a pulmonary clinic.

While all this was happening, I functioned like a robot in everyday life. School, study (about two to three hours a day, depending on the school's requirements), piano, tennis etc.

With dismay I realized that my access to the World of Reality had changed in a regressive direction – first slowly, then rapidly. I seldom reached the 'gate', and finally I didn't see other people's magical life-force or their soul-force-body. My deep, childish religiosity also vanished.

I'm no longer aware which predominated during those times: distress because of humanity's ignorance of the World of Reality, or distress because of the loss of my own capacities. I groped like a blind person in the gloom of the inner and outer void – but like a blind person who had once seen; who had once enjoyed the sweet fruit of bright light in abundance and now could eat only a tiny bite of it. I was a blinded, wounded person, constantly groping and tripping. Only the light of my dearest, holiest friend and teacher still flickered in the vital, awakening remembrance, like the weak glow of an eternal light in the deep darkness of a deserted church.

A change of place brought some relief. When I was sixteen years old, I went to live with relatives in the United States, where I went to school and, the following year, lived with a school friend. There isn't much to say about my inner life during this period, because it was similar to before the move. But because of the new and varied experiences, the almost unbearable privation of the spiritual aspects of life faded somewhat into the background. Furthermore, more joy and, above all, tranquillity returned to my everyday life. In the school I was, without exertion, a high-flyer, and I could spend the free time with my friends. Also, close proximity to the sea was a wonderful gift. An analysis of that period indicates that it was very easy for me to adapt to the current culture and lifestyle in which I happened to be placed. This had already occurred during my stays in other countries. I could be totally absorbed in all of them and, like an octopus changing its colours, become a part of my surroundings. So, I didn't consider what was foreign to be foreign, but enjoyed what was new in what I learned, and I could always find something with which to enrich the head or heart. The ability to adapt to foreign surroundings without difficulty was perhaps a result of my having the feeling that my actual homeland – which was at the same time the aboriginal homeland of all earthly places – lay beyond this earth. So, I was actually indifferent to where on this earthly world I happened to be. And yet, perhaps, the most striking result of that stay in the United States was that, for the first time in my life – in respect to my inner being – I recognized myself as a *European*. Previously, the countries that bordered 'my' country all looked drastically different from mine. But now I learned that they were all bound by the invisible but strong bond of a common, more than thousand-year-old, culturally and spiritually interwoven history, that had shaped the European peoples with each other in their sensibility and understanding of sensory and super-sensory concepts. I wondered how it could have come about that this cultural and spiritual history could have been so strongly anchored in me, although I knew so little about it and had lived such a relatively short time on earth. But it was so, although it remained a mystery for a long time.

***

So I wasn't all that sad to return finally to the Central European corner of the earth. Attending a German-American Community school in Berlin until High school graduation [Abitur], allowed my inner life to blossom again, in a new way. I encountered more understanding for my interests there – in the students as well as in the teachers. Among the students there were several who chose classical music or theatre as their future occupations. They quickly became my friends. There were also a number of musical activities and offerings in which many students participated. But there was also more understanding for the interests of other students, who were not enthusiastic for such activities, than I had been used to. In that school, the so-called 'school spirit' truly lived. In fact, in my first week, because of it, I – as a fresh newcomer – was elected speaker of my class, which was not due to my appearance or demeanour, but because of the friendly desire of my classmates to allow the new student, unconditionally and completely, to integrate within the community.

There was no animosity among the students – all were liked by all, or were at least accepted, each in their own special way. We realized that the teachers were real people. The atmosphere of agitated standing-to-attention that I had known before was now one of peace and tolerance. I also had the impression that, for the first time, the teachers really saw where my strengths lay and praised and encouraged them.

The high school subjects that were taught appealed to me more than middle school ones. And so, higher mathematics, which previously had been my weakest subject, suddenly became a revelation. But my greatest appreciation was for history and, above all, German and English literature.

In these I encountered something very strange, which I had already experienced in delicate beginnings. The phenomenon, that began as a kind of prologue, appeared first in German class. We were studying some of Goethe's works, first some early poems followed by the novel *The Sorrows of Young Werther*. While I was still intensely occupied with the poems, even as some of the other students were patiently explaining them at the teachers' bidding, something totally different happened when we came to *Werther*. I scanned the little book in about an hour. Not scanned in the sense of superficial, sloppy reading, but in the sense of a (spiritual) overview. It was all easily accessible and immediately clear to me. But the novel left the taste of a certain shallow sentimentality which alienated me, although I was also strangely electrified by reading it. The days dragged on in which we studied the material and laboriously picked it apart, as if it were a corpse that was being dissected. I had to control myself so that my inner unease would not show. I moved back and forth restlessly but imperceptibly on my chair. It was as if someone had given me only the first, introductory chapter of an exciting novel to read, then forbade me from reading the main part. Finally, we continued.

After we had learned about what a *Bildungsroman** is, we inspected some parts of *Wilhelm Meister's Apprenticeship* – as far as I can remember, the first, third, sixth and eighth sections. We had to write a report – for which we were given a few days – about how what we had read related to what we had previously learned regarding aspects of the *Bildungsroman*. What occurred to me about those texts could not be justified or explained by conventional logic. All of a sudden, I was 'stuck in the middle' of the work. And not only respecting the content, but in all the habits and the psychical-spiritual mood, in the specific milieu of its creation – not least due to my own understanding of it. I stood in the 'middle' of what was said *beyond* the words – the intermediate space between what was occupied by the words in order that they could carry the content – which did not lie in the story itself, but in the invisible bond of the words providing coherence to the thoughts and intentions of the author. It was as if Goethe were standing beside me as I read, with all his impulses and mannerisms.

And very suddenly they met with mine! Like an outsider, I watched how a spirit arose from within me which began to duel with Goethe's great spirit. This unexpected, aggressive spiritual side of me complained bitterly and excitedly about the lack of empathy of Goethe's spirit concerning what that spiritual side of me recognized, as if Goethe had expressed himself, his understanding of the world and humanity, in *Meister* – that he had overlooked a part of the characteristic nature of the divine, misunderstood, ignored – and this was the part in which I saw my spiritual side residing.

What flowed from my soul and pen in relation to this furore lay beyond the task of the homework that the teacher was supposed to grade:

This book, and especially Wilhelm Meister himself, is so relentlessly stuffed with the 'same-same', that the protagonist has no time to pause and think about the essential questions. He is so snowed under by the epic breadth of his own story and the proscribed amount of meaningfulness, that at the end one asks: Should the reader feel pity or compassion? Why didn't Goethe make his apprentice seek the meaning of life, or at least ask about it? [...]

---

* A novel dealing with one person's formative years or spiritual education.

Goethe's intention was to write a catalogue about the whole human being. Nonetheless, the singularity of the individual lying in the depths remains hidden, because only the thoughts, feelings and desires are described. [...]

With the 'beautiful soul' Goethe explains to us that such a beautiful soul exists and its existence in the world of today is permitted. But it ultimately stands beside the turmoil of real life and is, in a way, a pretty plant for which neither the busy worker nor the educated aristocrat has use, and around which both of them jump in order not to squash it as they go about their business.[...]

Where in all the hidden magic is the Godhead, which opens the heart with the loveliest, most graceful affection, and the spirit in earnest holy rigour?? It is all so reasonably described that it loses its deeper, inner meaning! There is no attempt to understand what it is and could be, but it is offered on a plate until it degenerates into a frivolous, burlesque, rural farce. One should eat with the spoon provided in order to be satisfied in the belly, even if it doesn't taste good. One realizes, though, how good it could taste, and that's what makes the story so appealing. [...]

The heavenly is always only in comprehensible [= earthly tangible] *ways sought and celebrated. But why doesn't he ask how it came to be included, so that the reader could know the truth? That is probably what Goethe wanted. Instead, the explanatory spirit is used as a spoon feeder who, bite by bite, turns the externally handsome food into gluttony. [...]*

Naturally! 'Meister' is a masterpiece. It is perfect. But how is it perfect? Despite Meister's meek nature, it is perfect in victorious splendour.

My paper was returned without a grade, but with an invitation to a private talk with my teacher, written on an attached note. During the discussion it became obvious that my work had irritated her greatly. How could an immature, overly clever schoolgirl dare to criticize the great spirit of German literature in that way? Nevertheless, she had somehow grasped my text, perhaps less because of its content than what spoke through it about my inner self. She was faced with an enigma – as was I. She wanted to know what I wished to express in the paper. I said, precisely what I wrote. She asked about my parents' profession; maybe they were literary specialists or something similar. We got no further. Nevertheless, being together in that way gave me a peculiar feeling. It seemed as if the relation between teacher and pupil was shifting, because through her irritation I sensed something like a special, respectful reticence toward the pupil, a kind of attention and interest arising from strange feelings of admiration. At the end, she told me she could not really give it a grade. (The grade was immaterial to me. I had forgotten that it was a work to be graded.) She was in sufficient agreement with me, though, to give me an 'A', 'anyway'.

This remarkable event caused me to ponder on myself, and afterwards I couldn't explain how I could have had such a strong reaction – although I still considered my arguments to be well founded. Above all, I was surprised because, until then, I had always admired Goethe greatly, and marvelled at his genius and greatness. I was also awed by Goethe's greatness in respect to *Wilhelm Meister*. But through this experience, the private Goethe somehow appeared to me between the lines. And not like in *Werther*, where Goethe in the person of *Werther* had made himself vulnerable, but in a somehow grandiose way. In *Meister* – who in truth was the apprentice and Goethe himself the master – he was the creative god of his creature, who always had to remain an apprentice because Goethe had penetrated his being before the figure could be presented to the reader. But that alone was not what annoyed me, for after all, that was applicable to all literary creators in respect to their literary creations. It was much more that, through the whole text, regardless of how awkwardly his *Meister* was presented, the creator had infallible knowledge of every aspect of Meister's soul, and at the same time – and that was the worst – he was obviously to be seen as some kind of representative of mankind 'as such' (including the minor characters mirroring his psychological facets). This meant that Goethe had set himself up as omniscient over the most diverse qualities of human souls by 'characterizing' one of them. For me, the unfathomable mystery of the individual divinity in the hidden human interior died away through this. Thereby, he had also nullified, virtually desiccated the magically-artistic poetic passages. It seemed to me that Goethe was ascribing to himself the greatness that others bestowed upon him. For me, *Wilhelm Meister* was not finished, and never would be, until Goethe himself reconsidered his role in it.

I had entered into a relationship with the affair on a level that I – two hundred years after the event (and not to mention with the immaturity of a school child) – basically could not have at all.

It simply was not a pupil's examination of literary material to be dealt with as homework. I was seized with a powerful anger at Goethe, who seemed to have betrayed a certain holy literary principle, which every honest heart, burning for the literary arts, would wish to defend with chaste ardour.

But Herr Privy Councillor Goethe still had more surprises in store for me. We went on to see the tragedy of *Faust*, Part One. I took the book and began to read. My heart started to pound with the very first sentence. The words, the sentences, one image after another, flew before my eyes. My heart beat faster with each sentence, until it raced. This was it! The *true* Wilhelm Meister!

But what I read was so familiar in a quite unfathomable way! I knew this already! Stop! Stop! It's too much! My heart, my head – it bothers them so much that both threaten to burst. It was an incomparable state. The material, the poetical approach – it all felt so deeply connected to my inner self that reading caused an unbearably bittersweet pain. It was as though I was already full from only one scene, from even one word; as if what I read touched upon something that had long resided within me, where it led a secret, long forgotten existence which I had totally forgotten. How could I have forgotten it: that world, which was inexpressibly precious to me, which I now discovered with confusion, shame and happiness!?

But this world within, which I had touched upon by reading *Faust*, was of a vastly enormous size. It was as though I had grasped the tip of a piece of cloth lying under water, which was then washed to the surface by a shallow wave, thus betraying its true great size. In reading the first lines of *Faust*, I had taken hold of the tip of the whole cloth. I put my head under the water and tried to open my eyes. The contours were too blurred to recognize, but I sensed that the cloth was as large as half of the sea. So a whole world was attached to *Faust*. *Faust* was the tip and the world was the sunken cloth, which grew ever larger and heavier the more I pulled it up.

But it was impossible to bring that world, as it was, to the surface. I sensed that a physical or otherwise appropriately trained *organ*, with the corresponding capacity and skill, was needed. However, this *organ*, which I couldn't readily locate, might exist in predisposition, but was too weak to raise the whole and inspect it, and too small to recover it permanently.

Was this world a part of a remembrance of my actual self, able to remember me and everything in me, with which, however, I could not, completely and lastingly, unite?

Sweet, nostalgic pain filled my breast. With every word I read, that forgotten kingdom, the front lawn of which I had just stepped on, urged me forward. Profuse thorn-hedges, which prevented my view, surrounded it. So my rediscovered Arcadia became an almost overwhelming power that my poor human self could not cope with. I slammed the book shut, threw it on the table and ran out of the house. I ran and ran and ran until a stitch in my side forced me to stop.

I had not gotten any further than *Eritis sicut Deus: scientes bonum et malum.* * Faust's attempt to grasp the concept of the 'Logos' was almost unbearable. It felt like my fingers itched – or rather my mind. I felt that I had the answer to his question within me, but I had first to emerge from my present, tightly bound cocoon if I wished to find it.

I could not continue reading without bursting asunder psychically, spiritually and physically! It didn't fit within me because it was already there, and much more. So I put the book aside and didn't pick it up again (for fear of not being able to bear the abundance of it and the joy).

Shortly thereafter, the exam we took contained the following question: *Describe Gretchen's inner conflict based on the scene at the spinning-wheel.*

I would fully understand if, when reading the following account of what happened at that time, one had doubts about the veracity of my account. But I can do no more than affirm that it is completely true. One would think that, given the task at hand, I might as well have just gone home, because I had not got around to Faust's first meeting with Gretchen, let alone the spinning-wheel scene. I had not finished the book. But in a miraculous way, the moment I read the exam question, I knew the contents of that scene and, through the assignment, was called into the *Faust* narrative. At first I didn't

---

* You will be like God, knowing good and evil.

know the content 'directly', in respect to its informative substance and progression, but I did know it in respect to the subtle nuances of the characters' minds and their respective relationships. From that emerged – as if by itself, in a second development step of the process – the outer course of the plot in its essential features. I received the highest possible grade for my work, as well as euphoric praise.

***

Such incentives from school revived my old ideals. I could turn again to the World of Reality with renewed strength. And I did so by trying to come into contact with it, and the spiritual beings permeating it (and the visible world), in a targeted manner. For this, two things were necessary. A noble and an honourable motive had to be present from the beginning of the path that led into that World. I found it to be easy to find my old, sacred ideals, for which I was fired up in a new way. And, it was necessary to respect the boundary that was marked by the gate of the view into my own being. I could not let myself be misled by taking a detour or a shortcut. I had to stay on the path – even when it was uncomfortable to follow – and continue on it.

In this respect, I also discovered a possibility to achieve a conscious contact with the spiritual world without having to wait for night's repose – that is, a consciously producible contact during the day. Besides – prompted by aspects of semantics and linguistics presented in German class – I had undertaken several experiments concerning the properties of words and sayings in the German language. It occurred to me that the spiritual concept associated with the physically producible and audible word could be detached from the spoken word to such an extent that one's habitual thoughts associated with the word's meaning were not precise enough. One had only to repeat words loudly (or also mentally) until the tone of the combined sounds seemed absurd. That was something one did as a child, but if you didn't stop there and continued the experiment, something astonishing happened – you entered the sacred halls of higher conceptions. Behind the facade of sounds was hidden the meaningful life of the word; the divine, perfect thoughts lying within it. And these perfect thoughts, which represented actual, true concepts, introduced a whole world of attributes which one usually could not recognize, because one strangled the word in a formalized shell by an egoistic and therefore personal way of expression. This is because the truly living word, or its essence on earth, is not understood with earthly understanding, but is usually used as a mere bearer of information.

From this experience came my newly discovered access to the World of Reality. In a quiet moment I sat on a chair and thought of a short prayer, for example *Hail Mary*, which I silently repeated many times until the content of the prayer was no longer in the foreground – forgive me, Lord, this expedient profanation! – although earthly reason, which was otherwise so easily distracted from concentrating on the essential because it always wanted to think about 'something' else, was occupied with the content of the prayer in the background, and in this way no longer constituted an obstacle for 'higher' thinking, which was in the foreground. So the same thing resulted as at night. Consciousness raised itself from everyday understanding and observed it 'below', or from without. Therein all kinds of impulses bustled about which – had one given them an imaginative shape – would have again had an appearance like something from a Bosch painting, but which, however, one could spiritually experience and recognize. Only then could one turn to the World of Reality, in which one could go on a journey of discovery.

I must however explain that the words 'journey of discovery' can easily lead to a misunderstanding, for it is only used, as has been explained previously, as an inadequate expedient. Therefore I will be precise: To go on a 'journey of discovery' in the spiritual world sounds perhaps like an enjoyable walk in the park which one can decide whether or not to take. But according to my experience at the time, that does not apply to the spiritual world. The soul must be prepared for it. But the determined, purposeful dedication to the spiritual world – if it is achieved in a sincere manner and the soul has been accordingly prepared – is only one side of the coin. The rest, which is basically the nurturing substance of higher knowledge, must be 'given' by the World of Reality. The great figures of cultural history also felt themselves endowed by gifts of grace from beyond the physical world and attributed such gifts to the Being from the World of Reality, as is attested to by innumerable letters and poems. Certainly, even a great mind would have had to expand, in a self-determined and purposeful manner, to gain such insights. And yet it would always have been an 'endeavour' – a struggle to make a little progress. He or she could only develop real insight into a significant question or sphere of knowledge with the cooperation of the Godhead. Perhaps one could say one's own Godhead, that is, the higher self, which lives in the World of Reality as a fully conscious component. But with only this – one's own higher divinity from the other side, so to speak –one can in reality do little. If one were able to master it well, one would already be a higher being. Nevertheless, during my 'discovery trips', the higher beings in fact 'showed' me that the human being can forge a link to close the gap between earthly and super-earthly consciousness. I also strove to achieve this.

Only years later did I realize that the repetition of words, sayings and mantras to achieve a deeper vision into the World of Reality was a generally applied method, especially in Buddhism.

During those years, between my seventeenth and twentieth years of age, my behaviour and thinking in the earthly world, and my related relation to the spiritual world, became ever more a 'path'. Because of the stimulation from school lessons, I came into contact with spiritual 'fields'. Within these fields I learned of different ideas developed by the cultural greats before our time, which had a most fruitful effect on my soul-spirit – and even on my physical sensitivity. I realized that certain 'sacred' thoughts that were oriented toward the true, the beautiful and the good, came to me from the magical life-force more often than previously. And in turn they awakened in me the force to 'produce' the true, the beautiful and the good. It seemed that a sacred production-circulation was actuated in this way – like a wonderful sensory and super-sensory economy that was not purely spiritual, but which also incorporated sensory existence. This was because, due to the impetus from spiritual life, the physical world could be transformed into the true, the beautiful and the good. Furthermore, this also had an effect on the soul-spiritual development of the human environment.

At that time, I returned to the mystical sources of Judaism, because they seemed to reach further into the origin of humanity than all the other sources known to me then. The Christian teaching, as it was taught by the Church, disappointed me. (At that time I knew nothing of the great early Christian teachings or of scholasticism; in fact, no meaningful Christian teachings or viewpoints had been made known to me at all. So, I had no idea of their existence and thought that what I heard in religion class and sermons was all that the Christian church had to say about the true, living knowledge of the World of Reality.)

I discovered the Kabbalah as a source of new insights, the contents of which were curiously familiar to me. To my great joy, I found conceptions in the kabbalistic traditions that were very close to my own discoveries and experiences – or I found some of my discoveries explained in a different way and even supported or supplemented. The concept of 'Adam Kadmon', the paradisaical primal human, seemed in a certain way to correspond to my idea of the higher self, the actual human-being-core – that higher state of existence which at some point we must have lost, for otherwise we would be able to remember 'ourselves' today. In that state of existence, according to the Jewish tradition, we corresponded to God himself, only in a smaller way. I had some difficulty with that though, because the sources at my disposal interpreted 'Adam Kadmon' as the human condition of man before his earthly corporealization. In that state, the human being was swimming in the divine unity (this, so to speak, was his natural state) – but didn't his Fall from Adam Kadmon to simply Adam have something potentially more uplifting than the original state? His corporealization brought imperfection and egotism, but through them also the ability to be conscious of himself (like a god) and, by impetus and determination, to find his way back to that state of an 'Adam Kadmon' – that is, to perfection – equipped, however, with a new consciousness of himself achieved by a path of knowledge based on pain and austerity. Why did Prometheus fight for man, if not for freedom to assert himself without the all-mighty Zeus – if not for us to develop our earthly self-consciousness? And why then – as though in a second step – did Christ become man if not to enable the self-conscious yet egotistic human being to acquire a higher insight and therewith the return to his full, spiritual consciousness? But I resisted thinking of God as an anthropomorphic, macrocosmic counterpart to the microcosmic human being, as the

Kabbalah did. For as pure and noble a state of being man as Adam Kadmon may have been, this model could only be seen as a divine preliminary stage. The 'venerable Light' was also not 'God' Himself, that is, the God of Genesis. A spiritual being in the hierarchy of divine consciousnesses, described as an angel, was not the all-embracing creative primal source of life, but a freely serving creature or representative of God, cooperating in the great cosmic plan. How could God be the macrocosmic counterpart of his own creation? Or rather, how could the being first created by God and out of God be the microcosmic counterpart of his creator if he could not (yet) create like Him? And, why should God only be able to work on microcosmic human beings through the ten Sefirot of the kabbalistic tree and not directly? Were all of God's abilities really contained in the Sefirot? Or, was it not also in his power to intervene *directly* in the cosmic world-plan or in his microcosmic creature, the human being, and not be dependent upon its emanations?

I assumed that the kabbalistic concept was seen from the perspective of the 'fallen' man's understanding of God and the creation of the world. Because, for the sensory or earthly man who was not able to unite with his higher self, God was really manifest via 'detours' (the Sefirot): about earthly conditions, nature, *Malchut*; over the magical life-force, *Jesod*; over the human soul, *Tipheret*. Only *Kether*, the living spirit in man, indicated a direct connection.

What especially delighted me was the kabbalistic tree of divine emanations and the considerations and viewpoints arising from it regarding the essence and effect of language, of words and tones. Accordingly, all innermost being led back to a certain quality of a divine-spiritual 'primal word' (*Ur-Wort*). This is what John the Evangelist must have meant in his Prologue!

This 'word' of the 'primal beginning' occupied me with a fascination that can hardly be described. Just as in a similar way to how *Faust* led me *to* my deeply buried world, the thought of the primal-being as spiritual 'word' also led me to that world. I sensed that this was a world in which my everyday comprehension-consciousness lay in silent slumber but was in reality in constant movement – like a primal fire blazing in my spiritual interior, as in a lava-chamber in the earth's interior.

I had previously overlooked these forces – which formed my real being – or I had not yet been able to see them, although they belonged to me. While temporarily leaving the physical body, my soul-force-body, in which ethical and reprehensible impulses, feelings and desires abounded, was unrecognizable as a part of my Self. Of course! For that particularly powerful part had to belong to the deepest core of my actual Self! And it was far beyond the castle's gate. I had been hunting for this 'actual Self' since the day of my earthly awakening. Since I had not been able to find or recognize it in its wholeness, I had not discovered this curious, primal fire-like aspect. It dawned on me that, in a certain sense, the teaching of the 'venerable Light' served one purpose: to find my actual whole Self. Perhaps it was all 'only' a preparation for it. Perhaps this occult teaching about the world and existence was the only way to lead me to 'myself'.

That was when I sensed for the first time that this, my actual higher Self's primal fiery part, which until then had remained hidden from my spiritual eyes in my deepest interior, could also be miraculously linked to the spiritual primal word (Ur-Wort). Sometimes, it seemed to me that it was born from the primal word, like one of the ten emanations which I understood as the spiritual primal principle of the creation. The 'primal-word' – which John the Evangelist called 'Logos' in Greek – this spiritual 'primal word' that stood, so to speak, behind the kabbalistic Sefirot-tree or above its crown ('Kether'), was perhaps, beyond the hunt for my actual consciousness-existence, the final goal of my search, because in it everything came into being!

When I thought such thoughts, which unfortunately cannot be adequately conveyed – thoughts which I also felt, feelings which I also thought – they seemed to involve my entire organism. It was as though a spiritual pillar of fire, merging above and below within me, flashed through my whole being – as if it were the thoughts themselves that suddenly unleashed a force that lifted me out of my body, only in the next moment to embody thought-beings, thought-facts within it, and return it transformed to the earth. Afterwards I felt my body having ascended to a higher level, materially rarefied, but at the same time potentiated, more alert, more powerful through fire – like a phoenix that rises from the burnt shell of its lower self on wings of fire; a thought-body, a truly lived-through place of action of light, spiritually divine thoughts.

Was this the 'procreative' Word in John's Prologue – as I later found it in Hegel? The procreative word, which directly intervened in man if he concentrated his most internal life-thoughts on the creative primal-substance of the Creator Mundi? If so, the thinking-will of the Most High must have been able to transform the substances of matter, to spiritualize them! The foundation of a new human existence!

The kabbalistic mysticism of numbers, which seemed to have been conceived from the spiritual contemplation of the Word – the words and tones – attracted me as if magnetically. Ever since I first learned numbers, I had the firm impression that they were 'ensouled', and that each one had its distinctive characteristic and purpose in relation to the *whole of all numbers*, which man with his mathematical abilities could never calculate and thus could never comprehend through mere intellectuality. I had always felt that 'real' mathematics was not just a means of calculating the laws of the world, because I considered 'real' mathematics as the basis for the super-sensible blueprint of a cosmos which could never be calculated. As a child, a number meant much more to me than an arithmetical tool for determining dimensions or values. For example, for me a number was either masculine or feminine (regardless of whether it was even or odd) – a few were also asexual. It also radiated a special effect, which made a colourful impression on my soul. Also tones, corresponding to a certain number, whose pitch and acoustic colours I 'saw' or 'heard' in their respective *colours* and *sex,* could call forth the same impression. But this special character that I perceived in numbers was degraded to mere 'values' in mathematics class. For example, I found the value of four to be not greater than three, but rather the opposite. I experienced four as an 'impossibility' – falling out of the natural sequence of one, two and three. It was a violation of the spiritual structure of the cosmos. For me, 'one' was a symbol of the creative Majesty. 'Two' arose from the impulse to create something 'different'. The unity had split into a duality. 'Three' was the 'child', engendered as the consequence of the whole having been broken into a duality, and which strives toward unification. So three, although completely new and independent, turned into a super-sensory gesture like a wondrous arc – which I thought I recognized anew in the written form of the number – then back again to one, the perfection of which seemed to be reflected in three, whereby two split in two could be overcome, enriched by the experience of the creative process of division and the inclusion of the new. So the sequence of one, two and three was in itself a 'correct' segmented whole. In the geometric form of the equilateral triangle, I saw a solid-shape metaphor for this living being – and becoming – trinitarian organism. And I could barely contain my joy when I discovered it again in the crown of the kabbalistic tree.

'Four' on the other hand was for me an over-extension of this organism, correct in itself and not needful of anything else – like an overbreeding or a perversion of two. I felt that because four was there, the dam was broken and the other numbers could follow. Some of them seemed – by their very existence and way of acting – to strive to make four so supple that it would not forever act as a wall, blocking access to the great triangle by all the other numbers which derived from one. 'Twelve', for example, did exemplary work in mitigating four by its threefold repetition, and therefore had to be in the service of the higher trinity.

This perception – really experienced by me – of the relationship between the individual 'essences' of the numbers, accompanied every assigned arithmetic task during my school years and – especially in the middle school – spoiled my enjoyment of mathematics because the lessons paid no attention to such relationships and misused the character of the numbers, which to me seemed alive, for its purposes. However, in the Kabbalah I found the numbers as glyphs of higher, spiritual principles giving the greatest possible purity and accuracy to a dead depiction of living qualities on earth.

The Kabbalah was for me the first encounter with a complex spiritual work in which I finally found ideas which seemed related to my own in respect to their nature and direction. And I was certain that its exponents would neither laugh at nor consider mine to be inventions. For several years, the Kabbalah was a lively source of inspiration through which I encountered the beliefs and thoughts of several people who specialized and differentiated the Kabbalah's wisdom. One of them, who lived within a different cultural stream, and worked, so to speak, parallel to the kabbalistic tradition of the ancient Hebrews that existed long before the Christ-event, was Plato. His knowledge of the origin of the world and its super-sensory nature corresponded with the basics of what I first learned through my study of the Kabbalah. I experienced Plato as a deacon of higher thinking in whom had permeated a purification of the psychical element of the kabbalistic worldview.

I found Éliphas Lévi and Arthur Edward Waite to be conscientious representatives of the Kabbalah. In respect to the latter and his concern to return to the primal source of knowledge regarding the divine world – in order to help the knowledge-hungry and striving souls of the nineteenth and twentieth centuries to rediscover the right path in their complicated materialistically minded world – I saw an honest intention. But it seemed to me that his understanding of the Kabbalah's original essence was not completely accurate. I probably had this impression because of Waite's (alleged) devotion to magical practices, which took place in one of the lodges he founded. But my research regarding all of that remained quite superficial. The philosophical part interested me a lot, but the eager dealings in magical practices were weird to me, which was why I never had a more intensive engagement with them. I myself had, after all, experiences (such as with the bottle-cap of my mother's hairspray) of how easily one could take a wrong turn if one misunderstood or even over-estimated one's present spiritual tasks and abilities. Thus my engagement with the hermeneutic Kabbalah in those years was nothing more than a pale sidelight in the brightly-lit firmament of ideas and impulses, which I encountered in great number and variety from all directions, including in school.

* * *

They were (for my inner life) productive years! There were so many new things to discover. Every crack into which I looked opened a fantastically winding cave system of vast breadth and depth, which harboured innumerable treasures of which one was more enchanting than the other.

In a philosophy course I studied Ovid's *Metamorphoses*. I had already encountered it in Latin class in my old school, but at that time my enjoyment of the content was a bit lost due to trying to find a correct translation. But now, in the translation in hexameters (a kind of verse you need to be in the right mood for), I began to see the deeper meaning of the poem – from the origin of the world, the circumstances of which I so yearned to learn and which had always attracted me, to the Deucalion and Pyrrha, as the only survivors of the Great Flood and thus the ancestral parents of the 'new' humans, who seemed to be the Greek version of Noah and his wife.

The principle of transformation awoke new interest in me and I tried to express my question about the meaning of *Metamorphoses* – especially about man's relation to the divine – and bring it to the spiritual world and explain it to the 'venerable Light'. When I succeeded I often experienced that when I brought a question to the spiritual world, as long as it was clearly formed in me, it seemed to become a torch which illuminated the spiritual 'space' and the question itself. If I say that when searching within the spiritual world, one's own question turns into answers, it sounds as absurd as it is convenient. But both presumptions are refuted if you imagine that, in that state of awareness, to *one* question you find *more* answers, sometimes not even remotely corresponding to each other, which in turn means even more *new* questions – creations of the super-sensible world, that is, the world of higher thoughts – which again are fundamentally different from the original question and are not quickly answerable. For there is a difference if you are thinking in the sensory world or in the spiritual world, with sensory consciousness or with super-sensory consciousness, as little as it may have been trained.

This peculiar reproduction of a super-sensory answer is a kaleidoscopic effect which, as I realized over time, arises because of the fragmented unity of contemporary consciousness, which has not yet reached a complete unification with its actual, higher self – that is, to resolve the fragmentation and achieve the calm knowledge of the whole. So I stood before the Augean task, to filter out the real answer from the undergrowth of my own unconscious – the real from the unreal.

Just as with everything that you want to master, *practice* is also necessary here if you would like eventually to obtain a tolerably 'accurate' result and not be satisfied by merely convincing yourself that the results correspond to reality. You shouldn't be discouraged by setbacks from further trials and more practice. I found that the answers to a question have to do with the 'character' of the question asked. If the question contains a trace of 'pushiness' or urgency, the probability exists that you are dealing with dead-ends which, however, do not always allow turning back right away, but become ever narrower the further you enter into them because of their conic shape. In this way, they mislead you into being held fast to them, which leads at first to one not wanting to turn back and finally to *not being able* to turn back any longer due to the loss of the mobility that is necessary to turn around. If, however, the new spiritually-oriented question, resulting from an answer received to the original question, remains 'cautious' and to a certain extent in the dark, you have a good chance of dealing with an answer that corresponds to the World of Truth. You should continue to follow it, although it could take years before the darkness begins to yield and the Light of knowledge starts to glimmer.

Success in practice depends, however, in how far one has come in ethical self-education, which must be proven in ordinary every-day life. The further one progresses in this, the less the kaleido-scopic effect occurs, until one day the spiritual eye begins to focus on the answer that truly corresponds to the question asked.

But even then one is still far from the objective. A new challenge then arises, which I also experienced for the first time. The only 'correct' answer is so complex that it becomes a kaleidoscope of answers. Even these are not all in apparent agreement with each other – which also might be because consciousness has not yet ascended to its highest level. (If one had reached the highest level of spiritual consciousness, one would no longer need to 'investi-gate' in the spiritual world, for then you would be acting intui-tively due to a wisdom-filled consciousness.) The difference with the previously described kaleidoscopic effect is that, in this case, the answers are only apparently contradictory, but in reality stand in an inseparable connection to each other, as together they all – and *only* together – form the *one* true answer. Still, one is obliged to examine further the apparently contradictory parts of the answer – to delve deeper – because only in this way can you produce the link between the individual parts that is necessary to connect them and to be able to see the whole. In this way, it is possible to have a cor-rect answer from the World of Reality, even when one is not a per-son who is permanently and intuitively acting with a wisdom-filled consciousness, but is only sporadically achieving enlightenment and acquiring a certain higher knowledge by means of super-sensible research. At that time, I began this kind of super-sensory investigation.

As confusing and complicated these 'mechanisms' – and the attempt to reproduce them – may seem at first sight, they nevertheless constitute a consistent and wise system that is offered to an individual from beyond the gate, so to speak, and with which you become surprisingly familiar and can manage, so long as you remain sufficiently attentive.

As the next and unfortunately final assignment of the philosophy course – the teacher moved and left the school – we were given a paper with a long list of great philosophers' names. Each student was to select one of them, give a synopsis of his biography and the direction of his thoughts and concentrate on one of his works or an extract of the same. I went rapidly through the list of mostly unknown names, and then went through them more slowly: Adorno, Anaxagoras, Arendt, Aristotle – I stopped. Aristotle. Of course I had heard of Aristotle. But I had never studied his writings. The name strangely struck a chord within me, which vibrated slightly by its repetition: Aristotle, Aristotle, Aristotle. The name resounded like an echo from the underground of my soul, and with it the sense of strange familiarity. A feeling of wistful, longing joy pervaded my heart, which normally overcomes one at the spontaneous thoughts of an almost forgotten loved person or place from earlier, happier times.

I went to the school library and picked out a book which looked like it had never been opened before: Aristotle, *Metaphysics*. On the back cover were three citations: a not particularly productive one by Kant: *'Metaphysics is necessary'* – and two from the author himself: *'All men naturally strive for knowledge'* – *'We seek the principles and the causes of the entity, insofar as it is an entity'*. Whereas whilst reading the first statement my heart skipped a beat, it was the second which held me, *'... insofar as it is an entity ...'* Did he mean the true and immortal life, the creative and fully conscious potency of the World of Reality as opposed to the semblance of the transitory earthly world? I leafed through to the table of contents, which I found on the last page of the appendix: *Introduction, Book I, Book II, Book III, Book IV, Book... XIV*. Not exactly revealing. I took the book to a seat and began to read the Introduction. I gathered from it that there were no fundamental discrepancies in Aristotle between the exoteric and esoteric, which have only recently been divided into two parts, but that his *Scientific Prose*, as it was called, did not only include the fields of Logic, Rhetoric, Literary history, Politics, Philosophical history, Cosmology, Psychology and Natural science, but also Ethics and Metaphysics.

I also found subtitles of the individual 'Books' in the Introduction. The first was *Philosophy as Science of the First Principles, the Four Causes of the Entities*. I trembled with hope and incredulous bliss. Was there once a person who considered the affairs of the World of Reality, the super-sensory world, with the same seriousness as natural science? The subtitle of the sixth book seemed to indicate that: *The First Philosophy as Science of the Being, insofar as it is a Being*. I had always counted the spiritual Being as the cause of all sensory being. And here someone described the cognitional seeking of it as the *first* philosophy, obviously meaning 'most important' or 'most fundamental' of all philosophies and naturally – as *science*! This was *it* then: the book which unburdened people of the mere *must-believe* in the World of Reality! Why was it withheld from me? And why wasn't the whole world talking about it?

I opened the first book and began to read: '*All men strive naturally for knowledge. A clear indication of this is the love of sensory perceptions. For aside from usefulness they are loved for their own sake and, above all, the sensory perceptions that come into existence through the eyes.*' After this sentence I already craved to know the whole book. One could only start writing such a book if one intended to entice the reader to reflect again about the fact, namely man's urge to know the sensory perceptible, to show that he also strives to know the super-sensory. A few sentences later, the author confirms referring to the wisdom obtained by means of the mere sensory phenomena of the world. '*Nevertheless, we think that knowledge and understanding are attributable more to art than to experience, and we consider the artist to be wiser than the experienced ones, as if wisdom followed them according to the amount of knowledge obtained. Nevertheless it is so, for some of them know the cause, the others do not. The experienced ones know what, but they don't know why. The others, however, know the why and the causes [...] And we think that they are not wiser because of their ability to act, but because they possess the concept and know the causes.*'

'... because they possess the concept ...'. The *concept!* His methodically strict procedure – which I came to know shortly by studying his *Metaphysics* – for the determination of a concept as the basis for knowledge about an entity or a cause, was for me something which might be compared to receiving a Gospel. The brilliant and refreshing precision with which Aristotle approached this was breathtaking and exactly what I had always craved without realizing it, because I lacked the corresponding concept. In due course I was also amazed that until then, in respect to certain views, I had followed Plato's ideas without knowing it. But now I saw that Aristotle, in one or another place, had pointed to aspects which Plato had not noticed or had not commented on, which first became visible through Aristotle's ability to organize concepts. In other things – such as his perception of the relation of ideas to sensory things, as he discussed in his views about mathematics – I was torn. On the one hand, I was entirely on Aristotle's side and through him also got to know the work of Socrates, which differs from Plato and here and there gives the foundation of Aristotle's views – which, however, did not seem so dialectical to me. On the other hand, it was initially difficult to accept the proposition that ideas are not the cause of change in sensory things, although I could accompany and approve of his way of justifying that affirmation.

On that day, when I discovered Aristotle's *Metaphysics* in the school library, I tore myself from reading with great reluctance and ran to the lending desk in order to take the book home, like a tiger who drags her valuable prey to a secure hiding place where she can enjoy it undisturbed. On the way home I thought about how I should proceed. The assignment for the philosophy course was due soon and there were exams in other subjects which I had to prepare for. Upon reading the first paragraphs, I realized that my occupation with *Metaphysics* would be a long-term affair. So I decided reluctantly to concentrate on an extract, as the assignment demanded.

I wavered between Book X, *The Entity and the One*, and Book XII *About the Principles of Being and Movement, about the Philosophy of First Things*. I chose Book X. It began with the words: *'That one expresses the one in multiple meanings has been discussed earlier in the treatises on the multiple meanings of words.'* Aha, 'previously' then. I leafed back to the beginning of Book IX: *'Furthermore, what is called "being" and to which all other statements about entities are traced back to, has been spoken of as being. For according to the concept of being, every-thing else is spoken of as entity: the quantum, the quale, which is spoken of in this way, that is, all we have described in the first considerations, must contain the concept of being.'* I leafed back again to Book XIII about *The Principles of the sensory knowable being*, and, having gotten that far, I decided that it would make sense not to ignore Book XII: *Considerations about Being.* But then I first had to contend with Aris-totle's concept of 'substance', and finally also with the underlying *Hypokeimenon.** In this way, I landed back at Book I, not without a certain satisfaction at having found a plausible reason for having to study *all* of it.

But I will not go into here about which ideas appealed to me most and for what reason. I experienced the study of this book more as a dialogue. So, all the chapters appealed to me, especially those about the question of the 'first moved beings' and about the quantity of 'non-moved' beings, which could only be the movers of the moved beings. In this way, he came to the nature of numbers. I wanted to go deeper into that, not least because the thought that the 'first' was possibly not unmovable at all, as Aristotle claimed, wouldn't go away. A certain movement was necessary for the creation of the movable things.

As far as the content of *Metaphysics* and my thoughts are concerned, I must interrupt my narrative here because of its enormous scope, but I still want to refer to a phenomenon that does not affect the book itself, but which I first encountered while occupied with it, and is probably one of the most unusual things I will describe. I started again with Book I, this time in secluded, quiet surroundings. What had already begun to some degree when I first found the book in the school library, appeared now in my secluded room with a great dynamic. It was similar to the state I experienced whilst reading *Faust*, but this time the content didn't seem to come as emotionally close as with *Faust*, but rather as – I cannot describe it otherwise – *spiritual* (more 'objective'). The reading approached me more spiri-

---

* *Hypokeimenon*, later often material substratum, literally meaning the 'underlying thing'. According to Aristotle's definition, something which can be predicated by other things, but cannot be a predicate of others (Ed.).

tually and less psychically. And so I did not lay the book aside, but continued reading. And during this continued reading of what had affected me so deeply in a spiritual sense, something suddenly happened which I had never before experienced and about which one would never even dream were possible.

The more I connected to Aristotle's living thoughts, which suddenly rose intrinsically before my understanding, the more the way of reading changed, in a 'technical' manner but evoked by that connection with thoughts. The realization of this process is easier to describe than the cause of the process. It was as if the words and letters in the outermost part of the printed space were rapidly collapsing toward a central point in the middle of the page, while all the other words and letters that made up the content of the text on the corresponding page and were the bearers of the meaning of the conceptual content, together with the actual, purely spiritual content, was swept away and vanished into an indeterminably small 'hole' – like a vortex, but without the typical spiral-forming movement, but with a ray-forming one, to be understood in a mathematical-geometrical sense. From each letter, and its task for the emergence of the meaningfulness of the text, a ray went out, which had its goal in the infinity beyond the 'hole' in the centre of the page and on which the 'meaningful part' of a respective letter or word, and its connection with the others, was carried through the eye of the needle of the central super-sensory 'point'. Beyond the super-sensory needle's eye, beyond the now barely visible, unimportant page of the book, was my inner self, the living thought-world of my actual human-being-core, as an 'infinite', namely immortal, spiritual-meaningful quality. It absorbed the concept-content through an imaginary point – the partition between sensory and super-sensory perception – and unfolded it to a living thought-blossom, so that the (original) text was clear to me – or rather to my higher consciousness – to an extent that it had never been before. Because it was my 'higher' consciousness which could observe the thought-blossom, this consideration of the comprehension process was detached from the temporal relationships to which our earthly discursive thinking is subject. This resulted in a completely new way of reading a page, so that during the inner process of comprehending the concept-context of the page, hardly any time passed. This was repeated for all the following pages, so that I read the whole of Book I in about a minute and a half.

While this astonishing process was taking place, I was studying how it came about, that is, what I should do to make it a smoothly running process. This was possible because I found myself, with my consciousness, in a state or a sphere in which time as we know it – limited by three dimensional space – does not exist; so I could, to a certain extent, 'simultaneously' enter various 'spaces' within this spiritual sphere without having to have previously left a different one. I realized that this wondrous process which I had set in motion could be optimized if the sensory perception of the letters, which stood at the beginning of the process, could be changed to a super-sensory perception by means of the substance of the ideas borne by the letters – by aiming my will at the conscious bundling of the I-like force which, during the normal visual process, passes through the optic nerve and from there via the retina through the vitreous humor and the lens, and toward the light reflected by the object being viewed. This demanded utmost concentration on the conscious suppression of all sensory stimuli, achieved by my constant exercises for the separation of concept and word during the quiet, meditative moments of the day, and which I discovered to be a proven means for the purposeful entry to the World of Reality. It was not my intention to establish a speed-reading record, rather that the smoothest way of reading led to the smoothest spiritual treatment of the material. And because the turning of pages was always accompanied by a certain disruption of the suppression of sensory stimuli, I had to repeat the will-impulse in order to achieve the same way of reading for every page, and tried in this way to make the will-impulse as flawless and hygienic as possible. When successful, this enabled a more rapid transition from sensory to super-sensory perception and therewith an almost undisturbed pursuit of the substance of thought. I also realized that Aristotle had created his ideas from out of the 'super-temporal' sphere and that subsequently he was successful in expressing his ideas in a comprehensible way, namely in 'concepts', and to develop these for the reader, so that it was also possible to follow his thoughts, which actually 'live' on a higher level, in a purely discursive way, that is, to be able to understand them. (Even if the lively thought-dialogue was not possible in the latter way.)

Independently of the phenomenon of the new way of reading inspired by *Metaphysics* (which, however, was only possible under the stated conditions), that book became definitively a new source of inspiration and in my opinion one of the world's best books (although I must add that at this point I was not yet familiar with many other works, especially those dealing with this field of inquiry).

Of the many stimulating works I encountered during those three years, at least two more should be mentioned. For one, my introduction to Shakespeare – the master of higher psychology – whose expressive literary work I studied in the original language in English class, which in reality was a literature and philosophy course for English native speakers. After we had spent the entire eleventh year with *Macbeth*, *King Lear* and various of the Henrys, we went on to his sonnets. The sonnets opened the entrance to the spirit of the English language for me, which I might never have encountered without reading them. The diverse, subtle allusions with which they were spiced were like powerful, and at the same time noble, magical steeds of differing colour and stature, which one could jump onto at any moment and be whisked away to the most distant, strangest and furtive locations, where one would be initiated in unknown insights and perceptions. What a difference from the human nature characterized in *The Canterbury Tales,* written a good two hundred years earlier, and with which we finished the school year. From these contrasts one had a feeling for the developmental process of human souls and spirits as well as the language and the use of words. A whole earthly era seemed to lie between *The Canterbury Tales* and Shakespeare's poetry. Something extremely crucial must have taken place in human souls and consciousness in the time in between.

In addition to the works by the American transcendentalists such as Ralph Waldo Emerson and Henry David Thoreau, which were also helpful, I would like to mention above all the Irish poet and Nobel Prize winner for literature, William Butler Yeats. I had a very special kind of spontaneous access to Yeats. His idiosyncratic poetry attracted me in a strange way. There were times when I never left the house without a book of Yeats' poems under my arm. With few words, Yeats was able to lead the mind from the grating uproar of everyday life to the shady meadows of the immortal moment. In this prevailing immortality – constantly threatened by transience – which he expressed in his poetry, I sensed his sublime inclination for the occult. It was only later I found out that he belonged to the same esoteric order as Arthur Edward Waite.

* * *

Toward the end of my thirteenth school year, a barely noticeable shadow lay over that relatively carefree part of my life – so rich in productive spiritual impulses – which announced the unavoidable appearance of dark clouds. The question of my professional future hovered in the atmosphere. At that time, the decision had already been made. It was clear that I was to study architecture. However, I could not yet say a wholehearted 'Yes' to this decision. Nobody forced me into this choice. But it was not what I felt drawn to with my whole soul. My interests were widely spread: philosophy, literature, theology, history, art, music, archaeology, anthropology, paleontology – all subjects which I could have studied. But they all had their disadvantages. Philosophy seemed to be too greatly influenced by the contemporary, nihilistic zeitgeist, and I could not see what could be done afterwards. (I had no interest in teaching.) A degree in literary studies seemed too uncreative, too unproductive, and only consisting of theoretical comparative studies of the achievements of others; theology would also have interested me, but I did not see within it that which most enthused my soul. History was one of my favourite subjects in school, which I had chosen for my so-called major, but to dedicate my life to history alone seemed like gazing eternally into the past, and this under the Damocles' sword of a more-or-less time-dependent, falsified perspective, which would necessarily have to arise if one denied the direct connection between the course of all earthly events and super-sensory effects and causes. Against fine arts and painting, for which I probably had the greatest natural talent, spoke on one hand that they were – as my parents pointed out – 'profitless arts', and also that my aesthetic sentiments were contrary to what was then considered 'mainstream'. Unfortunately, music could no longer be considered because I had had to decide years ago whether I would concentrate on a musical instrument or a general education, and the choice was for the latter. I found archaeology and paleontology exciting, but a professional life dedicated to them seemed too one-sided; and in an anthropology that was basically grounded in natural science, I missed the engagement with the human being as a soul-spiritual being, that is, the philosophical-theological aspect.

I tried to avoid the inner conflicts about this as long as possible in order to enjoy the last rays of sunlight, for I knew that there was basically no solution to this dilemma. The subject of study that I felt attracted to – with body, soul and spirit – did not exist. And I knew no name for it. Actually, it would have been a mixture of *all* the subjects named above, but in a truly lively way, that is, neither imprisoned in mere theory nor in a mere practice. Ultimately, it always came down to the consideration and recognition of the World of Reality by my fellow human beings, and I knew that – as in the past three school years – I could draw a certain satisfaction if in the future I engaged in this or that applicable incentive to enhance my personal association with the World of Reality. However, I would never lead a permanently fulfilled and meaningful life so long as this engagement would have to remain a purely 'private' study hidden inside me – if no one around me considered the World of Reality as a fact directly affecting earthly life. Furthermore, as I believed then, without recognition of the World of Reality by the social environment, there would be no appreciable possibility of using the achieved super-sensory insights in practical life – at least not professionally. So the joy of being accepted to study architecture at a renowned Berlin university the next fall semester could not completely hide concerns fermenting beneath my 'day-theatre-world' façade.

The beginning of student life could not have been worse. The family conflicts had reached such a point that a school friend in whom I had confided gave me an ultimatum to move out of my parents' apartment. So, to my mother's dismay, I finally moved out. She had an entirely different plan worked out for my future living and life situation. And since I had not followed it, corresponding sanctions were applied which, among other things, included a break in contact, under which I suffered greatly. This time, not only was my inner life ignored, but my outer life was downright sabotaged, which made things enormously difficult during the *Wende*,* which led to a price explosion in the housing market. Without a guarantor, it was hopeless for a prospective student to rent even the humblest apartment. I was obliged to live together with my school friend for a long time. We found quarters with his family, moving from A to B and from B to C. So I spent the summer vacation with organizational matters and a preparatory course in a carpentry workshop.

The study of architecture, on which I had positive expectations because of the good reputation of the university, turned out to be a great disappointment. Despite the privileged small group of only 50 students (reduced because of the demanding acceptance requirements), some of the teaching was shamelessly about the professors' own work and personality, and the material was – to my taste – poor. The subject of statics, obligatory for students of architecture from the first semester on, was for some inexplicable reason not taught for the whole first year. Already in the first semester I feared that I would lose ground to students and graduates of other universities and be branded as unemployable by the labour 'market'. But that wasn't what most depressed me. A strange attitude ruled in that university, which seemed to confuse cosmoplitanism and a creative alternative lifestyle with aloof nonchalance and negation of any aesthetic and stylistic standard. Clearly, most of my classmates felt comfortable in that atmosphere and therefore directly contributed to its being that way. But, as much as I tried to adjust, this time I was not willing to descend to the generality and to betray my (also artistic-aesthetic) ideals. The most important subject, design, where my objectively greatest strength lay alongside free-style drawing and architectural history, became a nightmare for me because of a despotic professor who, if at all, only had a good word for the work of male candidates. Also, for her, no worthwhile architecture seemed to exist before and after Le Corbusier. After a trip to Paris led by that professor, during which three other classmates and I dropped out of the group in order to see at least a few historical architectural objects of interest which Paris is rightly famous for – instead of exclusively Corbusier – I was on her blacklist. After the first two semesters, the atmosphere was so depressing that I crept towards the university as

---

* The collapse of the (Communist) East German Democratic Republic.

if to the scaffold. But I didn't give up. I never even considered it. I could only grin and bear it. And I didn't want to take a break. I just wanted to get the inevitable over with as quickly as possible.

For this reason I didn't take a whole semester for the completion of the obligatory half-year internship, but used all the semester vacations to work in a carpentry shop that specialized in building staircases. Soon I found myself in a financial crisis though, because the master craftsman paid me neither wages nor pocket money. I arose every morning at 4.30 in order to be at work by 6.45. In that carpentry shop, strict rules were followed, apparently influenced by the owner's pre-war attitude. Fastidiously, arrival time was recorded with a clock, for work began at seven o'clock sharp. Naturally, you could not start at five minutes to seven if you had to change and get to your work station! Often I went with them on assembly and didn't get home until seven or eight o'clock. I got along very well with the journeymen and considered this 'honest' work to be a great asset. I was the only female but was avowedly appreciated, not least because of my willingness to do my work with the same seriousness as all the others.

Soon the foreman took me under his wing. Although a 'simple' worker, he was one of the few people I had known until then who possessed a truly beautiful soul-force-body, which one could also perceive without activating super-sensory vision. That is usually called (most appropriately) *radiance.* He was a fine person who possessed a good knowledge of other people and could make definite and correct decisions in difficult situations. Furthermore, he was a very balanced and kind personality with great inner dignity and natural authority. Also his long experience, his excellent ability for working with his hands and his theoretical knowledge made him respected in the whole workshop. At the same time he was a fatherly figure and friend, because he had a wonderful sense of humour and took part in all the jokes. For inexplicable reasons, that supervisor was convinced that he had finally found in me a pupil he could teach to carve curvatures – those intermediate pieces which connect the handrails and meet from above and below in the staircase landing area. Due to the constantly changing angle of inclination of the handrail as well as its individual profile-form, the curvature always had to be carved by hand, first calculating its 'form', using a quite complicated calculation method, and then carving it out of the block of wood that had been glued together for that purpose, using a large amount of visual judgment and spatial imagination.

Equally inexplicable as the supervisor's confidence in my abilities was the fact that I actually satisfied those expectations. Although I had never before held a carving tool in my hand, from the start I managed to succeed in this arduous work. In time I also had a feeling for which wood to use. Because of its elasticity, alder was the preferred material for carving curvatures, while those made from ash, oak or still harder tropical woods like the quasi-black wenge, brought the most beads of sweat to our foreheads – also because the cost of the material, which made it necessary to succeed at the first attempt, and because of the frugal master's ever watchful eye, who had a window built from his office opening to the shop floor.

My dear, revered supervisor was a figure of shining light at that time. He never tired of giving me the feeling – and I think he even said so explicitly – that I was not someone who had fallen out of my time, but that most of the other people were the ones who had fallen out of time, in that they knew less and less about the really sustainable concepts and aesthetic goals of life, which they were potentially capable of achieving. Instead, their heads were turned in this or that direction or superfluous phenomena by the latest trend.

Once the internship was over, I was inwardly and outwardly in an emergency situation. I had to find a job urgently in order to keep my head above water financially. But it wasn't easy to find something appropriate that could coexist with my ever-changing study plans. But above all, the *inner* emergency was increasingly more dramatic. No noteworthy or constructive impulses came from the university, and those I offered myself remained largely unrequited or were rejected outright. But what especially depressed me was that my technically oriented subject of study – although one also requiring a high artistic inclination – was determined by people who, as representatives of their time, were dedicated to 'the consistent exclusion of the beautiful'. And because the relationship that I had entered into with my former school friend did not include a (conscious) partner in the World of Reality with whom I could exchange views about the essence of existence, the only comfort in my spiritual life was the aspect of beauty in architecture – if only the consistent exclusion of beauty in art had not been in vogue.

My friend's study of medicine required intensive work. In the first year leading up to his preliminary examination, he had to study continuously, and learn by rote, which demanded a lot of discipline from him, since he was not accustomed to learning by rote through instruction, such as I had experienced in lower and middle school. For this reason, he had to spend many hours in the university library each day. The contents of my studies were by no means demanding. I mostly finished my work in a short time and I didn't much like the university's atmosphere, so I grew accustomed to also sitting in the library and studying his subject with him, which I found more exciting than my own.

So I also studied (on the side) medicine – naturally without the classes and having to pass the tests. But not even this extra activity satisfied me, and it was clear why: because it was a sideline. What good would it be to have studied anatomy, physiology or biochemistry if I would never use it in my professional career? Instead, I was left with only the prospect of a profession that (and in this respect it was basically no different from any other) – should it take a similar form or proceed under similar atmospheric and practical conditions as my studies, and if my future employer had the same attitude about architecture and aesthetics as my professors and fellow students – would lead to a creeping, miserably protracted soul-spiritual death.

Why must I have only this inner longing for the spirit? What, then, were my inner experiences for – what were the years of instruction by the 'venerable Light' for if nothing and nobody in this world could and wanted to do anything with it? In their everyday lives, everyone seemed to be satisfied and fulfilled within their blinkered ruts. They didn't seem to miss anything at all, at least not consciously. I withdrew more and more. As soon as I finished at the university, I went home and fell on the couch. For several weeks this went on, but led to nothing. On the contrary, if it led to anything at all, it was that I was ever more desperate and depressed. The hopelessness of my situation, the absolute impossibility of changing the circumstances, gradually benumbed my will – my will to do or to think anything meaningful. Only my will was benumbed though, not my feelings.

I could stand it no longer. I put on the television. The afternoon programme reflected in full the concentrated desolation of the present German cultural landscape. I stared stunned at the complete de-spiritualization that appeared on the screen: talk shows of inferior quality, 'courtroom' dramas and other pseudo-documentary soaps – which today are called 'scripted reality' – family 'sitcoms' with artificial laughter every few seconds, cheap detective stories, cartoon films with ugly figures and horrible distorted beeping voices and, between them all, minutes-long commercials for the same products for an over-consuming, affluent society... I was gazing into the murky pool of horror, into the abyss of humanity. Who had thought of such things? And who watches such things?

I do! I had jumped into the abyss with my eyes open.

Day by day, week by week, I bathed for hours in the emotionally deadening scum of what the soul-spiritual abyss of humanity can bring to earth. For this, I didn't even have to use an impulse of will to expose it. It clung to me like a heavy, doughy, sticky mass and pulled me into its depths, with every passing day, inexorably swallowing all light, all ideas and every feeling.

The thought that had inspired me all my life, to be united with all the people in pursuit of a higher aim, had disappeared. I was dragged farther away from people, from my brothers and sisters. I began to detest them. They became disturbing objects, monstrous creatures, sputum of the lowest, and I didn't realize what was happening: that I myself was what I saw in them. My actual human-being-core, my 'I', threatened to suffocate. My neurodermatitis returned. And I began to have painful stomach ulcers. My life forces weakened. I had 'poisoned' myself.

Nothing mattered to me, till I couldn't even turn on the television. Finally, only now and then was the shattered wreckage of my heart contaminated with a feeling of bitterness at the world and everything human that crawled on it, which had robbed me of my higher Self and trampled all its inner potentiality in the dirt.

I lay in bed and waited for death – the death of a broken heart.

As I lay there, I found peace in total resignation. The pains subsided and the last thing I heard was a soft lamentation by the holy spirits for the fate of a dying soul, in whose requiem they joined, like the elegy in Handel's *Rinaldo.*

> Lascia ch'io pianga
> Mia cruda sorte
> E che sospiri
> La libertà.
> Il duol' infranga
> Queste ritorte
> De miei martiri
> Sol per pietà.
> Lascia ch'io pianga
> Mia cruda sorte
> E che sospiri
> La libertà.
> –
> Let me weep
> For my cruel fate
> And sigh for
> My freedom.
> May grief break
> The chains of my suffering
> For the sake of mercy.
> Let me weep
> For my cruel fate
> And sigh for my freedom.

Shortly before eternal darkness enfolded me, I pulled myself together. The pitiful remains of my misery had not let indifference reach its ultimate consummation. With the remaining, almost totally defeated, force of will I stood up and said to myself: If you don't pull yourself together now, you will never be free again. Not your body, but your soul will die, and you will be the murderer of your

197

spirit. You will have forfeited your life, the life of your actual being, over which God has so lovingly poured His grace.

What I had always known, even during my lethargic misery, was that man had *one* duty in that he became conscious of his earthly life – to preserve earthly life, including his own, to the best of his ability. With all the means still at my disposal, I began to convince myself that *my* life must also have a purpose. Hadn't I observed God's wisdom? I had not fully participated in it – of course not. But I did see its presence and limitlessness. In view of this, then, how could it be possible that one of God's creatures had fallen out of His inescapable cosmic plan, evading His all-knowing gaze? Didn't my own destiny remain inscrutable so long as I had not yet united with my actual Self – my self which was able to remember *me*?! Even if the sense and meaning of my existence were to remain hidden until the natural end of my days, I would like humbly to trust that higher wisdom, in order not to cut the holy bond between God and human – between the master's thinking will and the foreboding feeling of the apprentice – because of arrogant stupidity.

Help me, Lord, to take one step and, after that, another!

It was an arduous battle ridding myself of the disgust at my own baseness and destructive thoughts, and thereby knowing that the feeling of disgust at my own being is also destructive of this Being. Likewise, to recover true *feelings* and real *understanding*. Only in this way could my shame before the One who had taught me what true love is, gradually give way to the will never again to let myself go in this way, so as not to reject His love heedlessly a second time.

***

The first thing I did after the preliminary diploma was gain admission to a different university. I transferred to a more technically oriented, more demanding university and spent most of my remaining time working, which alleviated my financial situation somewhat. Meanwhile, my inner life did not soar to any great heights. It seemed to me most important that I was disciplined and true to my own words. I intended to do good work in the profession I had decided to make mine, and earnestly studied in order adequately to prepare for it. And so I stoically endured the company I found myself in at my part-time job within a large department store: talkative, gossipy sales girls, most of whom neither knew nor wanted anything else than the department store and its small world during the week, and the gazebo under the autobahn with barbecue and beer on weekends. I accepted all this as a given, without being bothered by it, but saw more and more the needs that people really had, although they did not feel it directly – which seemed to indicate how great the needs actually were.

In the new university I sought a place in the course on design. Three different professors were available. I knew none of them, so also didn't know what one or the other could offer. I simply picked one of the names. During the midday break, for no particular reason I mentioned the name to a fellow student as the one I had chosen. He shook his head and said it was hopeless to even try to sign up for that teacher's course, for it was surely already full. These words gave my decision the push it needed. The next morning I was enrolled in the course.

The course began in a way that I had not experienced before. What was said about the meaning and effect of architecture was, in a completely unexpected way, like pure rain on the dried up soil of my soul. It was unconventional, natural, creative and highly stimulating. The professor's joy and dedication to the subject was so authentic that his soul-force-body appeared spontaneously to my inner vision: an unforgettably radiant, sunny, golden glow.

As part of the course he brought a picture book about the art of Italian city buildings in which were featured a series of drawings by the baroque master builder and painter Giovanni Battista Piranesi, whose work completely contradicted the ideal of a Renaissance architect (such as Andrea Palladio with his strict symmetry) as well as the current baroque style. His 'Carceri', a series of etchings of fictitious dungeons in fantastic three-dimensional, seemingly unending angular rooms made up of all kinds of possible and impossible building elements – not nearly as eye-catching as the drawings of M. C. Escher and therefore much more mysterious – did not seem like a utopia to me, but a graphically implemented imagination of the labyrinth of the human soul. I was absolutely thrilled! Based on its impression, I had the idea for the implementation of my design assignment.

The fire of my enthusiasm was not hidden from the professor. He was not used to his students receiving his offerings 'so readily and thankfully', he told me years later. We got talking.

One day, at his wish, I took him and his two small daughters to a synagogue for the sabbath service, for he was very enthusiastic about Jewish rituals and religious songs. Because of the hopeless parking situation downtown, we decided to all travel in my car.

Two days later I was vacuuming the inside of my car at a service station – long overdue – when something blue was sucked out of the space between the handbrake and the passenger seat. It was a booklet with golden letters on the cover, not much larger than a cigarette pack. I opened it. On every page, arranged according to the weeks of the year, was a poetical verse of few lines:

> Erste Maiwoche:
> *'Ich fühle Wesen meines Wesens:*
> *So spricht Empfindung,*
> *Die in der sonnerhellten Welt*
> *Mit Lichtesfluten sich vereint;*
> *Sie will dem Denken*
> *Zur Klarheit Wärme schenken*
> *Und Mensch undWelt*
> *In Einheit fest verbinden.'*

> First week of May:
> *'I feel the essence of my being:*
> *So speaks sensibility,*
> *Which in the sunlit world*
> *Unites with floods of light;*
> *It would give warmth to thinking*
> *For the sake of clarity,*
> *And man and world unite as one.'*

My knees gave way. I slumped to the ground next to my car. Tears ran down my cheeks. Trembling, I pressed the booklet to my breast – I was *home*.

Whilst during my school days, as previously described, I had been overcome by that truly strange emotion when reading *Faust*,

200

what happened to me now must be thought of as being many times more pronounced. These words grasped me to such a degree that I was not able to read more than three or four of the 52 verses. It was impossible. The splendour emanating from them – the true, the beautiful and the good – were not at once comprehensible. But what completely overwhelmed me was the strangely *unique*, sweet familiarity of these words. More familiar than anything that had been familiar to me before!

I don't remember how I got home that day.

I woke up during the night. I went into the bathroom and locked myself in. I sat on the floor with my back against the wall and tried to think. An inner 'voice' had pushed through my dreamless sleep and to my consciousness. I felt that there was an unspoken but clear request within the room – that there was something I should do, a task, something to 'work through'. Suddenly my whole three-month-long collapse, two years previously, stood before my eyes. It was the first time I had looked back at that episode from a certain distance, which allowed me to penetrate what happened as such, and its hidden causes. That was the request! It was a 'call' from the World of Reality with the request to face those experiences with a higher clarity of consciousness.

The walls around me had disappeared, I no longer felt the hardness of the floor – time stood still. I was totally concentrated on what had happened then, and considered it with a very calm state of mind – with an almost 'unbound' state of mind – as if it had happened outside of my own being. Through my total concentration, I had reached a state that was necessary for leaving behind a corporeality full of unconscious passion, if I wanted to achieve deeper insights beyond the 'gate'. What had happened at that time? It was obvious that I had manoeuvred myself into an adverse state of mind through my desperation and bitterness at the blindness and barbarity of the world. Now, though, I 'saw' why I could not free myself from this situation for months. Something had alienated me from the world – had wanted to alienate me – by grasping my heart with a cold claw in order to strangle the living spirit, which always needed empathy – no, even more, a 'higher' feeling. By benumbing my soul with the sick spawn of the media, I could not form clear thoughts let alone receive a 'higher' thought in the sense of the World of Reality. But it is only such higher thoughts that provide humanity with the force of creation and willpower. Soon, another will had taken possession of me – a will that did not want my everyday self to touch my actual self, that did not want any thought from the World of Reality to get through from beyond the 'gate' at all.

All the moments of the past in which I had the experiences already described here, like those on the sunbed, arose before my inner vision. In the past, I had often felt the merciless pull of that enchanting force that arose in me and to which I had almost fallen prey. Whenever I followed the pull even a part of the way, I gave way to egotism, to indulgence in the summit of physical existence – drifting away from community with other human beings, forgetting selflessness, celebrating ego.

But what I had passed through, almost two years ago now, was something *different*! That something – so strong that it should be called *power* – led to egotism, to misanthropy, but in a different way, or even to a different kind of egotism. It didn't want to achieve my downfall by an indulgence in spiritual heights. It didn't want me to even think about the spiritual! By completely alienating me from the spiritual world and having me despise the soul-element, it had almost made me into one of its own creatures – not a creature of the bewitching 'heaven', but of the benumbing 'earth', although *not* like earthly nature or of the living earth-organism.

Just like there was a 'false' heaven, there was also a 'false' earth! A fossilized, dead, de-spiritualized, exclusively material, earthly world which attracted humanity's attention to itself. I had known about it before, but not with such clarity. This exclusively material earth, as seen through the 'eyes' of that power who was the ruler of this earth, represented no more than a barren space in heaven, with some hot or cold chunks of matter within it. Under its influence, even what was *not* visible was called *matter* ('dark matter'). Considered from this de-souled perspective, only certain 'natural' laws ruled in the heavens, but never spiritual powers. There was no soul, no spirit, no 'World of Reality'. But that power was itself a psychical-spiritual potency – of the highest rank – which knew the abysses of the human soul all too well, and used them to convince the human spirit that there was no soul! And when this was accomplished, the spirit could be nothing more than an apparatus, cynically mocking everything psychical and spiritual – a thought-construct directed only to earthly, material things. Whoever allowed this power to rule within them only had eyes for the sensory world, the de-spiritualized earth, as the sole scene and ground of all action. It destroyed everything that could remind the human being of his spiritual home.

This power was the opposite of that force which previously wanted to attract me to such seemingly pleasant heights of the soul – that force and its false heaven, from where the earth was seen as nothing more than an ugly illusion, unworthy and of no use for anything better than to be overcome as quickly as possible – for in the eyes of that seductive heavenly power, this earth was not able to communicate the higher secrets of divine wisdom. Was this not the snake's seductive tongue which, according to Genesis, promised the pure, still asexual human being, insight into higher secrets – the attainment of divine wisdom – by tasting fruit of the Tree of Knowledge from which, however, fallen man learned to know and loathe the earth as despiritualized matter before, much later, becoming accustomed to it? To become so accustomed that, presently, loving the earth so much he no longer felt any longing for his home; indeed, abhorred anything spiritual. The dark power had installed this awful attitude again within humanity, the same one through which I had almost 'voluntarily' consumed myself two years previously. The one likely derived from the other.

Now it was clear to me: There were *two* problem makers. The perspectives of *both* forces distorted reality into its opposite. Neither heaven was the human Elysium alone, for without attaining self-consciousness on the earth, he would have remained a creature of the all-mighty Zeus, unconsciously in the womb of the deity, directed by divine forces from without, a permanently *dependent* being for whom Prometheus would have fought in vain. And wasn't it only from the earth that man could *decide* to return to the Father by following the Son, He who fertilized the earth with divine pollen in death? Nor, on the other hand, was the *earth* El Dorado. For if one left heaven completely out of the equation, the earth would mutate, with everything living on it, into a dead object which, from under the natural scientific microscope's view, the ultimate secrets could be withdrawn – or the ore, as the only thing of value, could be blown out of its belly at any time without fear of consequences. Without *heaven's* spiritual life, man on earth would remain a death-bound zombie. He could never discover what true *love* is, and would only misunderstand and misuse it as a cold, selfish comedy. Every spiritual flight would be forbidden, he could not enjoy poetic thoughts, would be deaf to the mysterious whispering of spirits inhabiting the forests, and could never experience eternity in the moment.

Now I understood: one should be an 'earth-person' and a 'heaven-person', in equal parts, in order to be truly human. One should not revile the earth and one should not despise heaven. But if one did either of them, one would become a victim of a power which would form the individual into either a mere earthly person or a mere heavenly person. Both would cause ruin. So, one had to pass between the two without straying from the road. There was not only one fork in the road leading to the World of Reality, there were *two*! They led in divergent directions and ended, paradoxically, in one and the same abyss – that abyss which was diametrically opposite to the World of Reality and which I had already seen as a child during my excursions into the spiritual world.

As I was having these thoughts, suddenly Homer's image of Scylla and Charybdis arose in my mind. So I had apparently encountered *both* beasts, as Odysseus once did on his journey. On one rock, in the strait, lurked Charybdis, the monster that sucked in the sea, like that force to which my soul had been at the mercy (in the episode on the sunchair). Wasn't there also a date tree on the Charybdis rock to which Odysseus had held fast, as the sea disappeared into the maw of the monster? And wasn't it from the fruit of a fig tree that the seducer had the – once paradisaical – human being eat from, in order to corrupt him, as the Passover *Haggada* text teaches us? On the other rock, the larger one, lived Scylla, the monster that ate everything that came too near. Wasn't Scylla an archetype for that awful power, almost greater than the first one, and which, two years ago, had come close to killing my spirit-being?

Whoever wished to *live*, in a higher sense – whoever wished to capture the Golden Fleece – had to pass by both of them, through the straits, without deviating from the path, as Jason had to. I had experienced the reverse side of my wind-sword as well as the reverse side of my altar-root. The *Swan Wings* would have to manage the constant balance.

Nurture your Swan Wings and do not stop beating them in the calm rhythm of divine pulse, for only in the oneness of the trinity does eternal life reveal itself!

I thanked the venerable Light for the advice and, transformed, returned to bed.

***

It was as if that blue booklet with golden letters had touched something that allowed me to develop unimagined dimensions of spiritual activity. I protected the booklet like a precious jewel until the opportunity came to return it to its owner, from whose coat pocket it had fallen in my car on the day of the visit to the synagogue. Until that time (a few days later), I hadn't even read all the verses – I couldn't read them all. Even the reading of a single verse had such an effect that I became aware of innumerable new layers in the World of Reality which occupied me for many hours – without these layers, facts and discoveries necessarily being related directly to the contents of the verses. The verses were like a general key to so many rooms of the occult castle, beyond the gate, that even today it's barely possible to select examples of some of the treasures I found in it. I will try, however, to describe the process which led to these insights.

This process, and the discoveries and explorations beyond the gate to the spiritual world, proceeded in such a way that the verse's content and form, because of its vivid truthfulness, enabled me immediately to enter that state which I otherwise achieved by other means of concentration – or 'meditation' – after a longer period of preparation. This was possible because the verse itself was a super-sensory fact expressed in earthly-sensory words, which allowed the immortal vitality of that super-sensible fact – which otherwise led its life untouched in the World of Reality and could only be found there – into the earthly-sensory world. Miraculously, it did not let that fact become solidified, dead information. Something completely new

205

to me sprang out of it from the innumerable rows of dead words belonging to the thinking and speaking of everyday life. The content of the verse was itself living. It was like a lovely, green garden within an endless desert. And in this garden was a hidden portal, which readily opened to anyone who entered the garden with joy and devotion. Behind the portal two sphinxes, Scylla and Charybdis, guarded both sides of the way, readily bowing their heads when one surrendered his own and, with a pure heart, entered the immortal land of our divine home from which the true, the beautiful and the good flow through the human spirit and into the lost world of the desert.

Then I was led to a spiritual 'context', for which my consciousness had first to be raised in order to be understood. I had to learn to solve it. Like a delightful puzzle, it grew up before the mind's eye, like a plant with numerous blossoms, each of which contained a secret – a 'painted', living 'word'. One should learn to *read* these secret blossom-words, to 'decode' them. For this, one has the force of will – which one normally only senses when in the body – in order to consciously perceive it, and then to concentrate on it with one's consciousness in order to 'read' and to employ the blossom-secret words.

Once the individual blossom-secret words are decoded – each of which represents a higher insight of 'sensing' – the second step is to be mastered. At this point, one could pause or stop, but the 'words' would remain like a basket full of parables – parables of the actual element, the actual fact which is to be present in the World of Reality. But in order to better understand the word-picture which gives a parable-like answer, a second step must be taken: to achieve a *synopsis* of all the individual blossoms that have been decoded. For this, you have to be able to ask questions. This questioning within the World of Reality, however, proceeds differently than in the world of shadowy, everyday consciousness, in which one usually asks as many superfluous questions as one says superfluous things. In the 'day-theatre-world', one is so often mistaken about what is true because one adds one's own cluttered, inaccurate ideas to the world. One can ask any question, no matter how superfluous, ponderously indifferent or nebulous, and never run into a wall on which to beat one's head until it is awake. In the World of Reality, however, one must ask in a different way! For there, you *will* most likely run into a wall if, from the start, you do not ask in a *wakeful* and *precise* way. And this can only be done if one is clear about the purpose of the question, and where any answer could lead – to whom or to what it would be useful. In other words, which impulse within me leads to this question? Secondly, one should place the context of the question as clearly as possible before one's mind, and work hard to acquire this context through thinking. And thirdly, one should make a sincere effort to find the answer *oneself*, for only through such a diligent effort can an answer come.

When these three conditions have been met, one can finally, in the right way, ask the individual blossoms for the individual answers. The question must become a lamp that illuminates the map upon which, as a coherent whole, the marked paths appear. For this, the will must be clearly seen as a driving, higher force. One must raise the will to a higher level, oriented to the question sent to the blossom-tree.

If this succeeds, an echo resounds from that 'tree', and all the decoded blossom-words join, in perfect harmony, in a single 'melodious' echo, which comes from the actual 'context' to be investigated and gives a sonic image of its true nature, which is more faithful and complete than the parable-like, fragmentary answers provided by the individual blossoms. It is as though, only in this way, one recognizes the tree's artistically contoured, swaying branches, through which the blossoms were connected to each other. If one is satisfied with this 'resounding' image of the context to be investigated, then one has already gained a substantive impression of it, which can then be carried back to the world of appearance in order to add a drop of clarifying reality.

However, if you wish to investigate the essence of the entire tree, the actual element in its unveiled nature (and I want again to emphasize that 'tree' and 'blossoms' and so forth are merely metaphors for certain parts of a spiritual process), you must take a third step. For this you should do no less than the following (but it is nothing more than what can be managed by human understanding, so the words used here are just as simple as the process is itself in its entirety). You must bring together the previously cleanly separated thinking, feeling and will until all aspects of the personal fall away and only the pure substance of the impulse remains – which is able to let the question 'touch' the answer and the answer 'touch' the question. And by accomplishing this, one has transformed the echo which resounded from the tree – that is, from the element to be investigated – into a super-sensory language, which is now controlled by actual consciousness itself. In this moment, consciousness becomes the creator of the divine-spiritual 'language', in that it takes the symphonious words of the echo and transforms them into the instrument which it operates. Thus, consciousness, at its highest level, turns 'outward' and speaks to the tree. The purposeful universal language permeates the living thinking beings connected to the element to be investigated. 'Outer' becomes 'inner', and becomes *one* in harmony with the individual *many*; consciousness shares itself with them as they make themselves part of a consciousness that was once foreign to them, but is now known. This all takes place at a mutually supportive level: the highest form of *conversation*. By means of this 'conversation', the researcher has created the brightest lamp that leads him to answers about which now he knows that *they are true!*

(Nevertheless, one should not think that the answers given at both lower levels are untrue. But they are 'only' a part of the full truth, and thus susceptible to the possible errors of the investigator.) What appears at the highest level however, is the ability of the researcher to penetrate to the pure relationships of the thing – to attain complete knowledge of it. Now, one has also apprehended the trunk of the tree, through which its sap flows in order to cause the blossoms to bloom through its branches, and thus the *whole* tree. Now you can see how the blossoms, which you were only aware of on the first level, sprout from the branches that give them support, which you discover on the second level, and where they get their strength from – a realization of the third level. We see the whole structure of the living being and its elements, its higher and lower natures; we observe it from all its many sides, which were not perceptible before. One's own higher self speaks the language of the other being and lives in it, in heart and spirit, to the extent that this self passes over into one's own consciousness as a living essence of thought.

By this method of a step by step, three stage illumination of consciousness, I entered the World of Reality and continue to do so today – in order to seek the causes and relationships of earthly and spiritual existence.

***

The days and weeks that followed my finding the blue booklet were as full of inner spiritual activity as all the previous years put together. I advanced more quickly than ever before. It was as though a great floodgate had opened and, in a few moments, insights into certain relationships that had moved me inwardly for years flooded toward me. I would like to mention at least one of these, but one that is fundamental and absolutely essential for a deeper understanding of many other circumstances. What had unceasingly occupied me over the years was something which had already existed on my earthly awakening day, but which, over the years, had taken on new forms and new aspects. Now, however, the collected 'blossom-secret-words' came together as a coherent 'sentence structure'!

Once again, the day of earthly awakening stood before my inner eye. I saw myself on the floor of my grandparents' living room. But now I observed the scene from a distance – so distant that my consciousness could enter unimpeded, so to speak, into my thoughts. I 'saw' how the newscaster's sentence had woken me up. I saw, as the echo of that sentence slowly faded, how I had clung to a thought preserved from out of my old sphere of consciousness – of an echo thrown back in the night of earthly, intellectual thinking: *Remember yourself!* With this heart-piercing call, the hunt for my consciousness had begun – that consciousness which could remember my actual self, the hunt for my fully conscious *I*.

But how could the newscaster's sentence remind me of something I had not experienced? The full consciousness that I sought would also have to include *this* memory. If I found my full I-consciousness – if I found 'myself', I would also know why a sentence that had no relation whatsoever to my earthly life had awoken me.

Because of my experiences and searching beyond the 'gate' during the previous years, I thought that a *complete remembrance* would awaken me to an earlier *purely soul-spiritual* existence in the World of Reality. That is, to an existence which I must have led before my earthly awakening day – or before my earthly birth – corresponding to that purely soul-spiritual state, to which one also returns after earthly death (and to which, during the night or through meditation, I could to a certain level find my way during my earthly life).

Now, however, since I had been given the methodical means described earlier for a purposeful searching beyond the 'gate' on a *higher* level (which I called the 'third step'), my vision expanded to an absolutely decisive fact which put all my previous 'findings' into a logical connection with each other.

What the newscaster spoke of was a purely *sensory fact*. But why, of all things, should a sensory fact remind me of a life in the super-sensory? Could it not be that I should remember my prenatal life in the super-sensory, in order to be able to remember (by the full power of consciousness then available to me) something which had possibly met me at a completely different place than in the super-sensory world during my purely spiritual life in the prenatal? After all, the newscaster's sentence called me into my *earthly* consciousness! Could it therefore be a memory, which referred to earthly conditions, which had been present both before my earthly and even before my prenatal life in the spiritual world?

What I am formulating here as a question – in order to include it together with my various thoughts up until that day – now arose in my mind as a tremendously thundering answer. What had been there for a long time, but hidden under a thin veil, was now clearly manifest to my unclouded, fully opened eyes: *the fact of different, successive earth lives* of the human individuality.

In a past earthly life, something must have happened that was somehow related to the newscaster's sentence, and that had influenced my I-being to such a degree that it resounded into my present earthly life and consciousness!

But at that moment, when I became completely aware of the fact of so-called *reincarnation*, I did not seek with the 'lamp' – my super-sensory instrument – for the sentence's reference to some event or thought from a past earthly life. That—in a way very personal—aspect was not an object of my interest at that moment. I was much more interested in those spiritual aspects which determine the meaning and purpose of earthly existence, and which seemed self-explanatory by the fact of repeated earthly lives.

So, the total I-being of man includes the prenatal, purely spiritual existence, as well as previous earthly lives and, again, the intermediate purely super-sensory lives between those earlier earthly lives. This wonderful fact seemed to me like a cosmic breathing rhythm, a steady in-and-out, whose individual breaths were, however, never as identical as its cyclical form, but rather adding one to the other – constantly ennobling the human I-being through the new experiences and achievements of struggling souls. Man in his whole being and higher context is an immortal phoenix gradually rising to divine potency and beauty!

It dawned on me that knowledge of successive earthly lives was the indispensable water of life for human beings' self-knowledge. As Goethe put it poetically to humanity in his *West-East Divan*:

> *Sagt es niemand, nur den Weisen,*
> *Weil die Menge gleich verhöhnet,*
> *Das Lebend'ge will ich preisen,*
> *Das nach Flammentod sich sehnet.*

> Tell it to none, the wise alone,
> for the crowd will only mock,
> Tis the living I'll extol,
> Who longs to die a flaming death.

> *In der Liebesnächte Kühlung,*
> *Die dich zeugte, wo du zeugtest,*
> *Überfällt dich fremde Fühlung,*
> *Wenn die stille Kerze leuchtet.*

> In coolness of those nights of love
> Which begat you, which you begat,
> Strange feelings assail you,
> When the calm candle glimmers.

> *Nicht mehr bleibest du umfangen*
> *In der Finsternis Beschattung,*
> *Und dich reißet neu Verlangen*
> *Auf zu höherer Begattung.*

No longer do you stay enclosed
In the shadow of darkness,
A new desire pulls you now
For loftier mating.

Keine Ferne macht dich schwierig,
Kommst geflogen und gebannt,
Und zuletzt, des Lichts begierig,
Bist du, Schmetterling, verbrannt.

No distance is too far for you,
You come flying and entranced,
And finally, eager for light,
You, butterfly, are burned.

Und so lang du das nicht hast,
Dieses: Stirb und werde!
Bist du nur ein trüber Gast
Auf der dunklen Erde.

And as long as you reject
This: 'die and be reborn!'
You remain a gloomy guest
On the darkening earth.*

The acquisition of experiences from various, successive earth-lives and their spiritual reception during super-sensory intermediate lives, made up the sum of the human-being-core, of the whole human-I-being. Later, as I looked back on my human-being-core's various past earth-lives, I saw them as spheres that contained their own essences – the useless, the transient thoughts and feelings were eliminated and those that were beneficial for the growth of the higher spiritual human being, as well as all the good and bad experiences, were compressed into a small bundle. The teaching content of the various earth-lives was packed into a sphere which, when needed, could be made available again by opening that sphere – but

* The original German is replete with rhyme and rhythm; the English gives only the nearest meaning. (Translator.)

what forms the I-being was already recognizable from 'without', by the very nature of the sphere itself.

But on that day, when the fact of repeated earth-lives first dawned on me, various aspects of my previous concerns now came together through this illuminating vision. I also understood, against this background, why every person was an incomparable individual. Every I-being was unique because of the sum of the equally unique experiences and choices made and encountered during repeated lives, which made him or her what they were now. That meant that what these experiences and choices had made of the individual, of his actual human-being-core, was carried into the new earth-life. Genetics appeared in a new light. I inherited much from my parents: my stature, my talent at drawing and sports. But also *not* so very much – such as all kinds of spiritual *inclinations* which, since I already had them as a child, could not have been acquired during my present life. I also entered my physical body, in earthly life, with certain *qualities* of soul which were not present in my parents, which I must have acquired in previous lives, and which seemed to have fallen into my lap as, so to say, ripe fruit. But even the less pleasing qualities of my soul could not be explained solely by the laws of heredity or childhood trauma, as conventional psychology suggests. And of course, my clearly unusual relationship with the World of Reality, which constituted my inner life, must have been built on a certain foundation laid in past times.

Genes, received from parents, were a brilliant invention to enable the total individual destiny of the particular human I! They didn't *determine* the destiny of the human I; they *enabled* it.

I saw beyond the 'gate', how the parents' impulse (whether conscious or not) to beget a child resulted in the 'production' of a bodily dwelling, which remained freely available, so to speak, until the corresponding human-being-core in the sphere of the World of Reality decided – toward the end of its intermediate spiritual life – on a new incarnation in a respective bodily dwelling. I saw, in that (supra-temporal) moment, how innumerable human I-beings were preparing to occupy certain physical bodies that were just coming into being on earth, and how the decision for a certain physical body was made with the wise guidance of higher beings, so that the respective human I would occupy the physical body most likely to enable it to apply its soul-spiritual achievements and particularities, brought down from the spiritual realm during previous earth-lives. The material-physical-bodily shape, including even the physiognomy and the lines in the hand, became the expression not only of the idiosyncrasies brought forward from the past, but the self-chosen instrument for the fulfilment of one's own individual destiny.

Thus, for example, the deeper cause of Mozart becoming an exceptionally gifted pianist and composer was not due to him having inherited his father's musical talent. Rather, the human-being-core of the future Wolfgang Amadeus Mozart – who once lived in the prenatal spirit – met his future fate only because he was able to realize the physical preconditions that were made available to him by Leopold Mozart and his wife.

And also, personal hindrances not arising from external factors, but which resulted from disappointing decisions in past lives, had to come to expression in the physical shape inherited from the parents – for example, the predisposition to a certain illness, for which however the parents were *not* 'guilty', even if it was a so-called hereditary illness.

But, in this physical body, new decisions were also made and processes were initiated which were not determined by the power of destiny – that is, from what had been 'brought forward' – but by the human I itself. For the human-being-core was endowed by an impressive ability, the freedom and the force – perhaps not always to the extent necessary to make it externally visible in earthly circumstances, but in a higher sense – to become master of one's own destiny! Whatever the circumstances in which he found himself for reasons of destiny, nothing and nobody could hinder his inner process of ennoblement if he did not allow it to happen through weakness or laziness. I had experienced that myself during all those years. Although I had never found understanding, let alone solace or support, I continued along the path – stumbling occasionally –that inner experience showed. I had been led to the edge, to the point where the adverse circumstances of life combined with self-pity, resulting in the terrible error of believing that man and his destiny are ultimately at the mercy of circumstances beyond his control.

This illusion was – thank God! – only a temporary one, instigated by certain spiritual powers based in my own soul, and whose activity I had allowed for a certain time. I became aware that no matter how adverse external circumstance might be, even if one had to face one's own inevitable execution – an exterior circumstance could never gain the ultimate power over one's inner being. How I dealt with exterior circumstances, which were perhaps consequences of my actions during previous existences, was decided solely by my own completely free self.

Now I saw clearly what the ugly grimaces meant that sprang to my face as a child, and which seemed, the older I became, more and more like a multi-layered, gloomy figure – like a shadow of myself when my consciousness arose from out of my 'lower' components. They were the product of my previous actions, thoughts and feelings. My I-being had been formed by all my previously existing lives, in which I had sometimes performed good, noble deeds that were beneficial for the great cosmic plan, and sometimes bad, lower thoughts, feelings and deeds, that were damaging for the great cosmic plan and my own destiny. So I carried into each new earth-life a kind of rucksack filled with both intact and broken porcelain, which sometimes rattled noisily as I stumbled over the stony challenges of earthly life. Now it became clear to me what a great privilege this peculiar facility represented, that upon entering the World of Reality, one's own being was presented unadorned before one's mind's eye. Then one naturally had to think *ahead*! The fact that one had already lived through various earth-lives in the past was a sure indication that the present life would not be the last. Of course not! With the means at my disposal, I clearly realized that. The next life was preprogrammed. But why? Because in my present life I had again thought so many thoughts, felt so many feelings and carried out so many actions, that the soul-spiritual monster – which I would have laboriously to eliminate in order to walk in the spiritual world – had grown big and fat. This alone indicates a need for a future life. Furthermore, I had hardly been able to work on the 'component sheaths' of the shadowy monster of myself, which had arisen not only during the present life, but clearly through previous ones too, because their deeper-lying nature and origin had, thus far, been hidden from me. I saw all this clearly now, whereas as a child I could only sense it. It was humanity's task, in service to the cosmic plan, in service to himself, to *decimate* his soul-spiritual excesses and deformities (to which he often seemed more attached than to his virtues). For this, he had to mobilize his actual higher will, the wise will which was in accordance with the cosmic plan – with God – who made him what he *could* become: an independent, truly divine being.

I sensed this continuity on my earthly awakening day. The vague but certain feeling that 'it should continue' was, from the beginning, like a blurred reflection of the super-sensory and sensory law of development – 'die and become!' – pressing on my consciousness. This 'continuing' was not limited to entering the spiritual world after earthly death. It was 'the same' which should continue – my earthly life should link to a past earthly life and my present one was to link to a future one. But then this fact had existed only in my subconscious. That it strongly made itself heard there did not make my sympathy for the Christian teaching of an eternal afterlife any greater. This idea of an infinite heavenly existence after a single fleeting visit was never compatible with my idea of 'continuing'.

However, life as one in a long chain of many, had an incomparable meaning. The fact of repeated earth-lives provided the primal impulse in man to act ethically and to want to achieve the true, beautiful and good in his thinking, feeling and will – for the first time a truly causal motivation! The motivation to develop sustainably. (Finally, there was a real opportunity to assert oneself against Scylla and Charybdis in the future!) It was only worthwhile to work on one's inner improvement if one had the guarantee that there was a little more time available for a considerable change in one's lower nature than one short earth-life, from which a significant amount of time had already been subtracted, in order to become again accustomed to the rules of the world that had been forgotten by having been immersed in boring, earthly intellectual thinking. But insight into these laws did not imply that one wished to relax because so much more time had become available. On the contrary. The knowledge that one's own behaviour was the cause of limitations in a new earth-life, was the appeal by one's own soul to amend the behaviour which hinders the cosmic plan.

Insight into the reality of reincarnation led directly to an intensified feeling of responsibility and conscience. One could not do other than be serious about self-education, knowing how one's own behaviour directly affected the shaping of the future – not only one's own, but that of the people with whom one associated; indeed, the future of the entire human brotherhood and the earth with all its creatures!

What were the consequences of giving in to one's lower instincts and what were the consequences of resisting? How much one could change the world, the future that one prepared for oneself, if one substituted selfless feelings and deeds in the place of yielding to lower urges. The development of one's own being in harmony with humanity as a whole lay in the hands of people aware of the process of becoming.

Didn't great personalities – regardless of their professions and levels of education – have a healing effect on their surroundings? They could only have become as they were through past earth-lives – and perhaps working on themselves during the present one – and were thus now able to have a beneficial effect on their fellow humans and on their environment. How much more potential would human beings have if only they realized their higher I-being!

The bright glow of recognition generated by my consciousness was suddenly suffused by an even more intense, warmer, nobler ray of light – a thought that seemed to spring from a source in the innermost core of my being and, at the same time, from the immeasurable vastness of the divine being of the creative majesty: *This I-being, through which the human being was able to return 'to the Father', was the achievement of God's sacrifice on Golgotha!* – My beloved and revered teacher and master, *Christ*, was my saviour because he had given my I-being resurrection – the resurrection of full consciousness.

Didn't the Greeks of antiquity suffer awful fear when thinking of Hades? My spiritual view looked at the past, to the sensations of the souls living in those times. I experienced how the ancient Greek people feared that their life on earth must end – although Plato, who was already highly esteemed, advocated the teaching that by wandering through many lives their souls could be purified. Nevertheless, they were afraid, because they felt themselves at the mercy

217

of the fate that could befall them in the beyond (and in the next earth-life) and which they could not foresee in that in-between-life that awaited them beyond the 'gate'. For they lacked the light of knowledge about the forces of their own I-being. That light, the force of the I-being to lift itself within the limits of self-created destiny, to overcome the death of consciousness in the death of the body – that they could not do. Only Christ, the son of God, could achieve this gift and pass it on to man. Today, the human being beyond the 'gate', during his life in the World of Reality, could become conscious of his self. He could recognize the quality of his actions and judge them and, with this knowledge and the help of the entity accompanying him, Christ, could design the plan for a new life.

So, life after death could not possibly appear as 'hell' as long as, in earthly life, one was not completely blind to one's real being. Only in such a case could hell become a self-created hell of belated knowledge – the knowledge of one's real self with all its pros and cons. Knowledge that matured only in spiritual life after death instead of during earthly life. For this purpose, Christ had given human beings an I-being capable of being fully conscious. Self-created hell would be one's waking up to reality, the complete disillusionment about oneself. If, however, one suspected or recognized one's shortcomings before one's earthly death, then an objective view of one's real being in postmortem existence would, at most, be a purgatory. Knowledge of one's defects and weaknesses in full view of one's divine master would provide the most beautiful impulse for future moral actions!

And didn't Christ act in this way, as the renewer of physical bodies? For the moral impulse changed the soul-force-body as well as the magical life-force-stature, which had a direct influence on the physical body. In this way, couldn't the soul-force-body act on the physical body through the magical life-force-stature, making it either sick or well? Whoever doesn't think at all, makes his body 'thicker'. On the other hand, active thinking makes the body 'thinner'. But there are two ways of thinking: *bad*, that is abstract thinking, when the body becomes thinner and, barely noticeably but steadily, is taken away from the earth. And *good*, that is, spiritually substantial thinking, by which the body becomes 'thinner' by being *transformed*. If a person's thinking, feeling and acting core was thoroughly moral, the sheath of his appearance would be adequate for his inner being. He would receive a mystical, invisible, totally spiritual immortal body, as the spirit of Christ bore *after* his *Resurrection*.

In light of the Son of God's sacrifice, shouldn't one consider the physical body to be truly precious? (Plato, who lived in a time when the redemption of the I-being was not yet apparent, understood it as a prisoner of the soul.) It was the instrument for gaining knowledge, the valuable home of the soul and spirit in which, and through which, the spirit could advance to the ennobling of itself and humanity in the sense of the great cosmic universal plan. Through it, the high, spiritual, moral impulses could take shape on earth.

One had to be a heavenly person and an earthly person! And one could only really balance them within by understanding the rhythmic beating of the 'swan wings' as the ultimate consequence of 'die and become'.

Only in this way could the love of Christ be revealed – even in the seemingly cruel fate of a dying child or a destitute, careworn person – who wanted to lead his human brother to the crown of development by letting him gain the experience he needed for such development through various lives in the most diverse forms and circumstances. (But I also realized that the full love of Christ is only revealed through the people who helped their fellow humans with their destiny, but also leaving them free.) I 'saw' how every soul that appeared on earth must have fallen at least once into the earthly abyss in order to find its way to the heights of spiritual consciousness.

Neither arrogance nor pretension, neither status nor learning in the sense of earthly knowledge, elevated one to the peak of spiritual greatness. The descent into darkness and the will to ascend to God was accomplished by one's I-being, because it was the darkness that raised the human being to truly mature humanity.

I could not shine a light into all the corners of the spiritual space with the new level of consciousness I had attained, in order for all the answers about repeated earth-lives to become visible. Only the basic truths of the law of dying and becoming were then apparent. At that time I only perceived, as if from a distance, the fact that one day the time will have expired for mankind to become conscious of these conditions and to act accordingly.

As if from a distance, only indistinctly and for a short (timeless) moment, a strangely familiar being appeared to me, who seemed to point to the Apocalypse of John, as well as to a spiritual word, which I was not quite able to decipher. Only the impression of the immeasurable love with which it had spoken remained, as well as its inner 'gesture', which motioned: 'Do not delay!'

***

These experiences were accompanied by different new ones, but wonderfully entwined by the same bond that united them all. From that time on, the shadowy essence of my lower self became my own cosmos, which I took out of myself upon entering the World of Reality – or, in other words, I took myself out of it and observed it from the outside.

Thus I entered again with alert eyes, like an interested and compassionate visitor in a strange house who sees the same things inside the house as the inhabitant, but is attentive to those things and takes note of them – whereas the master of the house has long been accustomed to seeing them, and for this reason overlooks them as if they were not there.

By this way of seeing myself, what had already existed in my heart as a steadfast truth was now clear in a new, thoughtful way: our freedom is linked to a higher morality. And this higher morality is aimed at one's own selfhood. It would be quite a pathetic and short-lived freedom if one believed that it consisted of being able to do whatever you wanted. For such a freedom often restricts that of others. So, only by overcoming the base urge to do whatever you want leads to the attainment of true freedom – freedom from the dictates of one's own limited ideas and personal desires. And the grim image of one's own self is gradually transformed into a gentler beast. The human spirit, like Heracles, succeeds by its own power and without the help of artificial weapons to defeat its own Cerberus and bring it out of the underworld and into the light of day, that is, learns to control it in everyday life and thus diminish the power of Hades.

From that time on, if outer conditions permitted, I could see into my own being as clearly as I had been able to see previously into the being of others, perhaps even more clearly. Looking into my own interior was equal to looking into the interior of someone else. And this was the moment when the use of the process, the spiritual 'seeing' itself, changed. Previously I was quite often permitted to see compassionately into the spiritual bodies of people. But from the time of my crisis, when I was about fourteen-years-old, until the day I saw my teacher super-sensibly, that is, until I was about twenty-four years of age, this state hardly ever happened. And shortly after the end of my schooling, it did not happen at all. Now, it was suddenly possible again, but in a completely different way! Whereas in the past the vision of the different super-sensory bodies of people in my surroundings happened of itself, so to speak, by means, for better or worse, of an extreme 'eruption' of these bodies themselves, now super-sensory vision could be purposefully controlled. But this 'purposeful' generation of the spiritual vision required strict conditions. Thus, the generation and observance could not be achieved with the means of everyday, 'selfish' consciousness. A real encounter with the person in question had to take place, but not in the way we usually encounter hundreds of people every week – without *really* encountering the actual human-being-core – when we pass them by without paying attention, or the way we accept change from the hand of a person in a supermarket who is of little interest. From then on, purposefully guided, deliberate super-sensory viewing of the spiritual bodies of a human being – the most devoted, selfless perception of the individual nature of the human being in question – was required. All tempting, judgmental thoughts about the other, that is, every personal thought about the other, must be nipped in the bud – and the same for feelings – for only in this way can contact be made with the other person's actual human-being-core. Therefore, one must have great compassionate interest in the other's nature and impulses of will, to the extent of raising them to one's own soul in order to become an objective observer. Only then does a communal process take place, with the I-being of the other receiving the unadulterated love of the brother or sister approaching one – whether or not the other's everyday consciousness remains unaware of this – and consents to the encounter. Only then, when the completely affirmative reception by the other takes place and one returns the favour, can the objective spiritual vision be activated with the careful and lasting respect toward the person being perceived.

One can well imagine that under such conditions this activity seldom succeeded at first. But it is just these conditions that serve to protect the 'viewed' person, because these faculties can never be used to cast a curious, compromising observation of another. Furthermore, they are the impetus for the researcher to constantly purify his or her own impulses.

When I returned the blue booklet to its owner, I asked him if there was more to read by the same author. It is still a puzzle to me why I didn't just go to a library and find out for myself, which I usually did when something interested me. An inexpressible awe and the premonition of being overwhelmed by what might have been found, stood like temple guards at the entrance to the sanctuary. All the more urgent, then, was my request to the lecturer when he agreed to lend me a book by the author of the blue booklet. The next time we met, what he handed me was not a booklet with verses, but an actual book. It had the auspicious title: *Theosophy, An Introduction to the Super-sensory Knowledge of the World and the Nature of Man.*

I carried it home like a secret treasure and finished reading it through the night. I was in speechless rapture and at the same time thoughtfully alert. The book contained all the thoughts about the essential aspects of the true nature of man, as well as his relationship to the World of Reality, that I had borne within me during all the past years. The nature of man was described as threefold – namely of body, soul and spirit – whereby new thoughts were added which could finally explain some of my observations. For example, that the soul, in respect to its abilities and activities, was differentiated into three sub-aspects, and that – caused by the spiritual activity of the human being – the existing lower components were transformed by advancing into new components of being. Thus, the development of the present and future human being was described and made plausible – how, starting from his highest base of existence, the 'I', he can develop right down to his physical body. Here I encountered a characterization which agreed with my experiences of the four human components of existence, which I called 'physical body', 'magical life-force-stature', 'soul-force-body' and 'actual human-being-core'. Here, in this book lying open before me, they were called 'physical body', 'life-body', 'astral body' and

'I' or 'soul-core'. Additionally, it was pointed out that all three lower components, that is, the 'astral-body' (the soul), the 'life-body' and the physical body could be transformed into a higher form of existence through the corresponding activity of the 'I' (or 'soul-core'). I had also already observed and presumed this, but had not grasped it in such structural clarity, consistency and detail – human nature, in its complete configuration, as seven-fold.

Not only was the physical world and its connection to the world of the soul and the purely spiritual sphere discussed in this book. It was also about the reincarnation of the spirit and human destiny. It even spoke of 'the forms of thought and the human aura' – a chapter in which my observations of the human soul-force-body and the magical life-force-stature, up to the super-sensory 'colours' and 'forms' as they appear in respect to certain thoughts and feelings, were described. And finally, I even found an unsurpassed introduction to the 'Path of Knowledge', from which two essential factors emerged. Firstly, that research in the World of Reality (the 'spiritual world') deserved to be recognized as a science. The investigation of the non-material, of the spiritual world, was a scientific activity, because it was possible to observe and investigate the spiritual world. So, it was similar to scientific activity which relates to material existential conditions, but with its own preconditions and parameters, but equal to 'natural scientific' activity. The author named this research in the World of Reality, 'spiritual science'.

Secondly, for this *spiritual science* a basic fact applies, as it does for any other science – it can be learned (by anyone). In this respect, it was unacceptable to scoff at statements revealed by this science because of the assumption or conviction that such a field of spiritual research – with which 'spiritual science' was concerned – did not exist, and that all the statements about it were the result of delusion, presumption or even lunacy. And if someone did, nevertheless, make such assertions, it was only because they had not yet had any experience in the field of spiritual science. That person had clearly not obtained the relevant knowledge by study or through the corresponding practice. So it was, in fact, as I had always felt when my inner discoveries were rejected through ignorance, and I would have loved to call out to those people if they would expect a pre-school child, who didn't even know basic arithmetic because nobody had ever mentioned it to him, to understand Chebyshev's polynomials.

You can more or less imagine, perhaps, what happened to me upon reading this text when you realize that for almost 25 years – or 23 when you subtract the time before my earthly awakening day – I had stockpiled the many spiritual gifts bestowed upon me by the World of Reality in a dark, hermetically sealed chamber. During that time, I was close to the limit of my suffering more than once, because no matter how supernaturally strengthening and enriching the spiritual treasures were, they also weighed heavily because they were limited to a strict, occult existence within that chamber. And in 1996, during the crisis in my college days – after I had committed myself before the Most High never to let despair about outer circumstances go so far as to shut myself off from the world forever – the very chamber itself threatened to burst, with unpredictable results. But this chamber I carried in my heart – hidden from the outer world – was so heavy because what was collected in it did, fundamentally, belong to that world! Its purpose was not to remain there as the treasure of an individual.

I had always known that every individual holds within them the potential to gain insights into the secrets of their own higher nature and of its existence. For everyone is provided with a divine I-being. I could experience this during my Christ-experience, when I was within a circle of innumerable other human-being-cores, all equally embraced by the 'arms' of the All-High and motivated by His force. But even the attentive observation of other people could lead one to this certainty. This higher I-being gave man the sacred drive to do what Aristotle stated in the first part of his *Metaphysics*: *'All human beings by nature strive for knowledge.'* And this striving for knowledge also had to refer to one's own spiritual origin and spiritual capacity – things that natural science can never answer. So my inner experiences, and the knowledge gained from them, were the property of all the people on earth, because they apply to general, not personal, phenomena. And now, after all the miserable years of isolation, I had met a person who, with great determination, openly described all my spiritual experiences. All my life I had kept these experiences from the people around me, who ignored or even mocked them. He did this, although he had obviously had

224

the same painful experiences as I had, in an environment primarily concerned with material matters. But it was for this reason that he openly bore witness to the super-sensory facts, for on the one hand he saw the needs of present-day people – constantly depressed by exclusively materialist ideas – who longed for life-saving higher insights, and on the other because he was steadfastly sure (or hopeful) that one day people would become enthusiastic for knowledge of their true home and future.

The introduction began with an statement by Fichte and additional thoughts:

When in the autumn of 1813 Johann Gottlieb Fichte gave to the world as the ripe fruit of a life wholly devoted to the service of truth, his Introduction to The Science of Knowledge, *he said at the very outset,*

> *This doctrine presupposes an entirely new inner sense organ or instrument through which a new world is revealed having no existence for the ordinary person.*

He then showed by a simile how incomprehensible this doctrine must be when judged by conception of the ordinary senses.

> *Think of a world of people born blind who, therefore, know only those objects and relations that exist through the sense of touch. Go among them, and speak to them of colours and the other relations that exist only through light and for the sense of sight. You will convey nothing to their minds, and this will be the more fortunate if they tell you so, for you will then quickly notice your mistake and, if unable to open their eyes, you will cease talking in vain . . .*

Now those who speak about such things as Fichte does in this instance, often find themselves in the position of a normal man among those born blind. Yet these are things that relate to a man's true being and highest goal, and to believe it necessary 'to cease talking in vain' would be to despair of humanity. We ought not to doubt for one moment the possibility of opening the eyes of every earnest person to these things. On this supposition all those have written and spoken who have felt within themselves that the inner sense-instrument had developed, thereby enabling them to know the true nature and being of man, which is generally hidden from the outer senses. Hence from the most ancient times such a hidden wisdom has been spoken of again and again. Those who have grasped some understanding of it feel just as sure of their possession as people with normal eyes feel sure of their ability to visualize colour. For them this hidden wisdom requires no proof. They know also that this hidden wisdom requires no proof for anyone else to whom the 'higher sense' has unfolded itself. [...] It is not, however, only to researchers into the spiritual world that the observer of the super-sensory has to speak. He must address his words to all men, because he has to give an account of things that concern them all. Indeed, he knows that without a knowledge of these things no one can, in the true sense of the word, be a human being. [...] The feeling for truth and the power of understanding it are inherent in everyone, [...] This feeling, which perhaps at first perceives nothing at all of what it is told, is itself the magician that opens the 'eye of the spirit.' In darkness this feeling stirs. The soul sees nothing, but through this feeling it is seized by the power of truth. [...] for although not every physical eye can be operated on, every spiritual eye can be opened. When it will be opened is only a question of time.

Down to the very wording, I read my own thoughts and insights in black and white! There they were: my thoughts, my experiences, my discoveries – as if an invisible being had made a copy of them from out of my head, from my heart, and transmitted them to this book. That couldn't have happened, however, because the author had written the book in 1904. So there was no temporal correlation. I was absolutely stunned. There had been a person who, over a hundred years earlier, had spoken of the important things that lived and pulsated within me, and I had wandered ignorantly in the desert all my life, carrying my own little green garden on my back!

In addition, the author had been able to pursue many further studies and to unearth wisdom by means of a special 'tool' – one that had always seemed indispensable to me for working with super-sensory elements, but clearly I had not carved mine as perfectly as he had. For one thing depended on the other – the more perfect the self-made tool, the more precise and extensive were the 'findings' that one could extract from the World of Reality beyond the 'gate'. The tool had two equally significant aspects: living thinking and finding the appropriate concept. Even in my attempts to be clear about the various aspects perceived beyond the 'gate', I had noticed how essential (and challenging) the formation of concepts was for gaining real knowledge. This in turn required flexible but clear thinking. So, I was pleased to read confirmation of this in the chapter 'The Path of Knowledge':

It cannot be emphasized strongly enough how necessary it is for anyone who wishes to develop his faculties for higher knowledge to undertake strenuous efforts to cultivate his powers of thinking. This emphasis must be all the stronger because many people who would become 'seers' place too little value on this earnest, self-denying labour of thinking. [See Appendix 2, page 273.] *Absolute healthiness of the mind is essential in a 'seer.' There is no better means of developing this healthiness than genuine thinking.*

Such refreshingly clear and objective words about the 'how', as well as consistent statements about the actual contents (the human being and his relationship to the physical and spiritual worlds) – the 'what' – were not even remotely pompous or nebulous, like in the more recent esoteric literature I had previously come across and discarded. Here I found the opposite, that spoke to me from the depths of soul, from 'thinking'.

I found here that factual clarity that had already appealed to me as familiar and 'right' in the sages of antiquity, but here the contents were presented in a less 'heavy' way – perhaps more 'contemporary' but at the same time more comprehensive – penetrating even deeper into the mysteries of existence. The author had an overview of the super-sensory world like no other wise person known to me. And not least was this due to his extraordinary ability to find the appropriate concept to describe the facts beyond the sensory world.

The next morning, I took the book back to the lecturer. I can repeat what I said to him because it surprised him so much that he still talks about it. It wasn't especially significant, but obviously surprising, in view of the fact that when he saw me coming again 24 hours later, with his book under my arm, he said (with a slight tone of disappointment): 'Ah, well, that probably wasn't the right one' – to which I answered, 'It is the clearest thing I have ever read'.

During the same week, I received two more books by the same author, one after the other. One with the title, *Occult Science, An Outline* and the other titled, *The Philosophy of Freedom*.

227

The first one dealt, among other things, with the human condition. The evolution of the world, which was also described, included times and evolutionary conditions about which natural science has never been able to elucidate precisely, because it only observes conditions that are physically accessible. All those states of the earth, however – which lay so far in the past that no physical evidence of them exists – necessarily remain completely untouched by natural scientific research. In effect they do not exist. But for what the author called 'spiritual-science', they certainly do, and he showed, in a breathtaking way, how far the higher consciousness-force of the human spirit, when combined with the divine cosmic memory, is able to 'travel back' in the history of existence. I had not yet explored much of the depths of this primal-existence myself. My own explorations in this respect reached back only to a certain time when the earth was already a physical-material body – although in certain contemplations the earth appeared as a multi-layered spiritual organism in which certain characteristics or states appeared 'blurred' like spiritual deposits, which must have originated in a condition that I could not relate to the physical-material existence of this earth-body; as if the earth in its actual core-being, almost like a person, had written down its previous 'lives'. Here, an area was again touched upon which led to a question that had greatly interested me for many years: the origin of being, the 'Alpha', the Logos.

In respect to the origin of the world, however, the book also covered a number of cosmic entities or forces, whose spheres of activity became all the easier for me to understand, because each individual group was assigned a specific name. For the first time, I became aware that those spiritual forces or entities – which I recognized in my inner experiences due to their different development of consciousness in a hierarchical structure and to which the *venerable Light* also belonged in a special and somehow unique way – could be and were called *angels*. The names used for these forces were not really important, but they did refer directly to the scriptures of the New and Old Testaments, thereby closing a circle.

In reading this book, one astounding discovery followed another. Again and again, I found descriptions of the experiences that had been granted to me over the years. There was also an exact characterization of the three steps or stages which I took in entering the various 'layers' of the World of Reality, which were really the stages of my own consciousness, and which I have already described here by deciphering the secrets of 'blossoms', and so forth! The author designated the first condition or stage appropriately as *Imagination*, the second – also appropriately – as *Inspiration* and the third and highest, as *Intuition*. These three states or stages of consciousness beyond the 'gate' were methodically described, so clearly and accurately, that tears came to my eyes.

But there was more. An equally accurate description followed of my Bosch-like monstrosities, of my own soul abyss, which had become spiritually 'figurative' and shadowy by my disembodiment. They were described by the author (succinctly summarizing my own experiences) with the term 'doppelgänger' or 'Lesser Guardian of the Threshold' (the multi-headed Cerberus) – even a description of my venerable Light, here called the 'Great Guardian of the Threshold'. And, when I already thought that this state of stunned amazement and joy could not increase further, I read the following words: '*This* [Great Guardian of the Threshold]*) will now be his* [the spiritual student's] *model to aspire to. When this sensation arises in the spiritual student, he will have attained the ability to recognize who actually stands before him as the Great Guardian of the Threshold. For this Guardian is transformed in the spiritual student's perception as the Christ-figure...*' (See Appendix 2, page 273f.)

All the experiences and insights that had formed in me up until that day now appeared before my inner eye – how I had seen and experienced the Christ as a non-confessional being, how by means of His sacrifice two-thousand years ago He bestowed upon man the possibility of developing to his true divine humanity and therewith *to the Father*. And, through the resurrection of the spirit (the attainment and retaining of the human-being-core's higher consciousness beyond death and during postmortem existence), man had been given the potential ability to work down into his physical body, ennobling it in accordance with his ever-maturing human-being-core.

The venerable Light's infinite goodness and patience appeared to my vision – my dear, wise teacher, who had not left my side since my

Christ-experience, when I felt that unforgettable love so intensely for the first time, and which accompanied my childish nature at all times.

I had finally found the question of Christ, the fact of Christ, in relation to the evolution of the earth and man – and yes, with the evolution of the individual human being. Here was given the key, so to speak, to understanding the meaning of creation.

The contents of the other book, *The Philosophy of Freedom*, affected me in a totally different way. It surprised me very much. (Although the content of the other books pointed to the content of this one.) If one wants to do justice to this book, it is basically not possible, perhaps not even permissible, to attempt to provide a 'summary' of its contents, which I nonetheless would have to do in order to clearly explain why reading this book touched me so deeply. That I cannot proceed in this way here is due to two extraordinary circumstances. First, practically every paragraph of this philosophical contemplation contains a new discovery about the nature of the concepts which we must clearly understand if we wish to also understand ourselves, the world and the causes of our being and becoming, as well as the purposeful design of our existence. For example, 'observation', 'thinking', 'perception', 'consciousness', 'conceptualization', 'imagination', and so forth. The book also takes into account the results of other philosophers, whose achievements, but also argumentative and intellectual weaknesses, are used to clarify the new discoveries and views of the author. And it can dawn on us how little we are generally aware of the meaning of these concepts.

The second extraordinary circumstance is – and it follows from the first – that the statements with which the contents of the book culminate, result from the previously made observations, which in themselves already represent a multitude of new insights. Therefore, one must know the whole book – and 'know' here means to make its content your own by following the thoughts presented in it, step-by-step, in order to be able to judge and appreciate its value.

So, I will try to express the meaning of this book for me personally through a few aphorisms, which I hope will provide insight into my thoughts and feelings at that time.

As the title suggests, it is a wholly philosophical work, which does *not* contain the results of research in the spiritual world through the use of 'inner' (that is, super-sensory) tools – like the main elements of the book *Occult Science, An Outline*, for example, which I had already read – but strives for a deeper understanding of the spiritual processes which take place in man when understanding himself and the world, and through which results a new understanding of humanity as such.

The initial question reads: *'Is man in his thinking and acting a spiritually free being, or is he compelled by the iron necessity of purely natural law?'*

I felt that the way in which the author introduced his readers to the clarification of these aspects was a masterpiece of pedagogy, which could only be achieved because he was imbued with the profound knowledge of what it conveyed. That is not always a matter of course. I had read philosophic texts by various authors (also contemporary ones) when I was not always sure that they had thoroughly thought through to the last detail what they were saying. Already on the first pages, long before I'd reached the 'final answer' to the initial question, the author's methodical approach alone demonstrated man's intellectual independence (or his intellectual freedom through thinking), which the author sets out to prove in the further course of his explanations. The book was, so to speak, a methodology of knowledge with a simultaneous application of the method of knowledge characterized by it. And since the answer was so comprehensible and plausible, the method used seemed to be a direct proof of the findings.

Having read in the first book that was lent to me that, for research in the spiritual world (what I called the 'World of Reality'), 'absolute health of the soul' was necessary, for the care of which there is nothing better than 'real thinking', it seemed to me that the author could not have demonstrated the 'absolute health' of his own soul more vividly than with the philosophical compendium now before me.

In order to at least mention three or four aphorisms from this book (which, however, set my soul-spiritual being into an indescribable, wonderfully vibrant dialogue), here are a few of the author's statements. Man is unfree in the sense of the initial question so long as he doesn't know the cause of his actions, so that he should draw a clear demarcation line between his conscious and unconscious motives, and ask himself the question about the origin and meaning of thinking, because without knowledge of the soul's [or mind's] thinking activity, knowing the motives for actions is not possible. Or, that self-knowledge consistently causes the dualism of I and world, whereas the sensation of being a part of the (outer) world as a human being produces the impetus to bring both together. Or, the fundamental thought in the passage about the terms 'observation', 'thinking' and 'concept', that the concept cannot be obtained from observation, but when concepts are added to our observations, their difference to thinking arises. So the *observation* of a horse does not yet provide a *concept* of the horse. This can only be done by *thinking* about the horse, through which, however, a real horse could never be produced.

These aphoristic thoughts may indicate why I considered the book's contents to be presented in an easily understood way, which was of course due to the clarity of their formulation. This cannot be conveyed by my reproducing them, however, but only by themselves. For that reason I have included some original quotes in Appendix 2 (see p. 274ff.) so that the reader has the opportunity to share my experiences and my joy at that time about them.

The whole content of the book culminated for me in one statement, in which I saw summarized in a philosophically objective way the essence and the realization of my first and most significant initiatory experience, my Christ experience:

Only the morally unfree who follow their natural instincts or the accepted commands of duty come into conflict with their neighbours if these do not obey the same instincts and the same commands as themselves. To live in love towards our actions, and to let live in the understanding of the other person's will, is the fundamental maxim of free human beings.

This book was also a surprise in that it acted like an epistemological preamble to the 'spiritual-scientific' content manifested in the two books I had previously read. In fact, it was written before the other books, in 1893, when the author was in his thirty-fourth year. Of course, this book could simply be considered as an epochal work in the history of philosophy, and left at that. But then we would be ignoring the 30 subsequent years of the author's life and his life's work accomplished during that time, which includes the other two books. Furthermore, the expression 'preamble' is not defamatory. There are extremely significant preambles. Think of the Prologue to the Gospel of John. Unfortunately, to many people who are enthusiastic about its contents, the *Philosophy of Freedom* does not seem to be considered a preamble. For I later experienced how this book seems to be loved especially by those who are apparently surprised by the realization that there are no limits to knowledge, because the way of thinking in which they feel at home keeps coming back to the limits of knowledge they must bump up against, as they do not (yet) possess the 'super-sensory tools' needed to overcome these limits of knowledge. For what is to be investigated beyond the 'gate' is not described in the *Philosophy of Freedom*. How one advances methodically to investigate the super-sensory world beyond the gate is also not described.

Rather, attention is drawn to how, by means of thinking, one learns to advance to that point from which the 'gate' comes into view – but in such way that one sees how the author has drawn directly from the source situated behind the 'gate' – which makes it impossible to deal with the thoughts in this book in the same way that abstract theorists tend to do with abstract (dead) treatises.

Later, I realized that such people have managed to entangle themselves in these living thoughts in such a way that they attach their own (rather less than living), mostly abstract thoughts, which delight them, and through which they don't see the forest for all the trees. In short, they overlook the fact that this book is an introduction to an activity which the reader himself needs to carry out. This consists not only of the reception of its fundamental ideas, but also their implementation in practical everyday life, which the author calls 'moral technique', that must follow 'moral imagination', so that the latter doesn't remain unproductive or lead *ad absurdum*, so to speak. As always, one understands only what one wants to understand, and if a person doesn't want to understand the whole book, then he can only fulfil the first part of what the author calls the 'fundamental maxim' (although not in a true but rather an illusory sense), but not the second part, and so he therefore remains, in the sense of the book, an unfree spiritual being, not yet able to work towards the great, cosmic world-plan.

To live in love towards our actions, and to let live in the understanding of the other person's will, is the fundamental maxim of free human beings.

***

A new life began for me with the reading of these books – at first and above all internally, then gradually externally. Because of them, I knew that I was neither alone with my experiences nor had I developed completely inaccurate results from my inner work, for from then on I was introduced to the contents of many other books from a total of around four hundred volumes of the author's complete work (of which a large number consist of stenographic records of lectures), most of them containing descriptions and results of super-sensory research.

One may well wonder why I have not yet mentioned the author's name. I will of course name him from now on, but would like to explain why I chose to introduce him first by his works, in which one can meet him 'personally'. This is the way I met him (and this book, after all, is about my inner path). Of course, I had read his name on the book covers. But this said to me just as little as any other name of a person unknown to me. This way of learning the content, namely without connecting it to any more-or-less accurate information about the author, had an enormous advantage, which I now want to offer to my readers: the *unbiased perception* of the contents. For nothing is worse than the contents being tarnished or completely spoiled by one's own ideas or prejudices.

At this point, in the spirit of Goethe, I can finally speak to my now *wise* readers with no concerns – *Tell it to no one, only the wise, for the masses will only mock it* – that the author's name is *Rudolf Steiner*.

Nowadays almost everyone knows something about Rudolf Steiner, the founder of *anthroposophical spiritual science*. Unfortunately, what is 'known' about him and anthroposophy is, as a rule, derived from hearsay and rumours. Such rumours and prejudices are almost exclusively the result of *ignorance*. And, even though it was bitter for me to learn about such disparaging judgments by the ignorant and those who wished to be ignorant, it could hardly surprise me. For my own experience had shown – and was yet to show, in a much more radical degree in the future than in all the years of my life that had passed up to that time – that the *fundamental evil* of our present age is to mock a person's highest qualities: their *capacity for knowledge and ethical impulses* and the *cultivation* of those two qualities. But the forces which oppose anyone who speaks openly about the existence of a super-sensible world do not only appear where expected, but also where they are not expected. Thus, toward the end of his life, Rudolf Steiner founded a Society in the centre of which a free 'School of Spiritual Science' was to stand, and within which there are people who wish to 'nurture the life of the soul, both in the individual and in human society on the basis of a true knowledge of the spiritual world' and who are convinced that 'there exists in our time a genuine science of the spiritual world'; and that 'today's civilization lacks the cultivation of such a science', for which reason they wish to make this cultivation their task. According to the statutes drafted by Rudolf Steiner, this Society should in no way be a 'secret society, *but a completely open one*', a member of which can be anyone 'who considers the existence of such an institution justified' and must also 'reject any kind of sectarian activity'. However, the impulse for the founding of this Society, in its intended form and sense of purpose, was not understood then, and still isn't today. So, the Anthroposophical Society that exists today has regrettably become something which is unable to preserve anthroposophy's aspirations, namely to promote the capacity for knowledge and the ethical impulses of man. Still more, it has itself become soil in which destructive forces can find abundant nourishment, so that anthroposophical spiritual science, as it was understood by Rudolf Steiner, has been counteracted *from within*. Naturally, this development greatly contributes further to discrediting the nature and seriousness of spiritual science, as well as the reality of the spirit itself, in a world that knows and wants to know little about it.

One could say basically that the only reliable way to obtain an impression of Rudolf Steiner's work is to deal directly with that work, that is, to study the primary literature.

But now to come back to my experiences at that time, for I knew nothing about that then. It is certain that from then on anthroposophy didn't play such a great role for me because someone had recommended Rudolf Steiner or his anthroposophical worldview, but rather because I came upon them – accidentally so to speak – in a totally unbiased way and free of prejudice, and discovered that this view of the world and the human being was also my own. All of my inner experiences and resulting insights were in overwhelming agreement with Rudolf Steiner's. Thus, it was clear to me that this man spoke the truth, and with this truth – which my surroundings so lacked – I wished to continue to occupy myself, just as it had been my most ardent wish since my earthly awakening day.

So I had been occupied with anthroposophical spiritual science before I even knew it existed. I was doing nothing differently than before, except that from then on I was in contact with people who were convinced of the existence of the World of Reality and Truth, of a spiritual world, and who were willing to acquire the appropriate means for exploring this world in the sense of a (spiritual) *scientific path of study.*

I could hardly believe my good fortune when I found out that there were not only those books which opened up a whole inner world, in which I frequently encountered many things I had already experienced as newly unlocked secrets, but that a movement of people existed who were also occupied and inspired with questions about the spiritually creative primal source of being as I was. I soon learned that these people were concerned with achieving certain 'abilities' which (I hardly dared admit to myself) I already possessed. It had not been clear to me up to that point in time, and for an amount of time thereafter, whether my experiences – and especially my way of dealing with the spiritual world was what was called 'higher abilities'. I had already been aware, through my own experiences, that one could do various things – especially with regard to the 'handling' of the access to the spiritual world, that is, one's own state of consciousness – in order to achieve this or that result. During the past years, I had always made 'modifications' to this handling, whereby I truly made progress beyond the 'gate', especially in getting used to the World of Reality, understanding the unspoken, thought-and-felt language, or the search for a certain spiritual circumstance or context. (All this was always of course only possible with the approval and goodwill of the entities living and acting in the World of Reality, who always lovingly and patiently urged me to pay attention to the momentary 'composition' of my psychical-spiritual body or consciousness whenever this attention slackened, so that I could continue with my super-sensory work or begin new learning through the venerable Light. If one wished to achieve anything in the spiritual world, it was necessary to bring one's own will into unison with the all-wise will of the divine entities. And the best way to achieve this was to pay attention to the control of the soul-force-body during everyday life. Because of the fact that one is seldom able to bring one's own will completely into unison with the all-wise will of the higher entities, one was ever dependent on the help of the benevolent higher spirits.)

I already knew that one could 'learn' certain skills in relating to the spiritual world. I also knew that most people in my surroundings did not cultivate such relations with the World of Reality as I did, but rather ones that were subconscious or totally unconscious.

Some of these people – I realized this when observing by means of the 'other' visioning – were close to raising their relationship with the World of Reality to consciousness. But they had not yet developed that quality which – as I now learned – was called 'clairvoyance', although they were already 'clair-*feeling*' – but many of them were not fully aware of this either, because they held the strange opinion that only actual clairvoyance could achieve results that were correct. I found this attitude to be most unfortunate, because in this way they deprived themselves of quickly taking the next step to fully conscious perception of the World of Reality. The spiritual entities do their utmost to promote human beings' inner development, and we should contribute the little we have in order to accept their help. But all too many people who have already developed a predisposition for a higher consciousness esteem it little, because they have become obsessed by an idea of what 'real' clairvoyance must look like.

I soon realized that most people who have such ideas assign attributes to clairvoyance which are erroneous. These ideas are applicable to the earthly world and its phenomena and natural laws, and must therefore disappoint, because the super-sensory world is totally different from the sensory one. One must actually bid farewell to all that appears in the earthly world as natural laws. What we experience once beyond the 'gate' is in no way a loss. For the spiritual world with its own laws and relationships takes the place of what has been left behind – in an incomparably more elevating, genuine, structured and agile way. But many people who stand before the 'gate' do not seem to trust the spiritual world and their higher selves. The conscious decision to let oneself 'fall back in absolute trust' – which I described in my childhood notes – belongs to entering the spiritual world. But he who wants to take a safety net from the old known world to the other one, because he trusts that world more than the World of Reality and Truth, will never become 'clair' beyond the 'gate'.

And so I always hoped, especially for all those people in whom I recognized a special relationship to the spiritual world, that they would cultivate their inner experiences through grateful mindfulness and appreciation, so that the high spiritual entities could accept this as a starting point for their further development. When afterwards I finally came into contact with a number of people interested in the spiritual world and noted how much they wished to be able to do what I 'could' do, I began again to be silent about my own inner experiences. It was uncomfortable for me to possibly embarrass them by my own reports, which was quite possible, because in some circumstances they quickly felt inferior – although for no reason. And I also avoided talking about my experiences, so that these people would not undermine their own perhaps tender, but no less valuable, experiences by ideas about a 'correct', and above all more 'spectacular', clairvoyance.

At first I only opened up to my university lecturer, with whom my acquaintance had intensified, not least because of our shared interest in the World of Reality and anthroposophical spiritual science. He explained, in his sympathetic, somewhat beguiling way, that he had come to anthroposophy when he was hired as an architect to design an anthroposophical kindergarten and soon realized that, in order to do justice to the task, he would have to learn something about anthroposophical pedagogy. For this he attended an anthroposophical teachers seminar in Berlin where, among other things, fundamental insights into the nature of the human being as well as the spiritual world, and corresponding books by Rudolf Steiner, were studied. All this had so appealed to him, and convinced him, that he stayed with it – which was not surprising for such a differentiated and pleasantly creative person, who also possessed a decidedly good-natured character. For instance, while studying architecture, he risked his future for the benefit of refugees from the German Democratic Republic, whom he helped to escape to the West through the Berlin sewage system, shortly after the Wall was built – which finally cost him two years in an East German prison.

My acquaintance with him, even when he was no longer my university lecturer, became ever closer and friendlier. I also started to work in his architectural office, where I was entrusted with what I considered to be the supreme discipline of design work.

One day I found out that he attended a weekly evening course at the Anthroposophical Society in which certain aspects of philosophical and spiritual scientific themes concerning the World of Reality were examined. This living, thought provoking treatment of such themes is of great importance, because what is found beyond the gate indicates that earthly conditions are often not correctly judged, because 'the other side' – where most of the causes of earthly developments are to be found – is ignored. So we cannot be very surprised that so much on earth goes wrong. This alone should activate a sensitive person, who is not only interested in himself, to pay attention to the facts of the spiritual world, for they are directly related to the facts of the earthly world. Thus, many things here on earth could change for the better if we would recognize and be mindful of their spiritual causes.

The evening course was being run by the same person who had founded and led the anthroposophical teachers' seminar and was regarded, both within and beyond the Berlin anthroposophical movement, as a great and capable personality in the field of spiritual science. He was the founder and for many years the leader of the Berlin Rudolf Steiner School. He had initiated the Berlin Rudolf Steiner House and was the author of various books, including a widely admired one about Casper Hauser.

In answer to my insistent questioning, I finally learned the subject of the evening course. It was the consideration of certain aspects of human destiny through various different lives on earth, entitled *Karmic Relationships*. As I didn't give up, I was given a book containing a lecture course by Rudolf Steiner about this subject.

In retrospect, I must have seemed like a hungry wolf. In fact, after my outwardly spirit-deprived past, I soaked up like a sponge everything I could get my hands on in the way of spiritual-scientific literature.

In reading this book, I came across a theme which had repeatedly been on my mind during the previous years – the forces opposed to the principle of the inner ennobling of the human soul toward a truly (psychical-spiritual) human being. As is shown in my childhood notes, even then I had asked myself about the nature of the 'bad' and how it entered into action. Now I found that Rudolf Steiner spoke of a *duality* in this respect – a duality that ruled the inner human being so long as the 'I' did not attain to a conscious relation to them and, thus, learn to master them. According to his observations, there was not only *one* 'devil' – again a correlation (Scylla and Charibdis)! And finally, these 'adversarial forces' condition the new lives on earth. The description coincided exactly with what my own trials and work revealed. But between this duality the redemptive force of Christ intervened. So that the new life on earth was not a punishment but – on the contrary – an important possibility to freely decide for the principle of the middle or the 'third' way, in order to redeem the duality working in man and therewith, one day, to redeem himself. Then he would become the balancing force of the *centre*; he would become a Christ-person (not in the sense of a religious denomination). Thus, each person was placed in the karmic necessities which he himself had prepared as the result of his previous lives. But at every moment of his present life, he could add something totally new to the world and to his individual destiny, and thus – through and in Christ – become master of his own karma.

These statements – like so many others I got to know at the time – resounded in my soul in a way that is only possible with things that we have forgotten for some time and about which, when they are found again, we ask how we could ever have forgotten them as they were so dear and indispensable to us. For although I'd had my own experiences with these 'adversarial forces' within my soul, the descriptions now before me, in their precise and truthful way, were as mysteriously familiar to me as though I had read them before or, rather, internalized them. Again, everything corresponded with

240

what I already 'knew' but had not yet seen described with such clarity.

In respect to this revelation of the trinitarian force of Christ between the duality of conflicting forces, I had to think of my understanding of numbers – or my perception of them – during my childhood, when *two* had appeared to me as a duality tearing apart the unity of the whole, and *three* as the entity that dissolved this unsatisfactory duality, again inclining to *one*, and thus bringing about the unity of the *three, the trinity*. Now my feeling condensed into a deeply meditative, spiritual consideration of this trinitarian principle. I 'saw' the true human being, figuratively speaking, as something that I could only compare (again) to a kind of tree, whose highest spiritual principle was expressed in its crown, as it was similarly symbolized in the Sefirot tree. But this trinity, which appeared before my spiritual vision, was a wondrous transforming principle in which I recognized the earthly as well as the godly human being. It appeared as an unstable 'form', riddled by the psychical opposing forces, into which a third force gradually entered, flowing from below and creating order from the chaos caused by the opposing and competing forces. This third force flowed steadily from below to above, until it seemed to balance the two poles, and then the spiritual form that had become a triangle was transformed into an upright 'living triangle', in which the poles of the adversarial forces had become the supporting pillars of a higher trinity – the redeemed, healing, good, reverse side of themselves. The 'lower' trinity was the internally torn person who took in the love of Christ and thus received the force to rise to the higher trinity, to develop as the human bearer of Father, Son and Holy Spirit, in which the forces of the Father and the forces of the Holy Spirit faced each other ('altar-root' and 'wind-sword') and in the centre, the radiant Son's force (the 'swan wings'), so that the higher principle functioned from the centre of the new human being – karma weaving, karma healing, for the benefit of all humanity and the world.

Meanwhile, my now dear friend (my ex-university lecturer) – who for his part also seemed to like me – avoided, with all kinds of excuses, taking me with him to the evening seminar at Rudolf Steiner House. Although I didn't stop asking, he kept refusing. One evening I lost patience. I drove to the meeting place which, curiously, was in the neighbourhood of my parents' apartment and my primary school, separated by only a small park, and which I walked by with our dog innumerable times during my childhood and youth without realizing it. I arrived just as the meeting was ending. And when my surprised friend greeted me, many of the participants leaving the house asked who I was and if I was interested in anthroposophical activities. When I answered affirmatively, and told them of my wish to be allowed to attend the seminar, they assailed my friend, asking why he had never taken me with him, and saying that he should do so as soon as possible. Embarrassed, he promised to bring me next time. And he did. Later, he explained his strange behaviour to me. He feared that I would think him crazy and might leave him if I came into contact with a group of people who took the existence of a spiritual world for granted – people who asked questions about the super-sensory world with a seriousness which must have seemed ridiculous to most people. That was the moment when I began to tell him more about my inner experiences and my state of being, and he became my unconditional confidante.

We eventually lived together and, five years later, got married.

***

On New Year's Eve 1997, we went together to a lecture by the already mentioned seminar leader. These New Year's lectures had become an institution. They were a kind of annual spiritual review of current events from a perspective that encompassed spiritual reality and contained the lecturer's new discoveries and insights. Toward the end of the lecture there was a pause, and then the lecturer spoke about something I didn't understand. It was about the history of the Anthroposophical Society, about which I knew almost nothing, because up until then I had no interest in this history, but only in the spiritual insights of its founder. So the references by the lecturer to this history went in one ear and out the other, and I lowered my head and closed my eyes, intending to recapitulate the contents of the lecture I had just heard.

All of a sudden, I woke up! Two words reverberated in my ears and struck me within, like a bolt of lightning: 'the fire'.

The fire. I had no idea what had burned or when. And yet those words hit me so hard that I can only compare it with the experience on my earthly-awakening-day when the words: *They only awoke as the fire came through the roof* entered my earthly consciousness, and at the same time shook up my human-being-core and called upon me to establish a connection from my earthly consciousness to my *actual* consciousness, so that I *remembered*! But now the words themselves, the content of what was said, seized me in my innermost person. They touched on what I had not been able to unravel until then: *why* exactly those words from the newscaster – *They awoke only when the fire came through the roof* – had awakened me to consciousness of my present life.

My throat tightened. Tears came to my eyes. Only with great effort was I able to hold them back. I began to shake as if I had been standing for hours in the cold – no, rather, as if a merciless cold from the endless void came creeping over my suffocating soul, frozen with grief and unspeakable despair.

At home I learned about 'the fire' from my friend. At the initiative of some friends, Rudolf Steiner had a building erected near Basel as a worthy venue for the performances of the *mystery plays* he had written. For nine years, even whilst the First World War was raging, people from almost 20 different nations – hundreds of volunteers who felt attracted to anthroposophy – worked together, alongside professional carpenters, on its construction. While explaining, my friend showed me an album of historical photographs.

The building's base, in curved organic form, was made of concrete, whereas the rest of the supporting structure, as well as the facade and the interior, were made of wood.

All the wooden elements – hundreds of square metres – had been carved by hand by the volunteers and artists, using chisels and carving irons. It was indeed a unique building: two interpenetrating circular halls – a larger and a smaller one – topped by two enormous domes covered with slate tiles, shimmering almost celestially in the sun so that they appeared to the observer like a shoreless pool of silver coins or like a calm sea whose surface, rippling in a gentle breeze, shimmered with countless glittering waves, blurring the frontier between heaven and earth.

Light, according to the position of the sun, penetrated the interior through large coloured windows etched with mystical motifs, escorting visitors to the building into another world. The dome above the great hall was supported by two times seven mighty columns, whose architraves expressed a metamorphosis of the Earth's evolution; the dome above the small hall was supported by twelve slender columns, which seemed to me like the archetype of the twelve apostles. At the eastern end of the hall a space was left in its centre in which the thirteenth was to represent fulfilment. A statue over nine metres high was supposed to stand there, which showed the 'representative' of humanity, the Christ-being, made visible artistically between the duality of the conflicting soul-forces.

In a certain sense, for the student of spiritual science the building was a path of initiation and at the same time a reflection of the inner being of man. Although the visitors at that time perhaps didn't immediately realize it, it was conceived as a mystery temple consecrated to the trinitarian Being, in which the human being – by entering the building and leaving the material outer world – entered into his own threefold interior. Further, by means of the artistic realization of spiritual universal facts when passing through the building, an individual was able to experience initially – in the 'atrium' – the divine *magical life-forces* coming towards him. For, by gazing into the small-domed room – into the 'Holy' – he perceived the cosmic forces which pervaded his soul. Then, to finally arrive directly in front of the statue of the Redeemer, in front of the holy 'triangle' of the wooden trinitarian group – the 'Holy of Holies' – he recognized his own *spiritual I-being.* With this knowledge of himself, the human being was to leave the building and afterwards be able to rejoin the community as a conscious and healing member.

This wonderful building – the so-called first Goetheanum – created in honour of the creative Majesty and the human being becoming aware of him, burned down to its base in a few hours on New Year's Eve 1922. The cause was arson. The glow of the flames from the organ's melting pipes could be seen in Basel, about ten kilometres away.

The building could not be saved, because the fire had been set in the double wooden formwork, between the inner and outer walls, and had been able to spread unnoticed until the flames finally broke through the walls and ceilings at around eleven o'clock, whilst the people living nearby were awaiting the new year at home or were already asleep. Dozens, perhaps hundreds of people who had worked tirelessly on the building for years, stood stunned, helplessly watching the destruction of their life's work. In their midst stood Rudolf Steiner himself. We can hardly imagine what that night must have been like for him, because the deliberate destruction of that structure affected him more than just personally. It had been his intention to give to every interested person – by using artistic means of expression through that building – a non-intellectual sense of being able to find his own actual essence. Rudolf Steiner died two years later after a long, hard illness, about which he once said that, since that night, his physical powers had been taken from him.

The fire had shown in a radical way the internal state of a large part of humanity in its relation to the spirit, and the 'opposing powers' active within them.

I stumbled from the living room, it must be somewhere! I rummaged in a dresser in the bedroom ... There it was! – I ran back into the living room and with shaking hands opened a small, weathered notebook: September 1982 (I was ten years old). With a broken voice I read aloud:
(See facsimile in Appendix 1, page 266ff.)

Adonai! King of the World,

Last night I experienced something terrible. Surely you know about it, but it's bothering me so much that I want to write it down for you. It is also precious to me, I never want to forget it!!! A black ball of stars fell from the sky and rolled on the earth. It destroyed the most beautiful thing I ever saw. Namely a house. It was so splendid that I have forgotten what it looked like in reality. In any case it was big, and a little like a church in which You live. But not so easy to understand. All the secrets about the world were hidden in the house. Although they were also displayed in it, like in a living museum. I was also in the church and was looking at the secrets. As I was looking at them, they became living figures and went right through me. Each time when one of them went right through me I became lighter and had a happy tingling sensation in my stomach. Like when I passed a venerable Light's test. I think the house belonged to you, Adonai. A man was standing at the back. At first I thought it was my Lord Jesus Christ, because he streamed out so much love. My heart jumped with joy and excitement. I wanted to run to him, but then I saw: the venerable Light was next to him. Then I knew that one may not touch him. He handed out many little balls of light, which floated strangely about the room. I reached for them, as did other people.

But then something terrible happened. The people fought over the little balls of light and tried to grab them away from each other. The man's voice of light said: Don't do that! I brought enough for all! He was very disappointed and sad. I felt so sorry for him that I let my balls of light fall. I thought I couldn't keep them. But then he became even sadder. So I tried to gather the balls together again. They had become heavy and rolled around the floor. I ran after them.

Suddenly I was outside in front of the house.It seemed to me as if we had not been worthy to have permission to be in the house and to receive the little balls of light and love. And then punishment came. A huge black burning ball fell down from the sky and entered the house. No one noticed it. From outside everything looked the same, but God's secrets cried out in pain, and because they had gone right through me I also felt unbearable pain. I still thought that you can't have any pain in dreams. But then I only saw the beautiful house. It was hardly recognizable. It was engulfed in green and purple flames. The vapour blazed high into the pitch-black sky like steam from a witch's cauldron. It was black everywhere. Except that the mighty flames were so bright that they hurt my eyes. But I saw how the secrets, unharmed, flew back to the sky from where they came.

I had to cry and cry and cry and cry and cry... I wanted to fly with them. It was so terribly sad. The beautiful godly magical house burned down and all its secrets burned in me. I was so miserable in my heart, Adonai, that I wanted to die. But I knew that would be avoiding a responsibility. I looked for anything comforting. But all was only dark night. Then I remembered the dear beautiful man who had the Jesus Christ heart and the venerable Light. But both had disappeared. Then I lost all hope and thought that I couldn't have died after all because otherwise I couldn't have felt such painful sadness. I was so sad, that at first I thought I had died of it.

Then I woke up. My pillow was soaked from crying. My dear God, I think one can only have so much sadness about something real.

I wonder all the time if the magical house exists somewhere. Maybe You have shown me the future to avoid that it really happens. But where is it? And where and who is the light-man? And what were the little balls that he handed out? With the little balls he had filled my heart with so much heavenly love.

He was surely your emissary, Lord, or it was your son Jesus Christ himself disguised in a black costume. I think he was suddenly gone because the house had burned down. He had no house any more in which he could hand out the little-light-balls of love. Maybe he can be found somewhere else. Just as the Lord Jesus Christ was nailed to the cross and now we have to look for him somewhere else than then. We must first pull everything together in one, then dive through the truth-point. That is the gate to his world in which all is true and was true and will be true for all eternity. The venerable Light awaits us there with his test, and the real world exists behind him.

Now it's raining. Maybe the sky is also crying. But when you think about it, without these tears the plants would die of thirst...

It could be that suffering is important for something else that we don't think about when we are in a bad way ourselves. Such dreams always make me very tired! Whenever something important happens, your inner weaker self makes you lazy. But I will NOT forget it!

Afterword

This book is a very personal, intimate one.

Those who have already become acquainted with my other books or with me in person know that there is not much to learn about my private life. I have also said little or nothing about it in response to direct and repeated inquiries from many different sides over the past 12 years. (Therefore – to anticipate my critics' possible insinuations – this book was not written in order to draw attention to myself by relating certain unusual anecdotes. Experience has shown that it is unfortunately not improbable that such allegations will come from those who claim that I have not given enough information about my 'access' to the spiritual world.) What then is my reason for publishing such an intimate history?

In an epoch in which we have made such great progress in every conceivable area in such a short time, one area has faded ever more, silent and unnoticed, until at last its reputation has fallen into such disrepute that today one hardly dares to mention it openly for fear of being labelled hopelessly reactionary, naive or even insane by the predominant mainstream: the area of the *super-sensory* or *the creative, living spirit*. If the human being could make himself into an observer of his own self and the current situation of the world, he could easily conclude that this loss of the principle of spirit in our lives is no accident. And in my opinion, he would not be mistaken. Naturally one will not look for the causes if from the start one considers an immortal human individual spirit as non-existent. Not even first-class spiritual-scientific treatises will do much to change this.

The spiritual experiences which I have had, and which for a long time I have felt to be most intimate and holy and have therefore kept for myself (and in a certain sense still do), have shown me impressively, shaping my whole life, that it is decisive for the well-being of the individual, his fellow human beings and the earth organism that the human being finds the knowledge of a creative spirit, independent of matter, in himself and in the world.

Everyone who has experienced this with the intensity that I have would do everything possible to make his fellow brothers and sisters mindful of the spiritual world – but leaving them free and not in a missionary way, which would contradict what he or she has learned about the nature of the spiritual realm. But one can tell of what one has experienced in a way that doesn't impose one's story on anyone. By publishing it, it is left up to people if they wish to 'hear' in this way or not.

One can at least *share* one's own experiences instead of being silent.

Admittedly, it took me a long time in daring to take this step. At first I feared making myself vulnerable. After all, with the publication of such a book I am sharing my inner self with unknown people and also with those who are biased from the outset. This concern is proved unfounded, however, if one really internalizes and lives what has been consciously encountered as spiritual reality – namely, that the separation between 'me' and 'the other' is an illusion, a mere earthly egocentric perspective. Once one has experienced that the divine-spiritual world exists in the communion of *all* human 'I's – as individual as they and their ways of life and development may be – the sharing of one's own experiences is self-evident, because I share them anyway with all human souls in the spiritual reality in which we all live together. Now, with the publication of this book, the disclosure about my being and inner development is, strictly speaking, merely additional information for the everyday consciousness of my fellow human beings.

But it is just in this everyday consciousness that we are trapped in long stretches of our lives. We don't consciously experience *what reality is* – the spiritual potency of our actual core-being and the indestructible bond of love which conjoins us all. But I believe that there is a key with which the locked door to the World of Reality in each of us can be unlocked – if, for example, we are willing to open our own door wide enough for others to perceive the super-sensory home lying behind it. This can then become the key that fits one's own door, because something of the living Spirit of Reality flares in the everyday consciousness of one's fellow human beings and reminds them of the living Spirit of Reality in their own immortal core of being. Of course, this can only mean that the other person is *reminded* of his own relationship to the spiritual world. He must find his own creative spirit, his own human-being-core. So, he should not believe that he must detect in himself anything that is absolutely identical with my experiences, or that he must reject my testimony about the spiritual because he has not had such experiences himself. Each person's inner biography is of course completely individual – as are the spiritual experiences and invisible encounters of which it is made.

If someone thinks he has had no such spiritual experiences, that may be because these experiences don't attract his attention amongst the noisy, glaring sensory life – or simply aren't remembered. But he *has* them! It is enough to extract small events from memory about which you sense that something is there that cannot be explained purely externally – perhaps something not particularly extraordinary or mysterious, but simply an inner experience of some situation, or through some other person, that has touched you deeply – if only for a moment – or inspired you with new ideas. It is enough to connect to your deep inner self by remembering such encounters or experiences in order to convince yourself that a purely soul-spiritual 'element' can inspire us to higher, ethical impulses – even to our own improvement.

If you have been able to recall such an experience from the contemplation of memory, you may find that you have not taken your – supposedly unremarkable – inner experiences with the world of the living spirit very seriously. As a rule, little importance is given to them, perhaps because they have not sustainably changed or ennobled you. So, were they more of the nature of appearance than reality? Is it really important to pay so much attention to such passing episodes when you are confronted and occupied with sufficient 'tangible' things in everyday life? You may have already more or less consciously asked yourself this or something similar.

It's comparable to caring for a garden. Although this comparison may seem banal, it is nevertheless appropriate. You will only be able to sustainably improve yourself if you care for the many small and seemingly unremarkable soul-spiritual gifts – like the plants in the garden which, after all, we do not want to let wither. How much effort goes into the maintenance and flourishing of a beautiful garden?! (We snip and water and fertilize and rake.) And how much for the maintenance and flourishing of our higher soul-spiritual being-core, our actual I, with which after all we influence ourselves and the world every day? How vividly and thoroughly would our psychical-spiritual being and experience be developed – how capable would be our I in terms of ethical impulses and deeds in the everyday world – if we consistently paid attention to, appreciated and cultivated our seemingly unre-markable soul-spiritual gifts?

These seemingly small inner experiences and super-sensory expe-riences are our greatest treasure! To guard this treasure, to increase it and thereby to become inwardly richer, is probably the great-est virtue and at the same time the holiest duty of every human being, and especially of the so-called spiritual student. To 'get rich' in the spiritual sense is not only permissible, but – in contrast to the material 'getting rich', the accumulation of personal wealth at the expense of others' quality of life – it is morally aesthetic to the greatest extent, and enables the formation and maturity of the 'higher' or 'divine person' in us; that is, our *I*, and not the inflation of our selfish *ego*.

Such contacts with super-sensory reality – which make our I richer, healthier, more healing – are only possible through one's own expe-rience and not through theoretical knowledge. So, to return to the content of this book, my individual experience with the spiritual world cannot provide anyone else with their own new spiritual experience. However – and this is my deeply felt hope and wish – the completely open, intimate and confidential sharing of my spir-itual experiences might, in certain circumstances, make the indi-vidual reader's own living relationship to the spiritual world and higher self more clearly visible.

I have come to believe that this wonderful reciprocal spiritu-al-economical process – actually a kind of communion of 'I's – is most likely to occur through unreserved trust, a giving of trust. I would like herewith to give my innermost being to all people so that my fellow brothers' and sisters' trust in their own precious soul-spiritual experiences and feeling for truth in the World of Reality may grow.

May the reports of my experiences with the spiritual word *embolden*! Embolden trust in the divine spiritual word! Embolden common life with our fellow human beings, and for awe and reverent esteem for the divine-spiritual interior of every single human being, who would not be in the world if not also born of the living spirit like us!

May my remarks also be supportive for parents whose children seem to be a puzzle to them – to have the courage to discover in an understanding way their own children as free individuals. Not only the parents of small children, but also the parents of grown children – for even retrospectively or in later years much can be embraced, transformed and newly shaped. It's never too late, so long as we are together in earthly life and use the time to finally be able to enter the spiritual world with transformed hearts and spirits. May my remarks also relieve possible feelings of guilt by educators, in that they show that especially difficult conditions prevail nowadays for recognizing the other as the divine being that he is. And conversely, may my words encourage children to develop patience, forbearance, sacrifice and endurance. Moreover, may this book be understood as an appeal for the perception of the other's I, regardless of his age and the age of the person perceiving – an appeal for the sincere interest in our neighbour.

The unreserved disclosure of my childhood experiences with the spiritual world and the public testimony of the reality of Christ by the publication of my most precious spiritual experience from childhood, are meant to bestow courage and confidence. They are meant to say: Yes, it is true! In every one of us God lives – a higher spiritual entity who ceaselessly cares for us, who never forsakes us and in whom we can find the only soul-spiritual morality that shows us the right way in thinking, feeling and acting, and unites us with our human sisters and brothers! If only we would turn to him, if only we would direct our attention to him.

By sharing my intimate spiritual experiences, I can only dare to hope that I am able to stimulate this (for such a gift can only be given without conditions attached), but this was the impetus for the publication of these pages.

So let everything written here belong to my fellow human beings, to the *human brotherhood of the spirit*.

Judith von Halle
Berlin, August 2015–June 2016

APPENDIX 1

From the Child's Diary
(Facsimiles)

Gesternnacht kam wieder ein Lichtnachtstraum. Zuerst bin ich aus dem Körper rausgeschlüpft und weit geworden. Eine häßliche Fratze kam durch mich durch, die steckt in meinem Kopf. Ich hatte erst angst, daß sie mich nicht losläßt. Ich hab mich umgesehen nach dem ehrwürdigen Licht. Aber konnte es nicht finden. Ich hörte aber seine Donner= windbrausende Stimme. Es hersprach: Judith du bist noch Judith. So lange bleibt es hell um dich von der verkehrten helligkeit! Im Hellen kannst du mich aber nicht leuchten sehn. da mußt ich die Fratze loplassen und es wurde finsterschwarz. Die Fratze versank im finsterschwarzen und auf Einmal sah ich das ehrwürdige Licht das mit der Weg weiß. da war ich mir sicher, daß ich aus dem Körper wirklich rausfahr

Da führte mich dein ehrwürdiges Licht durch ein himmlisches Tor geradeswegs in einen alten Mann hinein. Ich war plötzlich ein alter Mann. der trug einen schweren Umhang aus dickem Stoff. Ich fühlte alle Gefühle von dem Mann. das waren meine Eignen. Und da kamen Worte aus dem Mund des Mannes in einer Sprache, die mit unbekannt ist. Es klang schön voll aber gleich= zeitig ziehrlich. Insgesammt viel wahrer, unge= künstelter als unsere Sprache. Es war vor langer Zeit, daß dieser Mann lebte. Seine Sprache war wie ein lebendes Bild. Wie ein sich bewegendes Gemälde. Manchmal war auch Latein dabei, aber

das hat er nicht so gern gesprochen hatte ich den
Eindruck. Der Mann, also ich, war auf dem Weg
zu einem Kellergewölbe. Vor ihm waren aber schon
viele Männer dorthinein gegangen und versammelten
sich in diesem großen Saal. Sie zeigten etwas an der
Tür vor, damit sie berächtigt wären hineinzugehen.
Der Kellersaal war gerappelt voll. Es gab sehr
schöne bunte Glasfenster, in die ich mich am lieb=
sten hineinversenkt hätte. das weiß ich, es war
etwas besonderes, sonst gab es eigentlich keine Fen=
sterscheiben. Die Männer redeten alle ganz aufge=
regt miteinander, wie die Hühner. Ich (in dem Mann)
hörte ihre Stimmen schon von draußen. Ich ging
über einen Hof und in einen Gang mit kurzen Stein=
säulen. In jeder Säule steckte eine Weisheit. Sie stan=
den alle genau indemselben Abstand zueinander,
so konnte die Harmonie entstehen. Jede war nämlich
anders gestaltet und gab einen eigenen
Klang von sich. Der Abstand war der Rythmuß
für die Klänge, durch ihn klangen sie alle gemein=
sam, wenn man an ihnen vorbeiwandelte. Richtige
Lesesäulen über die Welt waren sie. Nicht mit ir=
gendeine Baukonstruktion. Aber daß sie das Dach
trugen, hatte eben auch eine große wichtige Bedeutung
das Dach schloß den Kopf oder die Kopfkräfte
ab von den Menschen, die darunter an
Gott denken sollten, damit ihre Kopfkraft nicht
einfach in den Himmel auf und davonfliegt,
sondern schön bei ihnen bliebe.

Ich in dem Mann ging dann eine Treppe hinauf
(oder hinab. ich weiß es nicht mehr) zu dem Saal.
Hinter mir folgte ein junger Mann. Er war zu mir
wie ein erwachsener Schüler zum Lehrer. Ganz ehrerbietig.
Es war wie ein Traum, aber alles viel echter.
Dann standen wir vor dem Saal. Ich ging nicht
durch den Eingang, wo alle durchgegangen waren,
sondern durch eine kleine Tür vorne am Kopf des Saales.
Kaum war ich durch den Türbogen getreten wurde
alles wie auf einen Schlag still. Das fand ich
amüsant, und ich glaube der Mann auch. Der
Saal war so voll, daß alle stehen mußten, aber sie
standen ganz ruhig und lauschten gespannt, was
der alte Mann sagen würde.

Vorne bei mir stand ein Tischchen und darauf
drei Schalen aus dünnem Blech. Eine Schale mit
Getreidekörnern, eine mit Wasser und eine die leer
war. Der alte Mann hielt dann eine Ansprache
wie einen Unterricht, an den ich mich nicht mehr
richtig erinnern kann. Es war ganz schön
kompliziert. Eigentlich wollte er nur zeigen, wie
Gott wirklich ist. Aber da hatte er sich alle
möglichen Sachen ausgedacht, um das zu erklären.
Er wollte beweisen, daß das Wasser und
sogar die Körner aus dem Inhalt der dritten
Schale entstanden waren, die ja leer war. So
habe man sich das Göttliche in dem Himmeln
vorzustellen wie die leere Schale, aus der alles
kommt, was der Mensch für sein Leben braucht.

258

Wenn der Gotteshimmel in einer ~~leer~~ Schahle ist,
die leer ist, dann kommt auch der Mensch daheraus.

Es war noch viel ausfürlicher, aber ich konnte mir
das nicht alles märcken. Habe es auch nicht alles
verstanden glaub ich. So ein bischen wie die erwachsenen
Schüler in dem Sahl. Dabei steckte ich ja in den Gedan=
ken von dem alten Mann drinnen.

Zum Schluß sagte ich in dem alten Mann, daß
es besser wäre die Nase nicht nur in die Bücher
zu stecken, sondern am großen Fluß entlangzu=
~~spazieren~~ und sich einmal die Steine zu betrach=
ten, die am Ufer angeschwärt werden und sich
vorzustellen, woher sie kommen, welchen Weg sie
gereißt sind, wie sie ihre Form verändert haben und
wohin sie noch gehen. Da staunten alle sehr, als sie
den alten Mann so sprechen hörten, weil der Mann
dafür bekannt war alle Bücher der Welt zu kennen.

Ich war aber nur zu Besuch in dem Mann gewesen
und als ich wieder rausflog habe ich ihm noch wie
nachgeblickt mit fühlenden Himmelsaugen und
sah, wie er zu seinem Lehrer gehen wollte, wo er die
~~Der~~ Antworten auf seine Fragen herhohlte. Es ging
kurz in eine ~~so~~ große alte Kirche, aber dann wieder
hinaus und auch aus der betriebsamen Stadt bis
zu dem Fluß. Dort hat er geweint und sich platt
auf den Boden gelegt und ihn wie umarmt. Aber
da kam er zu seinem Lehrer und er war viiiieeel
kleiner vor ihm als seine Schüler vor ihm gewesen

dem
Naturlehrer

waren. da war ich glücklich, weil so alles gut
war.
    Wie mich die Prüfung vom ehrwürdigen
Licht wieder zurückgebracht hat, schreibe
ich morgen oder übermorgen auf. Jetzt
reichts für heute.

Heute nacht kam wieder eine Prüfung. Es war ziemlich anstrengend. Erst bin ich wieder eben durchgeschlüpft und dann ganz ruhig ste- dig in die schöne Welt ge- schwebt. Jedes mal ist es das schönste, zweischte Liebe Gefühl im Herzen, es ist tausendmal schöner als eine Freudenfreude!!! Die Prüfung war dann im Anfang ganz schön schwie- rig. Ich war nur noch wenig klein in einem Frei= en Liebesprächelchen zusam= mengequetscht. Und ich

wankte wieder auf das große ehrwürdige ruhige Licht. Das mir immer den Weg es leuchtet. Und zum kam es schon und klangvoll: "Komm zu mir, wenn du kommst!

Da wurde alles wie ein tiefes dunkles Thal ruhig und end= los. Es war so tief, daß man nicht ahnen konnte wo der Boden war. Und ich sah ein starkes Licht= chen selbe zum ehrwürdigen Licht hinüber. Ist es, es gut keine Brücke gebe es war Das war nämlich die

Prüfung! Schein mal hatte
ich es bereut! Ich sollte
über den Thala bgrund
gehen ohne dass es einen
Übergang gab
(freilich dummer Mensch
Das es bestand auf die Angst
zutun bekommen und des=
wegen wurde es in der Tiefe
noch dunkler und
bösartiger. Es kam auch
noch ein häßliches blutiges
rotes Grauen dann da da=
zu. Ich, das will ein
mal verschlingen. Es war
ganz hämisch rot ich
immer denke rot ist
feurig und weiß! Aber

das schmutzrot war rot
und hot. Es war ein
häßliche Farbe
Da merkte ich, das mein
Licht immer schwächer ge=
worden war.
Da dachte ich an dich mein
liebes Jesus= Christus und
daran, daß du mich im=
mer lieb hast auch wenn ich
was falsch mache. Und
mit einem mal wurde mein
Licht wieder ein bischen
größer und heller und das
häßliche Abgrund wurde
wieder
noch dunkel aber die Farbe
verschwand. Das schmut=

diese Stunde war sehr ge-
duldig und schickst immer
noch. Es wartete auf mich
Und als sie es wieder an-
sah schockte es noch poröse
sagte als Zweck, um mit
Mut zu machen. Es gab
mit die Prüfungsaufgabe:
du magst den Schritt
wagen. Aus wenn du mit
Vertrauen kann es dich
führen, _____ betrspreche
es mir.
Underhalb ich mich grade
entschlossen hatte unter
Schritt über den Abgrund
zu machen, obwohl keine
Brücke darüber da gab mir

das ehrwürdige Licht eine
Heimöde. Ich wollte in meinem Liebchen sprechen:

im Namen des Vaters
und des Sohnes
und des heiligen Geistes

Da habe ich diese Worte
herzgesprochen und als
ich mich traute den 1.
Schritt zu machen
ging es mit einem mal
ganz leicht. Ich hatte
meine Hoffnungen geschlos-
sen _____ von dem
Abgrund, aber ich konnte
sehen, daß das Unterst

diese Licht seine Lichtarme
ausgebreitet hatte und
sich freute, dass ich die
Prüfung bestanden habe,
Das war wohl in 59!

es ist ein bischen wie wenn
man die Augen schließen
muß und sich rückwärts
fallen läßt und das man
vertraut, das einen der
hinter einem auffängt,
Bloß dass man sich bei der
Prüfung irgendwie selbst
auffangen muß.

(natürlich hab ich auch diese Leute und am
Nr. 8 = das ehrwürdige Diener
Nr. 6 = der Eingang

Was habe und gebe, entwickelt etwas
wie eine Brücke (Nr. 4)

"nämlich zuerst gar es
nicht gemerkt. Nur wenn
man hatte die farbenvolle =
schöne Leuchtkuppel
durchdringt daß man
kaum Licht geben und selbst
werden. Dann wird
alles hell.

Meine Glaswand
reicht aus der guten
Tiefenwärme heraus.
Die Schwanenflügel können =
ohne keine Augen sondern
Fühler und tasten das
Herschlag sucht der
Wolf und man Wind =
schützt das mit auf =
steigt durch die 2 Essen.

Als ich draußen vor
sollte ich zurückweichen
und das erste mit dem
was hinter dem Ei. =
gang ist, vergleichen. Da
konnte ich herrsehen,
daß es vorne es nichts nichts
Dunkel war wie es am
Anfang. Und ich wurde
alles sehen wie es er wird =
Lichtkl aussieht. da
stelle ich fest, daß die
Brücke lugentlich die
Leuchte-Regenbogenkuppel
war durch die ich hin =
durchgeschwebt war
und die die andere Leute
anfaßt. Das hatte ich

265

Adonai! König der Welt

Heute nacht habe ich etwas ganz
schreckliches erlebt. Du weißt
es sicher aber es quält mich so
darum will ich es dir aufschrei=
ben. Es ist mir auch zu viel
ich will es niemals vergessen!!!
Ein schwarzer Sternenball viel
zum Himmel hinab und rollte
auf die Erde. Es zerstörte das schön=
ste, was ich je gesehen hab. Nämlich
ein Haus. Es war so
prächtig und dabei habe ich ver=
gessen wie es in Wirklichkeit aus=
gesehen hat. Es war auf jeden Fall
groß und es war ein bisschen wie
eine Kirche in der die lebendiglich
zerbrist. Aber nicht so einfach in,

verstehen. Es war wie ein Rausch=
Zauberschloß. Alle Geheimnisse
über die Welt waren mir in dem
Haus versteckt. Sowohl die waren
auch dann ausgespielt wie in einem
lebenden Museum. Ich war auch in
dem Kirchenschloß drin und habe
mit die Geheimnisse angeguckt. Als
ich sie anguckt wurden sie auf
einmal zu lebenden Figuren
und wurden den Formen und
gingen durch mich durch. Jedes=
mal, wenn einer durch mich durch=
ging wurde ich leichter und hatte
ein glückliches Kribbeln im Bauch.
Wie wenn ich eine Folgerung vom
ehrwürdigen Licht bestanden habe.
Ich glaube das Haus gehörte zu

Adam. Dann hinter stand ein
Mann. Erst dachte ich es ist mein
Herr Jesus = Christus, weil es so sehr
Liebe ausströmte. Mein Herz hüpfte
hüpfte vor Glück und Aufregung.
Ich wollte zu ihm hinrennen, da sah
ich das ehrwürdige Licht was bei ihm.
Da wußte ich, man darf ihn nicht
berühren. Es sind viele
Lichtkügelchen aus, die seltsam
durch den Raum schwebten. Ich
griff nach ihnen und die anderen
Menschen auch.

Aber dann passierte was furcht=
bares. Die Menschen konnten
sich von die Lichtkügelchen und
versuchten sie den Andern weg =
zuquetschen. die Lichtsäume

als Mannes sprach: Tut das
nicht! Ich habe genug für alle mit=
gebracht! Es war sehr traurisch und
traurig. Es tut mir so leid, so daß
ich meine Kugeln fallen ließ. Ich
dachte ich durfte sie nicht behalten.
Da wurde es aber noch trauriger. Also
versuchte ich, meine Kugeln wieder zu=
sammenzunehmen. Sie waren schwer
geworden und kullerten auf dem
Boden rum, sie rollten aus dem
Haus raus. Ich lief ihnen hinterher.
Irgendmal was ich draußen vor dem
Haus. Mit kam es so vor als hätten
wir uns nicht völlig genug gemacht,
um mich Berachtungen an dem
Haus zu tun und die Lichtliebes =
Kügelchen zu empfangen.

Und da kam auch schon die Straße.
Ein schwarzes brennendes Riesen=
Soll sackte vom Himmel herab und
ging in das Haus ein. Keiner
machte es. Von außen sah es aus
wie vorher, aber die Gottes-geheimnisse
schrieben rot Schmerzen und weil
sie ja durch mich durch und in
mich hineingegangen auf mir
auch alles genauso unverändert.
Ich dachte noch im Traum kann
man doch gar keine Schmerzen haben.
Aber dann sah ich nur noch das
schöne Haus. Man konnte es kaum
noch erkennen. Es wurde von grünen
und blauen Flammen verschlungen=
wie der Dampf aus einem
Feuerkessel loh. =

dessen die Dämpfe hoch in den
pechschwarzen Himmel hinein. Es
war überall schwarz. Nur die grell=
roten Flammen waren so grell,
daß es in den Augen weh tat. Ich
sah aber wie der Geheimnisse von
beschades zum Himmel zurück
flogen, von wo sie gekommen waren.
Ich mußte weinen und weinen und
weinen und weinen und weinen …
ich wollte mit ihnen mitfliegen. Es war
so furchtbar traurig. Das schöne
Gotteszauberhaus verbrannte und
alle seine Geheimnisse verbrannten
mit. Mir war so elend, im Herzen
drinnen, daß ich sterben wollte. Ach,
ich wußte, das wäre wie sich in eine
Verantwortung zu stürzen. Ich

suche nach irgendetwas Bestehendem.
Es war aber alles nur dunkle Nacht.
Da sieht mir der liebe schöne Mann
ein, der das Jesus=Christus=Herz
hatte und das schreibende Licht.
Aber beide waren verschwunden. Da
hatte verlosch ich alle Hoffnung und
dachte nur, ich kann gar nicht ge=
storben sein, weil ich ja sonst nicht
so schmerzliche Trauer empfinden
könnte. Ich war nämlich so traurig,
daß ich erst dachte ich wäre daran
gestorben.

Da wachte ich auf. Mein Kissen
war total nass vom Weinen.
Mein liebes Gott. Ich glaube, man
kann nur so viel Traurigkeit
haben, wenn etwas schönes, die

ganze Zeit überlege ich ob es ir=
gendwo dieses Zauberhaus gibt.
Vielleicht hast du mir die Zukunft
gezeigt, um zu verhindern daß
es wirklich einmal geschieht. Aber
wo ist es? Und wo und wer ist das
Lichtmann und was waren die
Kügelchen, die es ausgestellt hat?
Es hat mich dem Kügelchen mein
so viel Himmelsliebe ge=
füllt. Es war sicher dein Ge=
gesanntes, Herr oder es war mein
schmerzen Herzlein verbleibt
dein Sohn Jesus=Christus selbst
Ich glaube es war aufeinmal weg,
weil das Haus verbrannt war. Es
habe kein Haus mehr, in dem er
die Liebeslichtkügelchen verteilen

269

wird wohl auch, wer immer man sich überlegt, daß ohne diese Träumen die Pflanzenverdursten müßten... Es könnte sein, daß alles Leid & richtig ist, bis etwas anderes an das man gar nicht denkt, wenn es einem selber schlecht geht ⊗

Solche Träume machen mich immer ganz müde! Immer wenn was wichtiges kommt mache einen der wieder Schwierige und Anfänge — Aber ich werde es NICHT vergessen!

⊗ (Aber ob der Krampf in meiner Hand zu irgendwas gut ist frage ich zu bezweifeln.

---

könnte. Vielleicht kann man ihn woanders finden. So wie der Gott Jesus = Bißchen ja auch aus Haus abschlagen würde und jetzt muß man ihn ja ganz woanders suchen als damals. Man muß sagt alles in einem zusammen bilden und durch den Wahrheits-

Punkt durchtauchen, daß die zu seinige Wolke in der oder alles wahr ist und wahr ist und wahr sein wird in alle Ewigkeiten. Da ... Licht mit seinem das ... Licht

Prüfung und dahinter besteht die wirkliche Welt. Jetzt regnet es. Der Himmel

APPENDIX 2

Additions to the Text

To page 227:

They say, 'Thinking cannot help me to reach anything; what really matters is "feeling" or something similar.' In reply it must be said that no one can in the higher sense (and that means in truth) become a 'seer' who has not previously worked his way into the life of thought. In the case of many people a certain inner laziness plays an injurious role. They do not become conscious of this laziness because it clothes itself in contempt for 'abstract thought', 'idle speculations', and the like. But thinking is completely misunderstood, if it is confused with a spinning of idle, abstract trains of thought. This 'abstract thinking' can easily kill supersensible knowledge; live and vigorous thinking can become its foundation. It would of course be more convenient if the power of higher seership could be acquired while shunning the labour of thinking. Many would like this to be possible. But in order to achieve higher seership an inner stability is necessary, an assurance of soul to which thinking alone can lead. Otherwise there merely results a meaningless flickering of pictures hither and thither, a distracting display of phenomena which indeed gives pleasure, but has nothing to do with a true penetration into higher worlds. Further, if we consider what purely spiritual experiences take place in a person who really enters the higher world, we shall realize that the matter has also another aspect.

From Rudolf Steiner: *Theosophy*, Chapter, 'The Path of Knowledge' – Translation: Cottrell & Shepherd.

To page 229:

...whose Being and participation in Earth evolution has been made clear in the previous chapters of this book. The student is now initiated into the exalted mystery that is linked with the name of the Christ. The Christ shows Himself to the student as the 'great ideal of man on earth'. — If thus through intuition the Christ is recognized in the spiritual world, what occurred historically on earth in the fourth post-Atlantean evolutionary epoch — the Greco-Latin epoch — also becomes comprehensible. The way in which, at that time, the exalted Sun Being, the Christ, has intervened in the Earth evolution and how he continues to work within this evolution becomes the personally experienced knowledge of the student of the spiritual. It is thus a revelation of the meaning and significance of Earth evolution that the student receives through intuition.

From Rudolf Steiner: *Occult Science, An Outline*, Chapter, 'Knowledge of the Higher Worlds'.

To page 232:

We must imagine that a being with fully developed human intelligence originates out of nothing and confronts the world. What it would be aware of, before it sets its thinking in motion, would be the pure content of observation. The world would then appear to this being as nothing but a mere disconnected aggregate of objects of sensation: colours, sounds, sensations of pressure, of warmth, of taste and smell; also feelings of pleasure and pain. This aggregate is the content of pure, unthinking observation. [...]

Our next task is to discover by means of thoughtful reflection what relation the immediately given content of observation mentioned above has to the conscious subject.[...]

I do not merely see a tree, but I also know that it is I who am seeing it. I know, moreover, that something happens in me while I am observing the tree. When the tree disappears from my field of vision, an after-effect of this process remains in my consciousness — a picture of the tree. This picture has become associated with my self during my observation. My self has become enriched; its content has absorbed a new element. This element I call my mental picture of the tree. [...]

I should never have occasion to speak of mental pictures did I not experience them in the percept of my own self. Percepts would come and go; I should let them slip by. Only because I perceive my self, and observe that with each percept the content of my self, too, is changed, am I compelled to connect the observation of the object with the changes in my own condition, and to speak of my mental picture. [...]

I perceive the mental picture in my self in the same sense as I perceive colour, sound, etc., in other objects. I am now also able to distinguish these other objects that confront me, by calling them the outer world, whereas the content of my percept of my self I call my inner world. The failure to recognize the true relationship between mental picture and object has led to the greatest misunderstandings in modern philosophy.

From Rudolf Steiner: *The Philosophy of Freedom*, Chapter, 'The World as Percept'. (All quotations taken from the Michael Wilson translation.)

One of this book's main themes is the nature of 'knowledge', for this had occupied me since I noticed that many people had more and others had less of it. This didn't always result from what they said, but above all from how they behaved. And the question continued to occupy me as to why nobody in my immediate surroundings realized the same things that I did by observing and reflecting on purely spiritual facts and conditions (beyond the gate to the World of Reality). Then I found a differentiated approach to these questions:

In thinking, we have that element given us which welds our separate individuality into one whole with the cosmos. In so far as we sense and feel (and also perceive), we are single beings; in so far as we think, we are the all-one being that pervades everything... The fact that the thinking, in us, reaches out beyond our separate existence and relates itself to the universal world existence, gives rise to the fundamental desire for knowledge in us. Beings without thinking do not have this desire. When they are faced with other things, no questions arise for them. These other things remain external to such beings. But in thinking beings the concept rises up when they confront the external thing. It is that part of the thing which we receive not from outside but from within. To match up, to unite the two elements, inner and outer, is the task of knowledge. The percept is thus not something finished and self-contained, but one side of the total reality. The other side is the concept. The act of knowing is the synthesis of percept and concept. Only percept and concept together constitute the whole thing.

From *The Philosophy of Freedom*, Chapter, 'The Act of Knowing the World'.

Making mental pictures gives our conceptual life at once an individual stamp. Each one of us has his own particular place from which he surveys the world. His concepts link themselves to his percepts. He thinks the general concepts in his own special way. [...]

However, we are not satisfied merely to refer the percept, by means of thinking, to the concept, but we relate them also to our particular subjectivity, our individual Ego. The expression of this individual relationship is feeling, which manifests itself as pleasure or displeasure.

Thinking and feeling correspond to the two-fold nature of our being.

From Rudolf Steiner: *The Philosophy of Freedom*, Chapter, 'Human Individuality'.

It follows from the concept of the act of knowing as we have defined it, that one cannot speak of limits to knowledge. Knowing is not a concern of the world in general, but an affair which man must settle for himself. Things demand no explanation. They exist and act on one another according to laws which can be discovered through thinking. They exist in indivisible unity with these laws. Our Egohood confronts them, grasping at first only that part of them we have called percepts. Within our Egohood, however, lies the power to discover the other part of the reality as well. Only when the Egohood has taken the two elements of reality which are indivisibly united in the world and has combined them also for itself, is our thirst for knowledge satisfied — the I has then arrived at the reality once more.

From Rudolf Steiner: *The Philosophy of Freedom*, Chapter, 'Are There Limits to Knowledge?'

The last sentences quoted here confirm my own experiences.

Based on my observation that man, as a conscious being – in contrast to the animal, whose highest member of being consists of its soul-force-body – also has a fourth component of being, namely a 'human-being-core', over the years I became ever more occupied with the question about the human-being-core, about the 'I' on the one hand and the activity of this 'I' on the other hand. The potential which exists in the human I could, but did not necessarily have to develop. As long as this I-activity was not developed, however, the comprehension of the world, of all material as well as spiritual things, would have to remain incomplete. Only when I could again remember myself – had accomplished the fusion of my earthly being with my spiritual consciousness, for which there are no 'limits of knowledge' – could I realize the unity of the whole, the complete and everlasting fusion of the material and spiritual worlds, that is, the true reality; or (as I thought of it then) expressed differently: '... *Within our egohood, however, lies the power to discover the other part of the reality as well. Only when the Egohood has taken the two elements of reality which are indivisibly united in the world and has combined them also for itself, is our thirst for knowledge satisfied — the I has then arrived at the reality once more.'*

I cannot resist quoting one last passage here, not only because it approaches the answer to the initial question, but because for me it resulted in a clear twist of fate insofar as it again put into motion, this time pointing in a certain direction, the question that had tormented me since my unsatisfactory choice of study or profession, and about the meaning of my present life on earth and my individual task to be fulfilled:

The first level of individual life is that of perceiving, more particularly perceiving through the senses. This is the region of our individual life in which perceiving translates itself directly into willing, without the intervention of either a feeling or a concept. The driving force here involved is simply called instinct. The satisfaction of our lower, purely animal needs (hunger, sexual intercourse, etc.) comes about in this way. The main characteristic of instinctive life is the immediacy with which the single percept releases the act of will. This kind of determination of the will, which belongs originally only to the life of the lower senses, may however become extended also to the percepts of the higher senses. We may react to the percept of a certain event in the external world without reflecting on what we do, without any special feeling connecting itself with the percept, as in fact happens in our conventional social behaviour. The driving force of such action is called tact or moral good taste. [...]

The second level of human life is feeling. Definite feelings accompany the percepts of the external world. These feelings may become the driving force of an action. When I see a starving man, my pity for him may become the driving force of my action. Such feelings, for example, are shame, pride, sense of honour, humility, remorse, pity, revenge, gratitude, piety, loyalty, love, and duty. [...]

The third level of life amounts to thinking and forming mental pictures. A mental picture or a concept may become the motive of an action through mere reflection. Mental pictures become motives because, in the course of life, we regularly connect certain aims of our will with percepts which recur again and again in more or less modified form. Hence with people not wholly devoid of experience it happens that the occurrence of certain percepts is always accompanied by the appearance in consciousness of mental pictures of actions that they themselves have carried out in a similar case or have seen others carry out. These mental pictures float before their minds as patterns which determine all subsequent decisions; they become parts of their characterological disposition. The driving force in the will, in this case, we can call practical experience. Practical experience merges gradually into purely tactful behaviour. [...]

The highest level of individual life is that of conceptual thinking without regard to any definite perceptual content. We determine the content of a concept through pure intuition from out of the ideal sphere. Such a concept contains, at first, no reference to any definite percepts.[...] But if we act under the influence of intuitions, the driving force of our action is pure thinking. As it is the custom in philosophy to call the faculty of pure thinking 'reason', we may well be justified in giving the name of practical reason to the moral driving force characteristic of this level of life. [...]

Among the motives, we have just singled out conceptual intuition as the highest. On closer inspection it will at once be seen that at this level of morality driving force and motive coincide; that is, neither a predetermined characterological disposition nor the external authority of an accepted moral principle influences our conduct. The action is therefore neither a stereotyped one which merely follows certain rules, nor is it one which we automatically perform in response to an external impulse, but it is an action determined purely and simply by its own ideal content. Such an action presupposes the capacity for moral intuitions. Whoever lacks the capacity to experience for himself the particular moral principle for each single situation, will never achieve truly individual willing. Kant's principle of morality — Act so that the basis of your action may be valid for all human beings — is the exact opposite of ours. His principle means death to all individual impulses of action. For me, the standard can never be the way all people would act, but rather what, for me, is to be done in each individual case.[...]

The sum of ideas which are effective in us, the concrete content of our intuitions, constitutes what is individual in each of us, notwithstanding the universality of the world of ideas. In so far as this intuitive content applies to action, it constitutes the moral content of the individual. To let this content express itself in life is both the highest moral driving force and the highest motive a man can have, who sees that in this content all other moral principles are in the end united. We may call this point of view ethical individualism.

From Rudolf Steiner: *The Philosophy of Freedom*, Chapter, 'The Idea of Freedom'.

And from this consideration the answer to the initial question followed:

An action is felt to be free in so far as the reasons for it spring from the ideal part of my individual being; every other part of an action, irrespective of whether it is carried out under the compulsion of nature or under the obligation of a moral standard, is felt to be unfree. Man is free in so far as he is able to obey himself in every moment of his life. A moral deed is my deed only if it can be called a free one in this sense. [...] Acting out of freedom does not exclude the moral laws; it includes them, but shows itself to be on a higher level than those actions which are merely dictated by such laws.

From Rudolf Steiner: *The Philosophy of Freedom*, Chapter, 'The Idea of Freedom'.

'The human individual is the source of all morality and the centre of life on earth.' Man *as such* was not meant here, but the emphasis must be on the word *individual* in the sense of the single, unique, individual human being. What must have been meant here was the following:

Whenever the impulse for an action is present in a general conceptual form (for example, Thou shalt do good to thy fellow men! Thou shalt live so that thou best promotest thy welfare!) then for each particular case the concrete mental picture of the action (the relation of the concept to a content of perception) must first be found. For the free spirit who is impelled by no example, nor fear of punishment or the like, this translation of the concept into a mental picture is always necessary. Man produces concrete mental pictures from the sum of his ideas chiefly by means of the imagination. Therefore what the free spirit needs in order to realize his ideas, in order to be effective, is moral imagination. This is the source of the free spirit's action. Therefore it is only people with moral imagination who are, strictly speaking, morally productive. Those who merely preach morality, that is, people who merely spin out moral rules without being able to condense them into concrete mental pictures, are morally unproductive. They are like those critics who can explain very intelligibly what a work of art ought to be like, but who are themselves incapable of even the slightest productive effort.

From Rudolf Steiner: *The Philosophy of Freedom*, Chapter: 'Moral Imagination'.

And then the creation of a concept followed, the living content of which has, since that time, not released me and has become the guiding principle for my contacts with everyday life on earth. The creation of this concept, as the most condensed form of the previous deductive thoughts, made it clear to me that this author's edifice of ideas had a different philosophical foundation than most of the others known to me, and that one who entered the edifice did not wake up in a castle in the air and, from this imaginary place high up in the clouds, suddenly plummet down into everyday life, but that here an epistemological content was given that led directly into practice! So I was not left with a bunch of pompous thoughts, which was what happened after reading many philosophers (to mention their names without substantiating my impression would go too far here and would not be proper) but led directly to a new understanding of my own practical way of living, by thinking together with the thoughts presented by the author:

Moral action, then, presupposes, in addition to the faculty of having moral ideas (moral intuition) and moral imagination, the ability to transform the world of percepts without violating the natural laws by which these are connected. This ability is moral technique. It can be learnt in the same sense in which any kind of knowledge can be learnt.

From Rudolf Steiner: *The Philosophy of Freedom*, Chapter, 'Moral Imagination'.

And toward the end I came to a whole chapter about a fact which I observed in such a drastic way in my crisis during my studies – that man in his 'I' can never be made unfree by *external circumstances*, however decisive he may feel them initially to be.

Anyone who judges people according to generic characters gets only as far as the frontier where people begin to be beings whose activity is based on free self-determination. Whatever lies short of this frontier may naturally become matter for academic study. The characteristics of race, people, nation and sex are the subject matter of special branches of study. Only people who wish to live as nothing more than examples of the genus could possibly conform to a general picture such as arises from academic study of this kind. But none of these branches of study are able to advance as far as the unique content of the single individual. Determining the individual according to the laws of his genus ceases where the sphere of freedom (in thinking and acting) begins. [...] How the individual has to think cannot possibly be deduced from any kind of generic concept. It depends simply and solely on the individual. Just as little is it possible to determine from the general characteristics of man what concrete aims the individual may choose to set himself. [...] It is from individual ethical intuitions and their acceptance by human communities that all moral activity of mankind originates. In other words, the moral life of mankind is the sum total of the products of the moral imagination of free human individuals. This is the conclusion reached by monism.

From Rudolf Steiner: *The Philosophy of Freedom*, Chapter, 'Individuality and Genus'.

Thus the following statement was added to the above-mentioned *basic maxim of free human beings*, the content of which hitherto I had felt only in my inner being or had longed for as a reality to be realized, but which now seemed to me, in the unpretentiously clear form given here, like a liberation for the whole human race:

I differ from my fellow man, not at all because we are living in two entirely different spiritual worlds, but because from the world of ideas common to us both we receive different intuitions. He wants to live out his intuitions, I mine. If we both really conceive out of the idea, and do not obey any external impulses (physical or spiritual), then we cannot but meet one another in like striving, in common intent. A moral misunderstanding, a clash, is impossible between people who are morally free.

From Rudolf Steiner: *The Philosophy of Freedom*, Chapter, 'The Idea of Freedom'.

Books to challenge *your perception of reality*

A message from Clairview

We are an independent publishing company with a focus on cutting-edge, non-fiction books. Our innovative list covers current affairs and politics, health, the arts, history, science and spirituality. But regardless of subject, our books have a common link: they all question conventional thinking, dogmas and received wisdom.

Despite being a small company, our list features some big names, such as Booker Prize winner Ben Okri, literary giant Gore Vidal, world leader Mikhail Gorbachev, modern artist Joseph Beuys and natural childbirth pioneer Michel Odent.

So, check out our full catalogue online at
www.clairviewbooks.com
and join our emailing list for news on new titles.

office@clairviewbooks.com

C L A I R V I E W